LEGACY OF COURAGE

TRUE STORIES OF HONOR FLIGHT VETERANS

CHERYL POPP
& PETER BRONSON

www.honorflighttristate.org

LEGACY OF COURAGE: TRUE STORIES OF HONOR FLIGHT VETERANS

For further information, contact the publisher:

Honor Flight Tri-State

8627 Calumet Way

Cincinnati Ohio 45249

Chilidog Press

6367 Waverly Hill Lane

Loveland, Ohio 45140

ISBN: 978-0-69252115-1

Cover design by Andy Melchers and Cheryl Popp

Interior design by Andy Melchers, Creative Services Manager, Allegra Marketing Print Mail, Cincinnati, Ohio

Photos courtesy of Honor Flight Tri-State: Ambassadors, Ed Finke, Donna Hasselbeck, Larry Cole, Jennifer Otten, John Sullivan, Don Long, Cheryl Popp.

Printed in the USA by CJK Printing, Cincinnati, Ohio

Ernie Pyle columns provided with permission by the Scripps Howard Foundation, Cincinnati, Ohio.

Share your story with a future generation...

My Honor Flight

Date

Veteran

Guardian

Veteran's Address

Phone Numbers

Guardian's Address

Phone Numbers

Service History (where, when, battles, unit, rank, etc.)

What is your legacy?

Honor Flight Stories

Write your personal story for your family here...

"The book is an engaging, heartwarming adventure into the psyche of our program's heroes. What a thrill it is to see and feel the Honor Flight experience through the perspective of our nation's most senior heroes. They thought they were forgotten. They also thought the sacrifices made by their family and friends had faded from America's conscience. An Honor Flight trip proves just the opposite — their friends, accomplishments and their service will never be forgotten, will always be revered and cherished by our nation.

This book proves that an Honor Flight trip stands alone as the culmination of appreciation and reverence for who they are, what they stood for and the liberty we all enjoy today. This powerful and gripping book eloquently tells everyone what an unmatched privilege it is for all of us to be in the presence of living legends during one of the greatest days of their lives. Thank you, Cheryl, for capturing the essence of what the Honor Flight program and experience is all about."

—Earl Morse, Honor Flight Founder

Honor Flight gives us the opportunity to honor the greatest generation while listening to these veterans relive their memories of World War II.

These men and women's incredible acts of valor during our world's darkest days have given the rest of us the freedom to live in a better world.

Legacy of Courage sheds light on these personal stories of service and sacrifice and it is our duty to tell them over and over again so that the history of war will never repeat itself.

—Bill Keating, Jr., Cincinnati Attorney and Honor Flight Guardian

"As a young man I recall hearing my father tell of his wartime experiences. It piqued an interest in World War II that has lasted all my life. It was so different from the history classes that seemed to be more concerned by dates than the stories that really recounted the reality of the events that shaped our world. Legacy of Courage — True Stories of Honor Flight Veterans *brings back to life the importance of what was accomplished during the war, told by the members of the greatest generation."*

—Rob Reider, Son of World War II Veteran, Air Show Announcer

TABLE OF CONTENTS

ACKNOWLEDGEMENTS

To all the people who made this book possible, thank you.

Special thanks to:

My husband, Tom, with whom I share my love, my life, my values and my vision to bring these stories to everyone. We share a deep gratitude for the sacrifices of the World War II generation, and a determination to bring it to print before it is too late.

Peter Bronson, who shared our vision, our focus and our gratitude, and brought his unique writing talent to these pages. Thank you, Peter, for hanging in there with two novices, to guide us to complete this vision. We will never forget the time we have enjoyed together working on this project.

The Honor Flight Tri-State Board of Directors, who encouraged us to write down the experiences we have had together, to record and preserve the amazing stories and thank our treasured veterans for the freedom we have because of their sacrifices.

The medics who have taken care of all of us on these long and emotional trips – especially our "regulars," Chief Bob Klein, Captain Larry Cole and District Chief Ed Thomas.

All of the individual donors and sponsors, especially the Simply Money Advisors and media team, led by Ed Finke and Nathan Bachrach, who have taken us to goals we never knew were within our reach.

The ambassadors, ground crew and guardians too numerous to mention, without whom we could not make dreams come true for these veterans.

Andy Melchers at Allegra, who brought our vision to life with his creative book design.

Jennifer Otten, whose photography and video have supported Honor Flight.

Jane Wenning for her help with proofreading and copy editing.

CJK Printers, the fourth-generation Cincinnati company that worked with us to make sure "Legacy of Courage" was printed locally, in the USA, with the highest standards of excellence.

And our daughter and her husband, Wendi and Don Long; grandchildren Cody Bowling (who has been a guardian), Heather Long and Abby Bowling, whose ideas and love inspired us to write this book so that their generation will have a firsthand account of what makes America great. Now the torch will be passed to them and future generations. Let that light of freedom never be extinguished.

— Cheryl Popp

If you know any veterans in the Greater Cincinnati region — Southern Ohio, Northern Kentucky or Southeast Indiana – encourage them to apply on our website: www.honorflighttristate.org. All veterans age 65 and over are eligible, regardless if they served overseas or stateside.

Or if you know any veterans outside the Cincinnati region, contact the Honor Flight Network, which is the national headquarters for 133 hubs in 42 states. Go to the national website www.honorflight.org and click on your state for the nearest hub.

THE AUTHORS

Cheryl Popp's leadership as director of Honor Flight Tri-State has brought great success to the organization. Her expertise in fundraising, speaking, recruiting and media relations has made Honor Flight participation available to more veterans and increased awareness throughout the Greater Cincinnati, Northern Kentucky, Southeast Indiana and Southwest Ohio region.

Before joining Honor Flight Tri-State, she was the producer of the popular Blue Ash Airport Days Airshow for thirteen years and booked the aerial acts, arranged media coverage, supervised volunteers and managed the Airshow.

Since the closing of the Blue Ash Airport, she has led Lunken Aviation Days at Lunken Airport. As a private pilot she's also an active member of the Cincinnati Warbirds, which preserves World War II vintage aircraft.

She has taught and lectured on floral design and does freelance design for special events. She also has experience in media as a former magazine designer at *Cincinnati Magazine*.

She is a member of the Aircraft Owners and Pilots Association, the Experimental Aircraft Association, Warbirds of America, the Cincinnati Horticulture Society, Symmes Late Bloomers Garden Club and the International Council of Airshows.

She joined Honor Flight Tri-State as a volunteer guardian to show her gratitude to veterans like her father, who served in World War II, but passed away before he could take an Honor Flight. She and her husband, Tom, have two daughters and five grandchildren, and live in Symmes Township, a suburb of Cincinnati, Ohio. This is her first book.

Peter Bronson is the author of two books: *For Pete's Sake*, a collection of his newspaper columns; and *Behind the Lines: The Untold Stories of the Cincinnati Riots*. His company, Chilidog Press LLC, provides writing, editing, publishing and consulting.

The winner of numerous journalism and public service awards, he was editorial page editor and columnist for *The Cincinnati Enquirer* for seventeen years. Before moving to Cincinnati in 1992, he was an editor and columnist at *The Tucson Citizen* in Tucson, Arizona. He is a contributing editor and columnist for *Cincy Magazine*. He started his journalism career at weekly newspapers in Michigan after graduating in 1978 from Michigan State University in his hometown of East Lansing, Michigan.

He has served on several non-profits as board member and volunteer, including Casa de los Ninos home for abused children in Tucson; Northern Kentucky Children's Home; and Leadership Cincinnati. He was a producer and panelist on *Hotseat*, a public affairs show on WCPO-TV, Channel 9 in Cincinnati, and also on the weekly Tucson news show *Arizona Illustrated*.

He lives in Loveland, Ohio.

From One Generation to Another: Thank You

PETER BRONSON

We played army.

As soon as our bare feet hit the endless lawns of summer vacation, we grabbed our toy rifles, shoved baloney sandwiches in our Boy Scout knapsacks and went to war. We fought in sandboxes and hedges, in the woods and parks and tall weeds of vacant lots. Every tree-shaded backyard was a battleground. For boys of a certain age in the 1960s, playing army was all we did from a rushed breakfast of Cheerios to the third or fourth call to come home for dinner. Nothing else compared.

Little League? Hot, confusing, over-organized, getting yelled at by dads who were not even your father. Army required no adults, no bags of equipment, no "practice" and no rules except one: "Take your deads." If someone "got you," a dramatic flop was mandatory, followed by a full-Mississippi count to twenty-five.

Computer games were not invented. We used our imagination to see Tiger Tanks, P-51 fighters, pillboxes and artillery.

We mowed lawns or threw the Morning Bullhorn into bushes, but only to buy a new plastic canteen to carry Kool-Aid. Trading comics was for rainy days when you ran out of things to do with little green army men.

After supper it was time for *Combat!* and *Rat Patrol* on TV.

Dads preferred *Gunsmoke*. If you asked why, they would mess up your hair and give you that "You wouldn't understand, kid" smile, or say something like, "That's not what the war was like." If you asked them to tell you what it was like, they'd say, "Some other time. Go watch your show."

And when we came home to tell them about how Mr. Nelson had chased us out of his yard, they took *his* side. "Leave that man alone," our parents said, making it sound like the final warning before they grabbed a flyswatter or a wooden spoon. Rumor said Mr. Nelson was at Normandy. He'd seen more than enough boys "take their deads." We left him alone.

With all that backyard drill and summertime boot camp, by the time the next war came along we were ready… to burn our draft cards and grow our hair out like a platoon of Breck Girls. What in the name of Sgt. Rock happened?

Politics happened. The CBS Evening News happened, bringing bleeding soldiers into our living rooms and dragging us out to fetid jungles where little men in black pajamas were not playing fair. Even Saint Walter of Cronkite was against the war.

It dawned on us that war was not a game or a TV show. It was for keeps. If one of those guys in pajamas "got you," you could not count to twenty-five and get your legs back.

Sometimes a dad who had a few beers said, "Don't enlist. This is a rotten war. The politicians have screwed it up." My father, who joined the Navy and spent World War II in a San Diego hospital with scarlet fever, said something like that. So I didn't enlist and I got a lucky number in the draft lottery.

Many veteran dads were bitter at the way America's leaders abandoned the men who were sent to Korea, then repeated the same fatal blunders in Vietnam. My step-father, who won a silver star in "It'ly," would get mad enough to break something when he recalled the officer who told him, "Now go home and raise some sons for the next war." He was permanently bewildered at how he was busted back to Pfc. because his Jeep was blown up by German 88s. He had a low opinion of the high command.

Many other veterans supported the war in Vietnam with what little enthusiasm they could muster, because they saw how losing it would cripple American confidence. That was my father-in-law, who served on an escort carrier in the Pacific. It took me years to admit how right he was.

So most of a generation would not play army, and refused to support and honor those who did serve their country. Looking down the long hallway of history, that's not a flattering picture. We're still paying for it.

By shirking service to our country, we never learned to serve anyone but ourselves.

By refusing to risk our lives, we never learned that some things are worth more than life itself, and the lives we protected look flat without the high definition of sacrifice.

By refusing to fight for the most serious things, we fight instead over trivial sports and politics.

By mocking the battle against evil, we invited evil to mock us.

By allowing the blame-America, anti-war virus to infect our media and politics, we caught the flu of defeat, full of "exit strategies," limited war, confused purpose and callous amnesia about the lives we have sacrificed.

By rejecting honor and duty, we lost our way in a "Never Never Land" of permanent childhood, where we never grew into daddy's shoes.

We loved the cliché that war is hell, but wound up defined by another one: Those who stand for nothing will fall for anything.

But somehow, in spite of our me-generation stupidity, America is still blessed with young men and women who answer the call to serve, who are defending us right now, risking everything to keep America strong and safe.

They are the true heirs of the generation of the 1940s who fought the last "Good War," where good battled evil and everyone was united to win no matter what it took. It's the biggest war in history and remains the greatest story of America's courage, spirit and basic decency. That's why we are still fascinated by books and movies about our American Iliad.

Lots of dads and veterans such as Vito "Vic" Raniere, who was at Normandy, should have been in this book. But Mr. Raniere died suddenly at age 93 a week before he could be interviewed. His daughter Vickie said, "He had the time of his life on his Honor Flight. He thought it was amazing. I feel bad that more people didn't get to do this before they died. So many are already gone."

She turned his treasured yellow Honor Flight T-shirt into a pillow.

I can't imagine a finer testimonial to Honor Flight, whose purpose is to give veterans one of the best days of their lives before they are gone.

So when Honor Flight Tri-State Director Cheryl Popp called me one day and asked if I would help on this book, I said yes without hesitation. I can never do enough to repay all the veterans who fought for us in World War II, Korea and Vietnam, but I can tell their stories so that others can appreciate what they did.

Our veterans are a national treasure, an American legacy of history and wisdom. We owe them our gratitude and respect, to show them that what they fought for has not been lost. It's our turn to pick up the torch of freedom they have passed to us as they march off into the mists.

Besides, they are still my heroes. Meeting and interviewing the men who won World War II was a dream come true for that boy who played army.

Stories that Capture the American Spirit
CHERYL POPP

I did not play army but my brothers did.

We did "girl" things like playing jacks in the driveway and babysitting for the neighborhood kids.

My father was a World War II vet, who threw his uniform and duffle bag out as soon as he came home. He was finished with that part of his life and he never talked about it. Only much later, in the last chapter of his life, did he talk to my brother about the war. I asked him a few questions and in his quiet way he once again tried to protect me from it all. He told me, "War is for men and you should just live your life and have babies and bake cookies."

When I told him I had already done that and needed to make a difference, he just smiled.

Vietnam was "my" war. We lived it through TV commentators and headlines. I experienced it in a different way than my co-author, Peter Bronson did. I lived it through the anxiety that my husband would be drafted when we had a small child. We never protested the Vietnam War, but I cannot say that I supported it either.

The politicians were running it and that bothered me. But I hardly thought about it until our friends started returning home with blank stares.

We saw the aftermath with our friends who had served. Why were they so different? We didn't understand what they had lived through, how the black-and-white images of war had turned to living color in their lives. How it all fit together never really made much sense to me until recently.

On my very first Honor Flight trip, I became painfully aware of how our veterans felt. They never expected to be thanked for something that they did "because it was our job." I looked into their eyes and saw the lives well lived in spite of what they had seen and what they had endured for my freedom.

We have inherited their legacy, and I wanted to tell their stories before it was too late. I wanted to tell the next generation about their courage and overwhelming sacrifice. Not in clichés, but in real stories from the veterans and their families. Stories their Honor Flight has allowed them to tell, one last time.

This book is for people who care, who are finally ready to listen. These stories have stood the test of time. Many have been kept buried for sixty years or more, and were finally set free when the veterans were reunited on their Honor Flight. They are purely American stories, told by those who lived them.

We want this book to make a difference, so their *Legacy of Courage* will be told again and again, handed down from generation to generation, so we may never forget what they won for us and remember that it is ours to lose.

It is our turn, now, to take their example of citizenship and pass it on. We need to tell the next generations that the greeter in Wal-Mart is not just an old man. The hat he wears, with the insignia of his battalion or squadron from World War II, Korea or Vietnam, was not purchased in a gift shop. He earned it.

We hope that people who read their stories will stop and smile when they meet a veteran, and thank him or her for their service. A conversation, a silent salute means so much.

The brave men and women who serve our country understand all this. They have volunteered to defend freedom on our behalf. The legacy of heroes is carried on through them. They carry the torch of freedom for the world.

This *Legacy of Courage* is more than just a book. These stories from our heroes describe and define the spirit that made America the greatest nation on earth. It needs to be passed on.

We hope you enjoy this journey with us.

Cheryl A Popp

Red Tail P-51s escort
B-17 Bombers;
the bomber captain,
then and now; mission log.

Our Hero

DATE	MAKE OF AIRCRAFT	CLASS	TYPE	CERTIFICATE NUMBER	MAKE OF ENGINE	H. P.	REMARKS OR INSPECTOR'S SIGNATURE CERTIFICATION NUMBER AND RATING
11-5-44	BOEING	B-17	G	U.S. ARMY	WRIGHT	4800	MISSION # 1
11-6-44	BOEING	B-17	G	U.S. ARMY	WRIGHT	4800	MISSION # 2
11-7-44	BOEING	B-17	G	U.S. ARMY	WRIGHT	4800	MISSION # 3
11-8-44	BOEING	B-17	G	U.S. ARMY	WRIGHT	4800	PRACTICE MISSION
11-10-44	BOEING	B-17	G	U.S. ARMY	WRIGHT	4800	MISSION # 4
11-13-44	BOEING	B-17	G	U.S. ARMY	WRIGHT	4800	PRACTICE MISSION
11-17-44	BOEING	B-17	G	U.S. ARMY	WRIGHT	4800	MISSION # 5
11-19-44	BOEING	B-17	G	U.S. ARMY	WRIGHT	4800	MISSION # 6
11-20-44	BOEING	B-17	G	U.S. ARMY	WRIGHT	4800	NIGHT TRANSITION
11-22-44	BOEING	B-17	G	U.S. ARMY	WRIGHT	4800	MISSION # 7
11-25-44	BOEING	B-17	G	U.S. ARMY	WRIGHT	4800	PRACTICE MISSION

I HEREBY CERTIFY THAT THE FOREGOING ENTRIES ARE TRUE AND CORRECT.

SIGNED *Herbert M Neilson*

> *"Uncommon valor was a common virtue."*
>
> —*Adm. Chester Nimitz after the Battle of Iwo Jima.*

CHAPTER ONE
Legacy of Courage

Who were these warriors?

What kind of men could stand in bread lines to survive the Great Depression, then stand in lines that snaked around city blocks to enlist in the military and go to war after the attack on Pearl Harbor?

They insist they were nothing special. "The real heroes were the men who didn't come home," they say. "I just did my duty."

They did a lot more than that. They overcame fear, battlefield wounds, bitter cold, scorching heat and shocking, grisly death to overcome the enemy and win the war. They defeated the fearsome war machine of Germany and vanquished the fanatical brutality of Japan.

The Cincinnati region has a small army of its own who served in World War II with honor, distinction, courage and uncommon valor. These are a few of their stories.

Flak, Fighters and Raw Fear Over Germany

Herb Heilbrun, B-17 Pilot
Distinguished Flying Cross

It was Christmas Day, 1944. Herb Heilbrun was piloting a 27-ton B-17 Flying Fortress bomber at thirty-thousand feet over Czechoslovakia, on a mission to destroy a synthetic oil refinery in a small town named Brux. The cloudless sky was clear, the sun was shining and the air was smooth as his squadron approached the target.

Suddenly the sky erupted in a solid wall of flak – a square black thundercloud, lit from within by flashes of hell-red lightning.

It was a "box barrage" of anti-aircraft artillery from hundreds of guns on railroad flatcars that were rolled out of tunnels to meet the bombers. The German guns – 88 mm and 155 mm – each fired huge twenty-pound shells at a rate of fifteen to twenty per minute, targeting a designated rectangle over the refinery. Each shell was timed to detonate at precisely the altitude the bombers were flying. The B-17 pilots knew this run would be bad. They had groaned during the 6 a.m. flight briefing when the red string on their mission map stretched across Europe and pointed to heavily defended Brux.

"The cockpit turns into a chapel pretty fast," Heilbrun recalled. "Seconds turn into minutes when they throw that stuff up at you."

The American bomber crews had no choice but to fly straight into it as their lumbering bombers were hammered and shaken by flak bursts like geese being shot-gunned out of the sky. If they banked or changed altitude, they would disrupt their precise echelon formation, lose the protection of interlocking fire from their gunners, collide with other bombers or even drop bombs on planes in their own squadron.

As Heilbrun gripped the controls he breathed hard through his black rubber oxygen mask. He was layered in wool and leather to hold off the fifty-below chill of high altitude, so a crewmate helped him struggle into his forty-pound flak jacket and pull down his goggles. They flew straight, steady and level into the dark cloud of high explosives. "I stayed in my position."

In his Cincinnati living room 71 years later, he reached into a drawer and picked up a piece of jagged metal that looked like part of a broken stick; then another, slightly larger piece, with the same sharp, uneven edges and surprising weight. One of his crew had swept those pieces of shrapnel out of their plane that day after they landed. When they counted the holes in their B-17, they found 49 hits from the flak storm. Only one crewman had been wounded, in the foot. They were lucky. Merry Christmas.

Only a few years earlier, when Christmas still meant candy canes and presents under a tree, Heilbrun had been hooked on dime-store paperbacks about World War I flying aces. As boys growing up in the North Avondale neighborhood of Cincinnati, he and his friends were crazy about airplanes. They spent hours carefully building authentic models of those World War I biplane Spads and Sopwith Camels, stretching tissue paper over glued balsa wood frames. They painted their models with syrupy "dope," dried them in the sun to stretch the paper over the wings and fuselage, installed rubber-band motors and wound up the plastic propellers.

Then when his mother was gone, Heilbrun and his buddies would climb upstairs to a second floor window, set one of their colorful model airplanes on fire with a match and launch it out the window. "All that work was gone in a few seconds. But it made a spectacular sight."

Little did he know that he would one day sit with his hands on the controls of America's most advanced bomber, flying over Europe through a tornado of steel and smoke as he watched real bombers and fighters, carrying real men he knew, spiral and crash in flames like those models he launched out a window.

Heilbrun flew 261 hours and 50 minutes in combat. Although the requirement began at twenty missions earlier in the war, it gradually escalated as pilots and crews were lost. By the time he arrived in late 1944 at his airfield in Foggia, Italy, he was told by his commanding officer: "You will take your assigned airplane to Germany thirty-five times. If you can bring it back thirty-five times, you can go home."

"We dropped millions and millions of bombs," he said. "That's how you win a war."

'Dear God, let what we love be unchanged – not for my own gain, but so that those who don't come back will not have died in vain.'

The names of targets that caused cold sweats at briefings are now long forgotten: Moosbierbaum Oil Refinery, Austria; Blechammer Oil Refinery, Germany: Pola Naval Installations, Italy. But he can never forget the ache and weariness of nine-hour missions wrestling a 54,000-pound B-17 Flying Fortress at nearly 200 mph. "That's a long time to have your ass shot off and you can't go to the bathroom," he said.

During one harrowing stretch, while the allies were trying to shut down Hitler's fuel supply, he flew three consecutive missions against oil refineries, each at least nine hours. "Usually they would give you a couple of days off to rest. But not that time." The crews shook their heads in disbelief when they were told they would fly more than 27 hours in three days. When he finished the third mission, Heilbrun collapsed on his bunk, almost comatose from fatigue.

The B-17s were beloved by their crews for their amazing ability to take a punch and keep on fighting. "There was no other plane like it," Heilbrun said. On the wall of his living room is a lithograph of a Flying Fortress limping home from a bombing mission with nearly all of its tail shot away and gaping holes torn in the fuselage. Depicting a true story, it shows the crippled plane being escorted by a German ME-109 fighter plane, whose pilot did not have the heart to finish off the valiant bomber – a thrilling story told in the book *A Higher Call*, by Adam Makos and Larry Alexander. The German pilot, Franz Stigler, risked his own life to escort the shot-up, crippled B-17 and its wounded crew through German flak batteries so that it could return safely to England on December 23, 1943.

With a payload of six 1,000-pound bombs or a dozen 500-pounders, each Boeing B-17 was armed with four gun turrets – top, chin, tail and belly – plus two waist gunners. The forward guns encircled the pilot and co-pilot, making a deafening .50 cal. machine-gun racket in combat – which Heilbrun calls "a beautiful sound." The alternative – jammed guns, or guns silenced by wounded or killed gunners, meant the aircraft was defenseless.

A B-17 was as long as a semi-truck, at 74 feet, and had a 103-foot wingspan, mounted with four Wright R-1820 turbo-supercharged radial "Cyclone" engines at 1,200 horsepower each. When the engines were throttled up before takeoff, the entire airplane would tremble and shake with eagerness to get off the ground and get into the fight.

The workhorse bombers of World War II flew in geometrically engineered "box" formations, stacked in echelon so that each gun had a field of fire to cover the squadron – forming a "Flying Fortress." They were decorated with cartoons painted on their noses, often pinups or girlfriends in swimsuits, and had colorful names such as "She Devil," "Bronx Bomber," "Murder Inc.," "Calamity Jane" and "Hitler's Headaches." They accounted for nearly half of all the bombs dropped on Germany and its occupied territories in World War II.

But as the bombers were shot up and shot down, Heilbrun and his crew were assigned to different planes. On one mission, they had to fly a rolling wreck that was long overdue for service or the salvage yard. "It was an old airplane from the 8th Air Force. It had long hours on the sheet and nothing had been done with it. I thought 'You can't keep it going that long without doing something.'"

He knew the limits of those Cyclone engines. Before he was sent to flight training, he had worked at the Cincinnati factory where they were made, testing and building them.

As they flew their rattle-trap, high-mileage bomber to the target that day, the crew spotted smoke leaking out of the No. 2 engine on the co-pilot's

*Heilbrun's flying helmet, oxygen mask
(Courtesy of his personal collection)*

side. Then the outboard engine on the pilot's side started smoking too. They had to bank out of the squadron formation and turn back.

"We were over the Dolomites (mountain range in northeastern Italy). We were a long way from home and we were alone. I prayed, 'Lord, just get me over the Dolomites.' I didn't want to look at our altitude. We could bail out, but that would put us on the ground to be captured." To lighten the plane, they dumped their bombs, their 40-pound flak suits and both .50 cal. waist guns that could be easily dismounted.

Heilbrun's Distinguished Flying Cross was awarded for "heroism or extraordinary achievement" after he brought his crippled B-17 and crew home safely.

Somehow, they made it over the mountain peaks. Then oil started leaking out of a third engine.

Heilbrun prayed again. "Lord, just get me half-way down the Adriatic to friendly territory." Finally, as they got closer to their airbase, he radioed in, "Foxtail One-Two to Longstreet. Two engines gone, one leaking oil. I need clearance for a straight-in approach on One-Seven."

As they finally touched down and rolled to a stop, "Needless to say, the crew was pretty happy." A major raced up in a jeep to greet them as they climbed out of the plane and told Heilbrun, "Lieutenant, that's a pretty good job you did."

Heilbrun didn't stop to realize he was outranked. He was as hot as the bomber's smoking, oil-parched engines. "I got up nose-to-nose and told him, 'I used to test these engines. I know every working part. To send ten men up in a plane like that is criminal. What I'd like you to do is take this plane, run it up to 4,200 RPM and fly it up your ass."

He could have been court-martialed for insubordination. Instead, the major looked the other way, let the outburst pass – and recommended Heilbrun for the Distinguished Flying Cross, which is awarded for "heroism or extraordinary achievement."

The golden medal shows a four-bladed propeller on a sunburst square, attached to a blue ribbon with red and white stripes. It now sits on white satin in a box at his home, next to the canvas flying cap he wore and the black rubber oxygen mask that kept him alive in an unpressurized bomber at 30,000 feet.

He took the cap and mask with him when he left the Army Air Corps. "A few weeks later I got a bill for $15," he laughed. "I paid it."

Heilbrun keeps everything. He still has report cards, hundreds of shooting medals from his pistol competitions, black-and-white photos of his high school friends, even the center "Boeing" button from the steering yoke of the last B-17 he flew in combat, pried loose and presented to him by his crew. And he has the little worn and faded leather-covered diary he kept from 1944.

It still gives him goose-bumps when he turns to the pages he wrote on the day when he watched a B-17 twist out of formation after a direct flak hit. It was piloted by his best friend from Texas flight school. "I asked my waist gunner to keep an eye on it. He saw it hit a mountain. I asked if he saw any chutes. He said no."

Decades later, Heilbrun found out that his friend Lyle Pearson had bailed out, survived the crash and was held as a POW in Germany for the rest of the war. He tracked Lyle down in Minnesota for an emotional reunion. But at the time of the crash, he was sure his buddy was dead. The prayer he wrote in his diary that day said:

"Dear God, let what we love be unchanged – not for my own gain, but so that those who don't come back will not have died in vain."

Heilbrun made another amazing discovery 42 years after the war ended. He read in the local paper about a reunion in Cincinnati of the Tuskegee Airmen, the black pilots who flew red-tailed P-51 Mustangs, often assigned to escort B-17s. He decided to go and say thanks. "They had saved my tail so many times."

At the reunion, he grabbed the first pilot he saw and introduced himself. It was Tuskegee pilot John Leahr, also from Cincinnati. As they talked, they realized they had been on some of the same missions over Europe – including one to Brux. Leahr realized he had flown fighter escorts alongside Heilbrun's B-17.

As they got to know each other, they discovered they had grown up just a few blocks apart. They were the same age. They both had worked for Wright Aeronautical in Lockland, a Cincinnati suburb, before they went to war. And both had grown up dreaming about becoming a pilot.

They even attended the same grade school. When Heilbrun dug out his class picture from Miss Pritchell's second grade in 1928, he showed it to Leahr. They were both in the photo – standing right next to each other.

Their incredible story made headlines and they were invited to speak about their experience. They gave more than eighty talks together around the country and were awarded a medal from the Harvard Foundation for Intercultural Race Relations. Their story was told in a thrilling book, *Black and White Airmen: Their True History*, and they were featured in shows on the History Channel and PBS.

Herb Heilbrun (top) and
John Leahr (bottom)

John Leahr told audiences about buying his own ticket to Alabama and riding in the train's "colored section" to join the Tuskegee Airmen. He remembered being told by his commanding officer, "You boys came down here to fly airplanes, not to change society. If anybody gives you a hard time off the base, you're on your own."

Years later, Leahr still got angry to think that black pilots were good enough to die in battle defending their country, but their country would not defend them. The message he heard was, "This is the South and you are still black men. Your lives mean nothing to us."

"I'd always had dreams of flying, but there was no place for black pilots," he recalled in an interview before his death. "The military thought they'd show we couldn't do it and then close the program."

But they surprised everyone. Leahr flew 132 missions as the Tuskegee Airmen earned a reputation for valor, fierce fighting and combat victories. Among B-17 pilots they were known as the "Red Tails," whose distinctive colors stood out among fighter escorts. Those "little friend" escorts made the difference between life and death by battling the German Luftwaffe fighters that filled the skies over Germany and often waited like wolves on the other side of the flak curtains.

"Little friend, we're on fire," Leahr would hear on his radio as he circled above the flak clouds, waiting for the bombers to release their bombs and turn for home. "Little friend, we need help. We have 109s on our tail."

"We watched those guys go through hell," he told John Fleischman, author of *Black and White Airmen*. "We're sitting out on the side waiting for them to come out, and we could see them getting hit. If they got hit in the bomb bay, the plane just exploded into a great big ball of fire. The whole plane blew up and then it was nothing.

"When they came off target, that's when the enemy fighters used to really get them. These guys would come off the target all shot up. Maybe they'd have a couple of engines knocked out. Maybe on fire. That's when we would try to pick them up. They'd call us 'little friend.' 'Little friend, I'm going down.' Or, 'Little friend, I'm losing altitude. Can you see us? The pilot's dead.' Or, 'The copilot's injured. Stay with us. Little friend, stay with us.'

"In some instances, we were able to escort them far enough from the target so that they could make it on back. We would be running out of gas. We knew to the minute how long we had before we wouldn't make it back ourselves. The stragglers would be very slow, traveling on two engines, but we stayed with them long enough to get them out of range of enemy fighters."

The two Cincinnati pilots, who hardly even knew each other in second grade, had no idea they were side by side again in the skies over Europe. But once they got together, Herb and John became good friends, barnstorming the nation to tell their stories.

Leahr died in March 2015. But Heilbrun kept going, speaking to schoolkids, veterans' groups and other crowds, spreading the story of a friendship that spanned six decades, stretching from 30,000 feet over Germany to their own backyards.

At age 94, Heilbrun's memories remained as vivid as his amazing life that outshined even the flying aces from those boyhood paperbacks. He has had adventures that most kids only dream about. At age 20, he was presented with a factory fresh, polished aluminum B-17G bomber, with a nine-member crew, and ordered to fly it 7,075 miles to Italy. He filled his diary with daily reports in A-plus cursive penmanship, until one day he had to stop. Too many friends and crew members killed. "It just got to be too much."

Like so many veterans who won the war, he came home, started a family and went to work. He had a successful career in real estate and became president of the Cincinnati Real Estate Board in 1970. And he continued to serve his country, helping disabled veterans and delivering prayers at graduations of veterans who completed counseling and treatment at the local Veterans Court.

A few years ago, he flew again with his friend John Leahr, on an Honor Flight. "It was wonderful," he said. He became a leading ambassador for Honor Flight Tri-State, spreading the word and recruiting other veterans to share the experience of a lifetime.

"Anything I can do for Honor Flight is what I have to do. I want to help in any way I can. I want as many veterans as possible to enjoy a day like the one I received. It was fantastic. They cared. The word 'care' just means more than anything. They treated us royally. Anything we wanted they had ready for us – they would not even let us buy our own Coca-Cola.

"We came back after the war and never really thought we were anything special. But on Honor Flight day you can really feel the respect of the younger generation. Unless you are a veteran you cannot describe what it feels like to be honored like this – it is so emotional. We're brothers. It's that simple. Any man who puts himself in harm's way to protect our country is my brother."

The war is long past. But it's always with him. "It was the greatest experience and thrill I've ever known. I was glad to come home, but there was a bit of sadness mixed in. Some small part of me will always remain there."

When he came home from the war and met his family at the Cincinnati train station in 1945, his grandmother scolded him, "Herb, look at your shoes. Your heels are run down. You can't go out in shoes like that."

"Here I was just back from thirty-five missions, and she just had no idea at all." It was the kind of jarring collision with the world at home that veterans never forget. They find it almost impossible to describe what it's like to step from one dimension to another, from war-torn insanity and death into everyday, normal peacetime society. Maybe, in an unexpected way, that was the answer to his prayer: "Let what we love be unchanged." His grandmother's innocence; her blithe security to worry about something as trivial as the worn heels on his shoes – that showed "things unchanged," thanks to the sacrifice of men like Herb Heilbrun and the others who did not come home.

But don't ask him what it's like to be a hero. "The next time I find one I'll ask him and tell you what he had to say," he might answer. "There were no heroes in cockpits. Just ordinary men in extreme situations who did what they were taught to do."

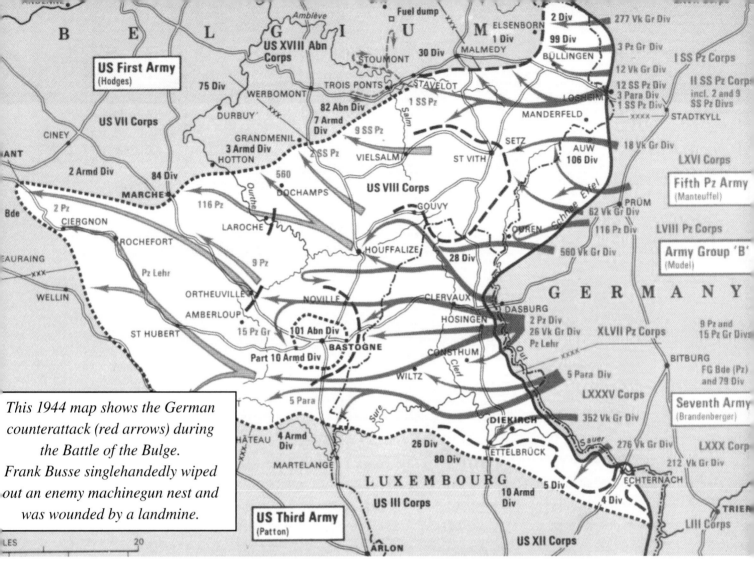

This 1944 map shows the German counterattack (red arrows) during the Battle of the Bulge. Frank Busse singlehandedly wiped out an enemy machinegun nest and was wounded by a landmine.

'It was colder than hell. Oh, it was cold.'

Capt. Frank J. Busse, U.S. Army

Bronze Star, Battle of the Bulge

Minster, Ohio is just south of New Bremen, west of Botkins, and about one hundred miles straight north of Cincinnati. In the 1940s it was practically next door to Germany.

"In the town where I grew up, everybody spoke German. There were four different dialects, and I grew up speaking them all fluently," said Frank J. Busse, whose German name and German language skills started causing him problems as soon as he was drafted into the U.S. Army.

It was 1943, and the war was raging in Europe. Busse, whose name rhymes with "fussy," was a pre-med student at the University of Dayton when his induction notice came in the mail. He found out he was good at handling all kinds of weapons – M-1 rifles, water-cooled machine guns and heavy mortars – and he breezed through Basic Training like a pro.

"The officers were suspicious of my name. And I could speak German," he recalled in an interview for the Veterans History Project at the Cincinnati and Hamilton County Public Library. "I told my friends I could speak German and I showed them."

They also noticed that he handled training as if he had been through it before. "I didn't have any previous training, I was just good at it. But I think the Army thought I was a plant."

He soon proved otherwise. Serving with the 78th Infantry Division at the Battle of the Bulge, he took on an enemy machinegun nest and was awarded the Bronze Star for heroism. Or as he put it, "I had the opportunity to destroy an enemy machinegun placement and neutralized four German soldiers. I did it singlehandedly."

Later that December in 1944, he was wounded when one of the men in his platoon stepped on a "Bouncing Betty" landmine. "The way they worked, you'd step on it and walk away and then it would come up out of the ground – boom! He was killed instantly and I got sprayed by it."

He was sent to a field hospital for two weeks of treatment, then rushed back to the frontlines for one of the most vicious, last-ditch counterattacks by the Germans, as Panzer and Tiger tanks backed by all the infantry and artillery Germany could scrape together broke through U.S. lines in Belgium, creating a huge bulge in the front. As the battle began on December 16, fog and overcast skies kept allied aircraft grounded for seven long days, neutralizing American air superiority as the German's "blitz" overran hundreds of U.S. troops who were captured and, in some cases, lined up and shot on the spot.

'I had the opportunity to destroy an enemy machinegun placement and neutralized four German soldiers. I did it singlehandedly.'

More than twenty years later, Busse had problems with his back. Two surgeons removed more than forty pieces of shrapnel from that Bouncing Betty mine. Pieces of it could still be seen in a blue shadow under the skin on his forearm in 2012. "To this day I still have never received a Purple Heart medal for being wounded," he said, shaking his head as he pointed to the bits of German steel embedded in his body.

During his brief stay in the field hospital, he had the rare opportunity to witness one of the infamous meltdowns by Gen. George S. Patton. A captain in the Quartermasters Corps (supplies) was also in the hospital, and Patton came looking for him. "He came in asking 'Where in the hell is my fuel? He was madder than hell. While he was there he dropped his pearl-handled pistols, took off his pants, changed his underwear as the doctors stood there, and all the time he was giving this guy hell, just madder than hell."

Later, in the Ardennes Forest, Busse was in another group of combat G.I.s who were encouraged by Supreme Commander Gen. Dwight Eisenhower and Gen. Omar Bradley. "They came out into the field to talk to us – not the field of battle, they stayed at the rear."

Busse was seldom at the rear. "I was always on the frontlines. When our chaplain would come around when the battle stopped for a while, he would use the hood of his Jeep as an altar and our helmets were our pews. We sat on our helmets."

He recalled, "We rode into battle on the back of Gen. Patton's tanks one time. It was colder than hell. Oh, it was cold."

The 78th Infantry Division, nicknamed the "Lightnings" was in the thick of the war in Europe. The Lightnings broke the vaunted "impregnable" German Siegfried Line that was studded with deadly pillboxes and "dragon's teeth" cement pylons to disable and block tanks. At the time, the *Stars & Stripes* newspaper of the U.S. military described what the 78th Division faced:

```
Ingeniously concealed concrete pillboxes guarded every square
yard of ground, firing slits covered all approaches. The ground
surrounding these 16 foot thick monsters was sown with deadly anti
tank and anti personnel mines. Concertina wire entanglements spiraled
across the countryside. Intricate networks of ground entrenchments
afforded the enemy movement and cover for forward firing positions.
The entire diabolical system was completely registered in by
artillery and mortar units which could lay down a murderous barrage
on any threatened point.
```

The Lightnings broke through and drove into the Ruhr Valley industrial heart of Germany, crippling war production and capturing their share of 300,000 soldiers of the Wehrmacht, the S.S. and the Hitler Youth who were forced to surrender after fighting tenaciously to defend every inch of their homeland, town by town, house by house, room by room.

The U.S. Army history of the 78th Division describes the bloody December of 1944, when the Lightnings were ordered to hold their ground "at all costs."

```
On the 13th these regiments smashed into Simmerath, Witzerath and
Bickerath and were fighting for Kesternich when Von Rundstedt
launched his counteroffensive in the Monschau area, 18 December. The
78th held the area it had taken from the Sigfried Line against the
violent German attacks throughout the winter. The Division attacked,
30 January 1945, and took Kesternich, 2 February, the town of Schmidt
on the 8th and captured intact the vital Schwammanauel Dam the
next day.
```

Capt. Busse led his own Lightning bolts through some of the most brutal battles of the war, as Germany dug in to the last man to defend its Fatherland. Finally, as the war came to a close and Hitler was forced to surrender, Busse began to think about going home to Cincinnati.

But then his German language skills said, "kein glück" – no such luck.

"I was ready to be shipped back to the states. The war was over and I had no other position or duty in Germany. Then I heard my name called. Being an officer, I knew that was bad news so I didn't answer. The MPs picked me up two days later and asked me why I didn't answer. I told them, 'You probably didn't pronounce my name right.'"

It was a nice try, but the Army had noticed that he spoke German and had a special new duty for him. "A Lt. Col. from West Point told me I was assigned to find Army Air Force people who were shot down. I told him I had no qualifications and didn't know anything about it. He said, 'There isn't anything to it. Just find the bodies, dig 'em up, identify them and re-inter them.'

"I told him, 'Colonel, you can take this job and shove it right up your ass.'"

That was verboten. Busse was court-martialed and busted from captain to lieutenant. And he was assigned to Graves and Registration for two-and-a-half years. "I never saw the colonel. He never came out in the field to see what we were doing."

Busse led a team of eighty – forty clerk-typists and forty soldiers who were always on the move, through Germany, Holland, Denmark, the Netherlands and Sweden. "Their dog-tags were how we identified them. Local civilians were often helpful in finding the graves where they had been buried. We dug them up, put them in pine coffins and re-interred them in France."

Ironically, a team from his family's business, Miller, Busse & Borgmann Funeral Home in Cincinnati, was sent to monitor his work. "But they had nothing to offer us." Nobody wanted any part of his assignment.

By the time he finally was shipped home, to return to the family business, Busse and his unit had recovered the remains of fifty thousand Americans and one thousand Canadians. He was awarded an Oak Leaf Cluster from Canada for his distinguished service. Thousands of American and Canadian families have Frank J. Busse of Minster and West Chester, Ohio to thank for finding their sons, brothers and husbands who otherwise would have been forever listed as missing in action.

It was very tough duty. "Officers were issued two bottles of liquor each month. When I became the company commander of Graves and Registration, they doubled my ration because of the job I was doing. I was drinking pretty heavily and I did become an alcoholic. I'm not proud of it. My lovely wife is what saved me. She got me to stop, and for that I can't thank her enough."

But finally, his German paid off. "The burgermeisters – that's the mayor – were often uncooperative. In one meeting, this burgermeister told his people 'We're not cooperating with these people." I told him, "Genug von diesem pferdscheise," Busse repeated in perfect German almost seventy years later.

Translated: "Enough of this horseshit."

The burgermeiseter's eyes popped and he ordered his people to cooperate immediately. "We went right to work," Busse said. "I think he was surprised I spoke such good German."

The 78th Division in World War II accounted for one Medal of Honor, 599 Silver Stars, 3,909 Bronze Stars and 5,454 Purple Hearts. Frank J. Busse accounted for one of those Bronze Stars, but never got his Purple Heart.

His courage under fire and stubborn standards of excellence in the aftermath of the war gave countless families a gift of peace, knowing their loved ones had been found at last and put to rest.

U.S. soldiers sit on a captured German Panzer Tank at the Battle of the Bulge.

Lt. Frank Busse relied on local civilians and dog-tags like these to recover and identify the bodies of thousands of Allied soldiers who were killed in action.

A Daring Mission

The Doolittle Tokyo Raiders was a group of eighty men from all walks of life who flew into history on April 18, 1942. They were all volunteers and this was a very dangerous mission. Sixteen B-25 bombers took off from the deck of the USS Hornet, led by (then Col.) Jimmy Doolittle. They were to fly over Japan, drop their bombs and fly on to land in a part of China that was still free. Of course, things do not always go as planned.

—www.doolittleraider.com

Twin-engine B-25 bombers were strapped down to the deck of the USS Hornet, then launched for the first time from the deck of an aircraft carrier in the daring Doolittle Raid on April 18, 1942.

The Raid That Punched Back for Pearl Harbor

Tom Griffin, U.S. Army

Distinguished Flying Cross, Doolittle Raid

Somewhere over China, Tom Griffin's plane ran out of gas and he bailed out along with the rest of the five-man crew. He jumped into a storm-battered night so dark he could have been falling through a soot-blackened chimney. He landed in a tree, but was somehow unhurt.

Narrowly escaping capture by the Japanese several times, the crew regrouped and made their way out of China, back to the U.S. Army – where Griffin was congratulated and sent right back to war in North Africa. The navigator from Green Bay, Wisconsin, who made Cincinnati his home after the war, was just 25.

"We were mad," he said years later. "We wanted to hit 'em back."

That's why eighty Army Air Corps aviators volunteered for a one-way mission that made them famous around the world as "Doolittle's Raiders."

"Suicide mission" brings to mind Japanese kamikazes crashing airplanes packed with explosives into U.S. aircraft carriers and battleships in the Pacific. But before there were kamikazes, while the surprise attack on Pearl Harbor was still an aching bruise to America's pride, the Doolittle Raid was about as close as Americans came to a suicide mission.

On April 18, 1942, Griffin climbed aboard an overloaded B-25 bomber that was sloshing with fuel and bombs, 1,500 pounds over its maximum load, and took off from the pitching, slippery deck of the aircraft carrier USS Hornet. They had just four hundred feet of runway to get airborne or crash into the sea. What they were about to attempt as their engines warmed up had never been done before.

Their twin-engine B-25 Mitchells each carried four five-hundred-pound bombs and five hundred gallons of extra fuel. Their radios and some of their guns had been removed to reduce weight. The .50-cal. machine guns in the tail of the planes were replaced with wooden sticks, painted to look like guns, as a bluff to discourage enemy fighters. But even all that would not be enough to get back – and they couldn't land a bomber on an aircraft carrier even if they could return to the Hornet.

Their trip was a one-way ticket. Just enough fuel to get to Tokyo, drop their bombs, then fly as

fast and as far as possible before bailing out or crashing. If the crews were lucky, they might get to friendly territory in China, perhaps refuel and fly on to a safe airfield beyond Japanese control. Attempts to negotiate a safe landing in Russia were rebuffed by Stalin's government.

That was the Doolittle Raid, which was celebrated by America as if the U.S. team had just won the World Series and the Olympics combined. It was named for Lt. Col. James "Jimmy" Doolittle, the renowned pilot who had set speed records before the war. He came up with the mission and led it by flying the first B-25 Mitchell off the deck of the Hornet just four months after Pearl Harbor.

"It really made us happy to see that first plane take off," Griffin recalled in an interview before he died in 2013 at 96.

Their flight was a one-way ticket. 'We had no more instructions than to make sure your harness is snug and count to eight before you pull the cord.'

The sixteen B-25s that took off from the Hornet that morning had to make an emergency launch after the carrier had been spotted by a Japanese patrol boat, which radioed a warning before it was sunk by one of the Hornet's escorts, the light cruiser USS Nashville. As the crews scrambled to their airplanes, they would have to take off ten hours early, adding another 170 miles to a flight that was already longer than any bomber mission before.

Those men knew they would probably have to bail out and might never see home again, even if they survived the mission. "We had no more instructions than 'Make sure your harness is snug and count to eight before you pull the cord," Griffin recalled.

By the time they ran out of gas, the mission had covered 2,250 nautical miles and took thirteen hours of flying time. Amazingly, fifteen B-25s reached China, and one landed in Russia, where the five-man crew was held as prisoners for a year. As the other crews crashed, ditched in the sea or bailed out, three were killed in action and eight were captured by the Japanese. Among those captured, some were tortured and three were executed, along with the friendly Chinese who tried to help them. One captured Raider died in prison, and four were rescued by American troops when the war ended in 1945.

The rest who bailed out over China made it safely back to the U.S., with help from the Chinese and an American missionary. Many of the Chinese people who had helped the Americans were executed by the Japanese.

Doolittle parachuted into a dung-heap next to a rice paddy in China. He thought his mission was a failure because the planes were lost. Instead, he was awarded the Congressional Medal of Honor.

Griffin's bomber missed its target, a tank factory, and hit a secondary target, a power plant. They flew as far as they could before the fuel ran dry, then jumped out.

The Doolittle Raid stands among America's most thrilling, proudest victories, an inspiring reminder of our nation's courage, ingenuity and sacrifice. It was an audacious, even reckless mission, but Americans were desperate for some shred of hope, some sense that America could strike back to avenge the shock and loss at Pearl Harbor.

"It was a tremendous success for American morale," Griffin remembered. Anyone from the World War II generation would agree.

What some may have missed, however, is the consensus that emerged among historians 50 years later – that the Doolittle Raid was also a key strategic victory.

Although it inflicted little damage on Japan's war-making industry, it shocked the people of Japan and sent notice that they had awakened the fury of the enemy they attacked at Pearl Harbor. It also provoked Japan's leaders into a reckless attack of their own at Midway Island. During the three-day Battle of Midway, which began June 3, 1942, Japan threw its "whole damn navy" into the fight, in the words of U.S. Navy fliers.

Thanks to timing, luck and a courageous attack by the U.S. Pacific Fleet, America won what has been called "the most stunning and decisive blow in the history of naval warfare." The U.S. Navy's carrier-launched dive-bombers sank four Japanese carriers and one heavy cruiser, while losing only one of their own carriers.

With the pride and strength of their fleet sinking in flames and fountains of black smoke, Japan's Navy was fatally crippled. "From that point on, they were in the defensive mode. We started the ball rolling," Griffin said.

Japan's losses also included 248 aircraft and more than three thousand deaths – including some of its finest pilots who could not be replaced. As the war came to a close, Japan was so desperate for pilots, it forced poorly trained recruits to launch suicide attacks – the kamikazes.

Surviving the Doolittle Raid and making it home from China would be more than enough of a war story for any veteran. But it was not the end of the war for Tom Griffin. He was sent to North Africa, where his plane crashed into the Mediterranean, and Griffin backstroked for an hour and a half to pull a wounded pilot to shore.

Over Sicily, he was shot down again, this time in a B-26 Marauder. As he floated to earth at the end of his parachute harness for the second time, a German pilot in an ME-109 fighter buzzed him repeatedly. Griffin was sure the pilot wanted to shoot him, and assumed his guns must have jammed. Later he found out the pilot was taking propaganda pictures of a downed American flier. "Boy, would I love to have that picture," Griffin laughed.

That was the end of combat for Griffin. He was captured and spent the rest of the war in Stalag Luft III, which was the German prison camp where the original "Great Escape" took place, that later became a hit movie starring Steve McQueen.

Griffin was awarded the Distinguished Flying Cross and the Air Medal with three Oak Leaf Clusters, as well as medals from the government of China.

After the war, he came home and went to work as an accountant, living with his wife and two sons in Cheviot, a Cincinnati suburb. He was among the last of the Doolittle Raiders who met for annual reunions until 2013, the same year Tom Griffin died. That was the final year of the Raiders' toast. Silver cups representing each of the eighty men were turned over as they died, and the remaining men would read their names and drink a toast of rare cognac to their departed crewmates. The last Raider died in 2015.

"I went through the war and never got a scratch," Griffin often said. "The good Lord has been very good to me."

'He was an only son. I wrote the letter.'

Capt. John Sullivan, USMC
Okinawa, Saipan

"My first real encounter with war was on Saipan. We were doing mortar fire training. We took a break and I walked over to an abandoned farmhouse. There was a shoe on the path. I kicked it and it was heavy, so I looked in it and there was a foot still in it. That was my first real introduction to the ferocity of war."

As a lieutenant and later a captain with the 8th Regiment of the 2nd Battalion in the Second Marine Division in the Pacific, John Sullivan saw a lot of the ferocity of war in some of the most horrific battles: Saipan, Okinawa and the Marianas Islands.

He died in February 2012, less than a year after his Honor Flight. "We had the best time of our lives," said his daughter, Kathy Davidson, who served as his guardian on the flight. "I still keep a picture of us together on the Honor Flight on my bedside. His story is taken from her recollections and his interview with the Veterans History Project of the Cincinnati and Hamilton County Public Library.

He enlisted in June 1942, while he was a junior at the University of Cincinnati. He was told to finish college so he could enroll in Officer Training.

"Paris Island (boot camp) was quite a change," he said. "Quite a change. If it doesn't move, paint it. If it moves, salute it. Physically, they pushed you to the limit. One night we ran all night. I was in the best shape of my life."

Assigned to lead an 81mm mortar platoon, he handled the biggest weapon in the battalion. "We could stick one in his hip pocket. You had to kill or you would be killed. But along with that there was this fatalistic attitude that if your number is on a bullet, it will get you no matter where you are. So we had some who would get up and walk around, completely disregarding the enemy fire. I thought about that often. Those two feelings together were very strange."

*'There was danger all around. You didn't know where it was.
You just don't sleep. You don't sleep.'*

After Saipan was secured, he shipped out for the invasion of Okinawa. "We got aboard these little Higgins boats and just circled around off the south tip of the island. We kept on circling around and we sucked the whole Jap army south. We were a feint, a diversion, and it worked."

While the Japanese rushed to defend the southern end of the island, other divisions of Marines landed at the waist of Okinawa and cut the island in half. When kamikaze airplanes began to target Sullivan's boats, they withdrew back to Saipan. "We were told we were the reserve to the reserve to the reserve. I thought, 'How much safer can you be in wartime?'"

Mail Call at Saipan;
The scene on the beach after the landing.

(Courtesy of John Sullivan's
personal collection)

But then orders came down and they were rushed into battle. "There we were, on the line. We had our hands full. We were pinned down with enemy fire. I wrote home to say I was perfectly safe as long as I kept my head down. But you never knew if a band of Japs would come in. We had to be on guard at all times."

As Lt. Sullivan took his unit to set up a defensive position, they discovered a Japanese pillbox. "I hollered 'Come out!' in Japanese, but nobody came out. So we threw a phosphorous grenade in there. They still wouldn't come out. So we got a satchel charge and dumped it in there."

That cleaned out the pillbox.

After they dug in at their position, his BAR (Browning Automatic Rifle) man suddenly opened fire. "A Japanese soldier had crawled up to within four feet of our trench, and nobody even saw him." The next morning they spotted a Japanese patrol in the morning mist and killed 17.

One morning he was awakened by one of his men who said, "Lieutenant, don't move.' 'What's the problem?' I asked. 'Snipers,' he said. I laid there and we figured out they were firing in volleys, and there were three or four seconds between shots as they worked their bolts. So we made our move. One of my men, Joseph Manarino, picked up his pack, threw it over his shoulder and the sniper cut his finger off and shot him right through the heart. Killed him on the spot. He was an only son. I wrote the letter."

Sullivan told about another death that haunted him. As his men were pinned down by heavy sniper fire, they hunched down in their foxholes. A Marine next to Sullivan had several shots ricochet off his helmet. When the firing finally stopped, he decided to check the damage. He took off his helmet, said, "Look at that," and was instantly killed by a sniper shot to the head.

Casualties among the Marines on Okinawa climbed to 50 percent. "There was danger all around," Sullivan said. "You didn't know where it was. You just don't sleep. You don't sleep. On Saipan, one infiltrated and came into a tent, looking for food or whatever it was. There were Marines in there, guys who had been through battles, and one of them was sleeping. He went out of his mind, it frightened him so badly to wake up and see this engine of death over you. They had to take him away."

After surviving Okinawa, Sullivan was among the first Marines sent to Nagasaki almost immediately after the Japanese industrial city was flattened with an atom bomb. "When our Higgins boat came onto shore, I was standing next to a .50 cal. machine gun. We didn't know what to expect. I saw bodies floating in the bay. There were these bags of rotting soybeans piled up all around and it smelled so bad you couldn't catch your breath.

"I looked around to the horizon, and all the way around as far as I could see were aircraft carriers, battleships and cruisers. That was a proud, proud feeling to look at that array of warships, all their guns armed and cocked. Magnificent."

As they moved into the city, nothing was left standing by the bomb, only rubble like snowdrifts, as deep as a man's waist. "There was a radio tower, bent over, the tip was touching the ground from the heat and the blast. As far as I could see there was not one stone left on top of another. The whole city was wiped out. There was no sign of life at all. What civilians we found were in desperate condition. Everything was in chaos."

Radioactive fallout was not well understood at the time. Nuclear explosions were entirely new. "Nobody had any Geiger counters, so we just said, 'I'm alright.'"

His platoon was assigned to find enemy ammunition and take it out to be dumped in the sea. They found a temple booby-trapped with thousands of gallons of gasoline and a stockpile of gas masks – ominous signs of what they might expect if they had been forced to invade Japan. As they destroyed the gas masks, Sullivan and his men cut away the leather parts and gave them to the local Japanese to make shoes. Years later, a Japanese family sent him china as a token of their appreciation.

The Walnut Hills High School graduate came back to Cincinnati after the war as a Marine Captain, finished college and law school, became a partner in a law firm in Carew Tower, then started his own firm with his son. Before he died, he looked back on the Pacific war with mixed emotions.

"I learned a lot by going into the Marine Corps. The discipline is something I follow to this day. I still wear my Marine Corps watch. I have a Marine Corps flag at home. In many ways it was a magnificent experience. It was hard. Tragic. Awful. But it did something to me that stayed with me for my whole life. I never regretted joining the Marine Corps."

Battle scene photographed by Capt. John Sullivan, 1944

Airport Crash Fire Rescue salutes
veterans with water cannons

I never knew it
would mean so much

What a day with my Vet

"Our debt to the heroic men and valiant women
in the service of our own country can never be
repaid. They have earned our undying gratitude.
America will never forget their sacrifice."

— President Harry S. Truman

CHAPTER TWO
Legacy of Honor

Every Honor Flight has its own personality, its own magic. Each is as
different as the weather in May, August and October. But some things
are as predictable as misty eyes at Arlington National Cemetery and a
longing to linger at the Iwo Jima Memorial. There's the look of surprise
and disbelief on the faces of veterans when they are greeted with fire
engine water arches, salutes, bands, hugs and spontaneous gratitude
from strangers. There's the sadness and heartache that passes over like
the shadow of a cloud as memories come flooding back at the World
War II Memorial. And there's the question that comes up over and over
on every flight: "All this for us?" The thrill of an Honor Flight can only
be appreciated by being there – as a guardian or veteran or volunteer.
But the next best thing is to go along with us, as we share the story of
one Honor Flight in May 2015.

Flight log:
A day in the life of an Honor Flight

At 5:15 a.m., Cincinnati still sleeps. Highways that will soon be choked by rush-hour traffic are all but empty, but a dozen veterans have already gathered at Cincinnati/Northern Kentucky International Airport (CVG) and reinforcements are on the way. The Honor Flight day is about to begin.

Some of the World War II and Korean War veterans have been up for an hour or more, coming from local suburbs and cities throughout Southwest Ohio and Northern Kentucky, even as far as Louisville, Dayton and Lexington. They are dressed comfortably in khakis, loose jeans and slacks. They wear gym shoes, mall-walkers and lace-up boots. A few pull on their Honor Flight T-shirts over sport coats or sweatshirts. Their baseball caps don't advertise colleges or golf courses. Their favorite teams are "Army," "Navy" and "USMC," often embellished with gold scrolling and unit insignia that name specific divisions, battles or ships. Many carry canes. More than a dozen roll past in wheelchairs, and are escorted to the front of the room.

One veteran's jacket has a message on the back: **"Fallen Heroes: The nation which forgets its defenders will itself be forgotten."**

A WWII veteran wearing a USMC cap with a globe and anchor on the front is welcomed with a hearty, "Semper Fi!" and replies with a big grin and a crisp salute. At the sound of those two proud words, his face lights up like sunshine emerging from the clouds.

The first people to greet the veterans are members of the Honor Flight Ground Crew. They've also been up for hours so they can arrive early enough to direct everyone to the check-in tables in the departure area, to confirm identification and make sure everyone on the passenger list gets aboard. Ground Crew members can be easily recognized by their neon-green shirts and big smiles. As each veteran arrives, they are given a name tag and T-shirt that says "Honor Flight Tri-State" on the front, with another message on the back:

"If you can read this, thank a teacher. If you can read this in English, thank a veteran."

The men who were drafted or enlisted to fight World

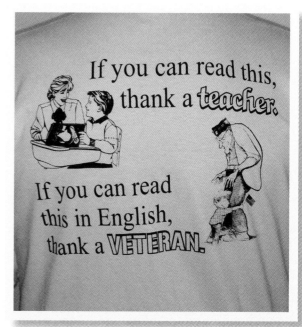

Back of Honor Flight Tri-State T-shirt

34

War II in the 1940s are now in their late 80s and early 90s. Korean War veterans on the Honor Flight are not far behind. Limited by age and infirmities, most have not been very far away from home in months or even years. Many have never been to Washington, D.C. And those who have been there often say they haven't been back since they were soldiers, sailors or young fathers. Some veterans have not been on an airplane in years. A few have never been on an airplane.

As the flight assembles, there are 70 veterans, 70 guardians, three medics, five board members and one writer. Faces of the veterans are pale and uncertain. Heads droop. Shoulders are hunched as if warding off a chill. They look a bit lost and confused, unsure what to expect, uncomfortable so far away from the security of familiar surroundings and reassuring routines.

Near the check-in tables, TV reporters with varnished hair and catalog-model suits do standup interviews as their cameramen roam the crowd. Big Band music and service hymns from the 1940s play on the speaker system. Commercial airline passengers just around the corner crane their necks to see what's going on as they wait in lines for airport security screening.

By 5:45, dozens of rows of chairs are nearly filled and volunteers who paid their way on the flight as guardians are making their first contact with their assigned veterans and getting acquainted. "Where are you from?" "Where did you serve?" "What branch of the military?" "What was it like?"

Family members, who came to participate in the Honor Flight opening ceremony and see off the flight, stand around the edges, filling the open spaces around the chairs as they snap pictures with phones and pocket cameras.

The guardians were briefed a week ago about what to expect, and everyone is ready for a trip that most veterans have waited decades to take – to finally visit the memorials that were built in their honor in Washington, D.C.

Many veterans are traveling with a son, daughter, grandchild or other family member as their guardian. Everyone on the flight has been assigned to one of three color-coded buses they will board after landing in D.C. The excitement is contagious as the crowd waits. The welcoming ceremony is about to begin.

At 6 a.m., the buzz of the crowd grows quiet, silenced by the soft, keening cry of bagpipes in the distance. Gradually, it draws closer. Even the TSA lines come to a halt as travelers stop and stare as the rugged pipers in kilts and sashes march past. The pipes send an electric chill through the crowd as the procession comes into view, as solemn and dignified as their haunting music that echoes from ancient battles, raising hair on the neck and bringing old warriors to their feet. There's a call to stand for the pledge, but the veterans are already on their feet, grabbing their hats off their heads as the rest of the crowd hesitates, then gets the cue and follows the lead of the veterans.

A Transportation and Safety Administration Color Guard leads the way for the pipers, taking a place in front of the room where everyone can see the flags they carry. As the Pledge of Allegiance begins, the veterans' voices are strong and deep, a baritone choir that can be heard clearly over the rest of the crowd. These men don't mumble or whisper or go through the motions. Their pledge is no empty ritual. It's a solemn oath, packed with meaning; a reminder of their deep loyalty to those who were left behind; a testimony to the steep price they have paid to defend "One nation, under God, with liberty and justice for all."

They salute or hold their hats over their hearts, standing ramrod straight at attention. Old shoulders that have been bent under the burden of eight decades are thrown back again; their chins rise up; eyes that have witnessed a lifetime of joys and sorrows, in war and in peace, are locked on the flag that means so much. For those few moments, they could be standing again on the parade grounds at Basic Training, watching the colors being hoisted skyward through the morning mist at reveille.

"The word 'hero' is used all too cheaply today," says Korean War-era veteran and Honor Flight Tri-State Board Member Ed Finke in his welcome speech. "The heroes to me are the veterans in front of me, and we need to remember that." Ed also says that he has heard from many veterans that going to war "was a million dollar experience, but they wouldn't give you a nickel to go through it again." He reminds them that, "Boot Camp was a combination of fear of the unknown and excitement." And that appropriate description also summarizes the feelings of many in the crowd: fear of the unknown and excitement. It puts the day into perspective. After Boot Camp, this will be easy.

"I would like to end with the most important thing I can do when addressing a group of veterans – my salute to you." Finke salutes. The veterans silently return it.

Cheryl Popp, Honor Flight Tri-State director, follows with a prayer:

As we begin our journey together, may God bless our trip today.

May the sun shine, cool breezes blow and the friendships begin, as we bring our treasured veterans to see their memorials.

Lord, please bless the guardians – who have paid their own way, taken time off of work and away from their families to help us honor these brave men and women.

And to our treasured veterans – may this be the beginning of a wonderful day, filled with memories. And may you be blessed all the days of your life. You have given us the freedoms we now enjoy, so please let us take care of you today, as a small gesture from a grateful nation.

Lord, please hold in the palm of your hand those who have gone before us and have given the ultimate sacrifice – and protect those now serving our great nation today.

And Lord, please bless all of the Honor Flight volunteers, board members and medics who work so hard to make this a safe and memorable trip for our veterans.

As everyone says "Amen," Cheryl's husband, Tom Popp, steps forward and calls for a team of guardian flag bearers to come forward. They line up in parallel rows and carefully unfold an eight-by-twelve foot American flag, as Tom recites a poem written by Johnny Cash in the 1970s, "Ragged Old Flag."

I walked through a county courthouse square,
On a park bench an old man was sitting there.

I said ,"Your old courthouse is kind of run down."
He said ,"Nah, it'll do for our little town."

I said, "Your flagpole has leaned a little bit,
and that's a ragged old flag you got hangin' on it."

He said, "Have a seat," and I sat down.
"Is this the first time you've been to our little town?"

I said, "I think it is." He said, "I don't like to brag,
but we're kind of proud of that ragged old flag."

"You see, we got a little hole in that flag there
when Washington took it across the Delaware.

"And it got powder burned the night Francis Scott Key
sat watching it, writing, 'Oh Say Can You See.'

"And it got a bad rip in New Orleans
With Packingham and Jackson tuggin' at its seams.

"And it almost fell at the Alamo
beside the Texas flag, but she waved on, though.

"She got cut with a sword at Chancellorsville,
and she got cut again at Shiloh Hill.

"There was Robert E. Lee, Beauregard, and Bragg,
and the South wind blew hard on that ragged old flag.

"On Flanders Field in World War I,
she got a big hole from a Bertha gun.

"She turned blood red in World War II,
she hung limp and low by the time it was through.

"She was in Korea and Vietnam.
She went where she was sent by her Uncle Sam.

"She waved from our ships upon the briny foam, and
now, they've about quit waving her, back here at home.

"In her good land she's been abused —
she's been burned, dishonored, denied and refused.

"And the government for which she stands
 is scandalized throughout the land.

"And she's getting threadbare and wearing thin,
but she's in good shape for the shape she's in.

"Cause she's been through the fire before
and I believe she can take a whole lot more.

"So we raise her up every morning,
take her down slow every night.

"We don't let her touch the ground
And we fold her up right.

"On second thought — I DO like to brag.
'Cause I'm mighty proud of that ragged old flag."

As the poem ends, the flag is fully unfolded and raised high over the heads of the flag team, then slowly passed, hand-to-hand like a blessing, over everyone in the crowd, first down one side of the room, and back to the front along the other side. Everyone on this Honor Flight has a chance to touch it and pass it along, in a moving ceremony that symbolizes how all Americans serve *under* the flag. Each hand that touches the flag unites veterans, guardians, Honor Flight volunteers and family members in an emotional connection.

To some the flag is a reminder of the country we love. To others it might symbolize the ideals of an exceptional nation as formalized by the Congress: white for innocence, red for valor, blue for justice, and stars representing our divine inspiration. For many veterans, it represents the sacrifices of so many Americans who have given their lives to make sure that our star-spangled banner still waves.

As nearly everyone in the crowd wipes their eyes and clears their throats, the TSA Color Guard and the bagpipers lead everyone to the gate area to the sounds of pipes and drums. Just before boarding, there's another photo-opportunity for veterans and guardians, and then everyone lines up to find a seat, supervised by HFTS board members in red shirts, who are also the tour directors on each bus in the Capital.

The charter flight jetliner taxis to the runway, while passengers point out the windows and call out their amazement. A rainbow of water is arching over the plane. It's a water-canon salute from the airport fire department. Such salutes are usually reserved for retiring airline captains, but this one honors the veterans. "Is that for us?" some ask in disbelief.

Breakfast and beverages help the one-hour flight pass quickly. The conversation is animated as strangers become friends. "Where did you work?" "Do you have children?" "Have you been to the Memorial?"

"I was in a tank," a veteran says. Another one comments, "This really means a lot. Nobody today wants to pass the torch. I sat in the front row today as they passed the flag over us and just cried."

A guardian mentions her service in Iraq and Afghanistan – making an instant bond with her assigned veteran, who served in the Army 70 years earlier.

The arrival at Reagan National Airport (DCA) is greeted again by two airport firetrucks spraying another water-cannon salute as the plane taxis to its reserved gate. Baggage handlers on the ramp and other airport ground crew members offer their own salutes. It's becoming clear: This is no ordinary flight arrival.

As the Honor Flight passengers emerge from the boarding ramp into the airport, there's another touching surprise: Men and women in uniform, airport workers and travelers have formed a flag-waving reception line, welcoming every veteran personally with smiles, hugs, handshakes and sincere gratitude. "Thank you for your service," the greeters say. Many veterans are so overwhelmed they can hardly respond. Some say, "Thank YOU!"

As a small band plays patriotic music and service hymns, families hurrying to catch a plane stop and urge their small children to go up to the veterans and thank them – a lesson that might last a lifetime. Many in the crowd become teary eyed when they see how the heartwarming welcome has brought tears and smiles to the faces of those tough old warriors. It's the ticker-tape parade, the conquering heroes' welcome they never had. It's a homecoming, in a way, too – this city, the center of American government, the home of our national treasures and history, landscaped with sacred monuments to all the founders and defenders of the nation – this is their place. Their citizenship has been ratified by their service. They are in a special category of those who know what it means to be Americans because they earned it and can never take it for granted.

"Overwhelming," says one of the veterans. "All that for us!"

And the gratitude has just begun.

Once everyone is aboard three tour buses, the first stop is the **U.S. Marine Corps Memorial**. It's a powerful work of art. Six struggling soldiers desperately clutch the flagpole together as they fight for footing on the rocky summit of a mountaintop on a tiny island that would be insignificant if not for their victory at the Battle of Iwo Jima.

As they raise the tilting flag. Their strong hands and straining bodies stand for an entire nation's battle to raise the flag of freedom in a titanic battle of good against evil. The flag is never completely upright; the battle is never finished.

The statues are larger than life, 32 feet high, alive with energy and action. The combat Marines carry rifles slung over their shoulders as they push their flag to the top of Mount Suribachi, claiming victory in one of the bloodiest battles of the Pacific War. Their hands grip the flagpole, their arms

The U.S. Marine Corps Memorial depicts the flag-raising on Mt. Suribachi during the Battle of Iwo Jima. Three of the six Marines who raised the flag were killed as the battle raged on for days.

and legs in a tangle on the volcanic rock. The monument seems to move and come alive. As the buses approach along a circular driveway, the angle of the flag gives the optical illusion that it is slowly being raised to a vertical position.

Someone tells the story of the 13th hand on the flagpole – representing the hand of God. It's a myth, but it has survived the decades because so many believe the hand of God was there with the soldiers that day.

For many years, this emotionally moving sculpture was thought to be the World War II Memorial. But it was dedicated by President Dwight D. Eisenhower on the 179th anniversary of the US Marine Corps, to honor the sacrifice of Marines since the 1770s. It stands on a hill, with the top of the flag reaching 60 feet over the surrounding landscape and the outskirts of Arlington National Cemetery nearby.

The rocks on which the Marines stand were brought from Mt. Suribachi. The scene was modeled after a Pulitzer Prize winning photo by Associated Press photographer Joe Rosenthal, taken on February 23, 1945, when the mountain was finally captured from the Japanese.

The Battle of Iwo Jima was one of the worst of the war, with 23,000 Japanese and 22,000 American casualties. The victory marked a turning point, as it provided an airbase for B-29 Superfortresses to bomb the Japanese mainland. Iwo Jima quickly came to symbolize the war in the Pacific, as Rosenthal's photograph was used to sell war bonds and support the troops. Of the six soldiers depicted in the scene – five Marines and a Navy Corpsman – half were killed in action on Iwo Jima in the days after the photograph was taken.

Honor Flight's Marines have a special attachment to the Memorial. On one flight, a Marine veteran lingered as the buses were loading. He sat in his wheelchair by himself, gazing at the statue. When asked if he was OK, he replied, "I left my brother on that rock and I have never seen the Memorial before. It makes me feel closer to him and respect what he helped accomplish there." He was proud of his brother and needed just a few more moments to be alone with his memories.

From the Marine Memorial, it's a short ride to the gates of Arlington National Cemetery. On the way, the tour buses pass the Pentagon, where a plane crashed into the building on September 11, 2001, killing 184 people working inside the unmistakable, massive headquarters of the U.S. Defense Department. Fifty of those victims were buried in Section 64 in Arlington, which overlooks the place where the hijacked plane crashed. Near the crash site is the Pentagon 9-11 Memorial.

Arlington National Cemetery is a place set apart. It immediately commands respect and quiet contemplation. This is the hallowed ground Lincoln spoke about at Gettysburg.

At 624 acres, by the most common measure, it's the largest military cemetery in the United States. It was established during the Civil War, when the property was still owned by Confederate General Robert E. Lee. The estate was seized by the government and used first as an artillery emplacement, then as a cemetery when the first soldier was buried there on May 13, 1864: Pvt. William Christman, 21, of Pennsylvania, killed by sickness, not combat.

Gen. Lee's stately home, Arlington House, still stands in the Cemetery and is open to the public. His wife, Mary Ann Custis Lee, whose family tree included George Washington, was rousted from her home and her beloved gardens at the beginning of the Civil War, when Union officers ordered burials to circle the Lee home out of spite, to make it forever uninhabitable.

In 1877, General Lee's grandson, Curtis Lee, sued for the return of the land to his family. He eventually won the lawsuit, but a year later he sold it back to the United States government for only $150,000, and Arlington National Cemetery began to accommodate the overflow from the U.S. Soldiers National Cemetery in Washington, D.C.

Arlington has changed over the years. Along with the many heroes buried there are 3,800 former slaves, Confederate soldiers, military nurses, generals, admirals, privates, Medal of Honor winners, sailors, airmen, 1940s bandleader Glenn Miller, actors and war heroes Audie Murphy and Lee Marvin, astronauts Roger Chaffe and Gus Grissom who were killed in a fire on Apollo 1 in 1967, civil rights leader Medgar Evers, Presidents John F. Kennedy and William Howard Taft, and the Civil War Union general who started it all by ordering graves to be dug in Robert E. Lee's garden, Gen. Montgomery Meigs.

Soldiers listed as missing in action are remembered with crosses. A section reserved for Confederate soldiers can be spotted near the Confederate Memorial. Pointed headstones mark those graves, the legend says, "to keep Yankees from sitting on them."

During the long stopover at Arlington, veterans and guardians are free to stroll around the grounds and visit individual graves and memorials. It's a beautiful setting. In springtime, rolling hills and green meadows are sprinkled with the confetti of pink-white cherry blossoms that drift like snowflakes into the headstones. Shaded here and there by ancient hardwoods, the linen-white headstones stand in ranks and files, an army of the dead on review.

Generations apart in life, they lie almost shoulder to shoulder in death.

*Headstones mark the graves of Americans who paid
the ultimate price, at Arlington National Cemetery.*

Looking out upon the lush trees and waves of green hills dotted with thousands of simple white headstones, it's impossible to be unmoved by feelings of sadness mixed with honor and deep gratitude for the sacrifice.

All those beautiful sons, brothers, husbands, fathers. Each one was a blessing from God, a treasure to his family, the smile on his father's lips, the mist in his mother's eyes, the love of his wife, the hero to his own sons and daughters – but now the light of love, life and laughter in their eyes is shuttered, put out by a bullet or a bomb or a tiny split second of high velocity steel that shattered a universe and sent shock waves rippling through the world they left behind. The families that loved them and prayed that they would come home safely were never the same again. So many. What an incalculable loss.

Arlington remembers. They rest in a place of highest honor, their names a silent testimony to the price of American liberty. Even those who never made it home for burial are honored at Arlington. If the word "hero" has been devalued by athletes and movie stars, Arlington reminds us all of the real meaning of the word "tragedy." By a strange arithmetic, every name in Arlington is a loss that diminishes us all, but still makes our nation greater.

The veterans quietly move to the Tomb of the Unknown Soldier for the changing of the guard and wreath laying ceremonies

The Tomb of the Unknown Soldier holds the remains of soldiers from several wars.

The United States lost approximately 77,000 killed in World War I. Many were buried in military cemeteries in France. One soldier who was unknown was chosen to be buried at Arlington, the first in the Tomb of the Unknown: *"Here rests in honored glory an American soldier known only to God."*

The Tomb of the Unknown Soldier is guarded 24 hours a day, 365 days of the year.

Since World War I, the unknown soldiers have been chosen from among the unidentified dead by fellow soldiers. The first was singled out from among four caskets when a sergeant silently placed white roses on one of them, then stepped back and saluted the fallen soldiers from World War I.

At the close of World War II, thirteen unknown Americans who had been killed in battle were exhumed from American cemeteries in Europe and Africa and shipped in identical caskets to Epinal, France. Major General Edward J. O'Neill, U.S. Army, chose one at random on May 12, 1958, to be buried in the Tomb of the Unknown.

Other sections of Arlington are set aside for the remains of other unknown soldiers from World War II.

Of the 54,260 Americans who were killed in the Korean Conflict, four identical caskets were exhumed from the National Cemetery of the Pacific in Hawaii. On May 15, 1958, Master Sergeant Ned Lyle, U.S. Army, chose the one that would be moved to Arlington by placing a wreath on the casket.

The most recent soldier in the Tomb of the Unknown was chosen by President Reagan as he stood before the casket of an unidentified casualty from the Vietnam War. "Thank you, dear son, may God cradle you in His loving arms," Reagan prayed as he awarded the unknown soldier the Medal of Honor. Years later, DNA testing identified the remains as Air Force 1/Lt. Michael Joseph Blassie, and his body was claimed by his family. The Medal of Honor stayed at the Tomb of the Unknown Soldier.

The most famous feature of Arlington is the Changing of the Guard at the Tomb of the Unknown Soldier. The veterans and guardians file into place to see this moving ceremony that has been played out seamlessly by generations of Sentinels.

The Tomb has been guarded by the 3rd U.S. Infantry Regiment since 1948 when they took over from the U.S. Army. It has been guarded 24 hours a day, 365 days a year since 1937, regardless of weather or circumstances. Guards remained on duty through the terrorist attack of September 11, 2001, and have stood their posts through snow, ice storms, pelting rain, blizzards and gale-force winds.

The ceremony begins as the Relief Commander appears on the plaza. He marches to a precise spot and announces the Changing of the Guard. He describes the sacred ceremony and asks everyone to remain silent and standing. When the new Sentinel arrives, the Relief Commander conducts a thorough inspection of the new Sentinel's uniform, then a white-glove inspection of every part of his rifle. Then the Relief Commander and the new Sentinel meet the Sentinel on Duty at the center of the black rubber path in front of the Tomb, as they salute the Unknown Soldier.

The commander orders the Sentinel who has been relieved, "Pass on your orders."

"Post and orders, remain as directed," the Sentinel replies.

His replacement responds, "Orders acknowledged," and steps into positon for his duty watch. The commander and the retiring Sentinel walk in cadence, at 90 steps per minute, to exit the area.

During Sentinel duty, each guard marches exactly 21 steps, turns to face east for 21 seconds, turns to face north for 21 seconds, then marches 21 steps back and repeats the process. When the Sentinel turns, he will move his weapon from the inside shoulder to the outside in a "shoulder arms" to keep his weapon between the spectators and the Tomb at all times. The key number 21 represents the high military honor of a 21-gun salute.

Sentinels not on duty wait in guard quarters below the Military Display room of the Memorial Amphitheatre, where they study, clean their weapons and help other guards prepare for duty.

Sentinels also act as hosts to Honor Flight Tri-State veterans on rare occasions when permission is granted to lay a wreath at the Tomb of the Unknown.

The Changing of the Guard ceremony is deep with meaning, solemn and silent, interrupted only by the click of steel-plated heels and barked commands. It comes from an earlier time and a warrior culture that has become unfortunately unfamiliar to most Americans. The guards epitomize discipline and respect – and they demand the same from all visitors.

Now and then, Sentinels have to remind the public to behave. On one Honor Flight, the Sentinel on duty paused his cadence, stepped off the black mat that marks their path, did a crisp half-turn to face the crowd, and scolded a noisy group of teens: "It is requested that everyone maintains an atmosphere of silence and respect!" The crowd was instantly silent, and the teens quickly left.

At about noon, the Honor Flight veterans and guardians board tour buses again.

The Air Force Memorial is the next stop, for a boxed lunch in the shade, on the grounds of the newest of the Washington memorials, dedicated on October 14, 2006 by President George W. Bush (who flew the F-102 Delta Dagger in the National Guard). This prime location overlooks the Pentagon, the Potomac River and all of Washington, D.C., offering a breathtaking view.

Everything about this Memorial evokes flight and draws everyone's eyes to the sky. The stainless steel spires are spectacular, graceful curves that trace the trails of jets "soaring to glory." It's a lonely place – all that empty blue above the clouds seems to reach all the way to the outskirts of heaven. The sad emptiness is a reminder of all the pilots who never landed again at home.

The design was based on the "bomb burst formation" of the Air Force Thunderbirds. The

The stunning Air Force Memorial draws all eyes to the skies, echoing the flight of jets "soaring to glory."

44

columns climb variously from 201 to 270 feet, with one "plane" missing from the formation – representing the "missing man" maneuver used for Air Force funeral fly-overs. The Memorial is surprisingly powerful, changing its appearance with the seasons and time of day – sometimes blue, sometimes mirror-like, sometimes stark in silhouette against a sunset.

Nearby is a paved "Runway to Glory" at the entrance; a color guard depicted in eight-foot bronze statues; and a wall that bears the names of Air Force recipients of the Medal of Honor. On a wall, the three core values of the Air Force are engraved: "Integrity first, Service before self, and Excellence in all we do."

The Air Force Memorial was dedicated the same year Honor Flight Tri-State began its mission to honor veterans from World War II: 2006.

The World War II Memorial started it all for Honor Flight.

Here is a monument shaped like a medal for World War II veterans, on a magnificent scale, as huge as a high-school stadium. The round Memorial is decorated with giant bronze wreaths and eagles symbolizing victory; polished stars and fountains symbolize the loss of America's fine young men and the ever-flowing grief of their loved ones. Rows of pillars echo ancient temples; a larger fountain in the center of the Memorial pulses with the living water of American freedom.

As they arrive at the main event of their trip, veterans are assembled for a group photograph. Then they enter the World War II Memorial, led by an Honor Flight Board member who carries a glass-and-wooden case holding an American Flag. This same flag has been draped over the coffin of a departed veteran, and is placed, in its case, on the pillar representing the State of Ohio.

Columns representing every state encircle the WWII Memorial; Sculpted into the wall is the story of the war.

The World War II Memorial is a marble and bronze eulogy for more than 16 million who served in the Armed Forces during the war and more than 400,000 who perished in the Pacific and Atlantic Theaters. Worldwide, more than 70 million died in the Second World War. When you step inside, the Memorial envelops visitors and takes them back in time to the Second World War, leaving the modern world behind. The sheer size of it makes everyone feel small, like the soldiers who fought during the war – supported by their fellow soldiers but alone with their own feelings.

Dedicated in May 2004, it's situated on the National Mall between the Lincoln Memorial and Washington Monument. Its size fits the global war it honors: 7.4 acres, 337 feet long and 240 feet wide. The center plaza and fountain are surrounded by 56 identical white pillars, each 17-feet tall, engraved with the names of the 48 states at the time of the war, plus the territories of Alaska and Hawaii (before statehood), the District of Columbia, the Commonwealth of the Philippines, Guam, Puerto Rico, American Samoa and the Virgin Islands.

Fountains at both ends of the plaza mark the Atlantic and Pacific Theaters of the war. Between are relief sculptures on the walls that depict wartime scenes: recruits getting physicals, combat, burial of the dead, farmers harvesting crops at home to support the war, homecoming of soldiers. Above the plaza are additional columns supporting archways decorated with massive sculptures of American eagles holding laurel wreaths of victory.

On the west wall facing the Lincoln Memorial and the reflecting pool is a Freedom Wall, decorated with 4,048 gold stars, each representing one hundred American casualties.

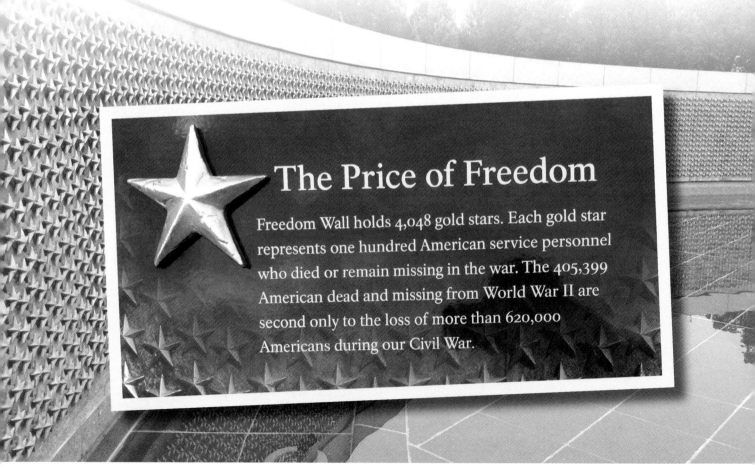

The Price of Freedom

Freedom Wall holds 4,048 gold stars. Each gold star represents one hundred American service personnel who died or remain missing in the war. The 405,399 American dead and missing from World War II are second only to the loss of more than 620,000 Americans during our Civil War.

Each Honor Flight group stops and gathers, to lay a wreath at the Freedom Wall of Stars, to remember all of the Americans who gave the ultimate sacrifice for their brothers and their country. There's a deep silence of sadness and memories as the veterans think of friends they lost. "Those were the real heroes," somebody whispers. Nearby, families who visit the Memorial have left pictures, notes and flowers to honor loved ones, lost in the war or more recently.

A visitor's view of a "baldachino," or granite canopy, that contains four 20,000-pound bronze eagles gripping a victory wreath.

Photo courtesy of Jennifer Otten.

On a bench is a photograph of a handsome young man from the 1940s: Mel Price of the Santa Fe Division, 35th Infantry, Battle of the Bulge. Next to it is a photo from his life before the war: a Western Swing band, "The Santa Fe Rangers," decked out in fancy cowboy boots, western shirts and hats, with Mel Price holding a fiddle.

These spontaneous expressions of love, loss and remembrance are powerful evidence that the World War II Memorial is finally honoring those who served their country in the greatest war in history. The Memorial was a long time coming – it took more than 60 years after the end of the war.

President Harry Truman, a World War I veteran, said it well in a quote that is carved into the wall of the Memorial: "Our debt to the heroic men and valiant women in the service of our own country can never be repaid. They have earned our undying gratitude. America will never forget their sacrifice."

With cards, old photos, wreaths, flowers, hugs and lots of tears, America remembers. The veterans stand in silence to honor all of the real heroes who didn't come home.

The Korean War Veterans Memorial is just a short bus ride away. At the beginning, Honor Flights were nearly all World War II veterans. But as they have faded away, more and more Korean War veterans are taking part. A typical flight now is only forty percent World War II veterans and sixty percent veterans from the Korean War.

The Korean War Memorial is approached up a long sidewalk. It suddenly emerges as part of the landscape, almost lost in the woods, taking visitors by surprise. Ghostly-silent soldiers in bronze sculpture patrol through bushes and groundcover in a park-like setting that suddenly seems haunted

A ghostly patrol of soldiers seems to step out of the woods at the Korean War Memorial, creating a haunting image and a reminder that "Freedom is not Free."

by a hovering threat. It's visible on the faces of the soldiers – they look lost, forgotten, their faces showing fear, stress and anxiety. One platoon, all alone – 19 young soldiers representing the thousands of men who were sent to a strange, faraway land to fight a cruel war that was mostly ignored at home and quickly forgotten by their nation.

They wear ponchos and carry rifles and radios, gesturing to each other, looking over their shoulders, scanning the ground ahead for threats; spread out, on full alert.

The Memorial demands silence and reverence. Conversations are almost in whispers.

"That's them," says a veteran of the Korean War. "I don't see any M-1 carbines. Oh, yeah, there it is. Yes. And that's a BAR (Browning Automatic Rifle). With three radio guys."

"It's so real," is a frequent comment. "Like being there again."

The bronze soldiers are seven-feet tall and represent various branches of the armed forces that served in Korea – fourteen are Army, three Marines, one from the Navy and one from the Air Force. They also represent the Americans who served: Caucasians, African-Americans, Hispanics, Asians and one Native American. A Pool of Remembrance is engraved with the words, "Freedom is not Free."

The Memorial was dedicated on July 27, 1995, by President Clinton and South Korean President Kim Young Sam. There are always fresh flowers at the Memorial, laid by Korean businesses or the South Korean Consulate. The Korean people remember what America did for their country and are forever grateful. Many of the Honor Flight veterans of the "forgotten war" say that when they visit they can see for the first time that what they did was remarkable and is finally remembered and appreciated.

The walkway is inscribed with the number of casualties of U.N. troops, 628,000, and American casualties, 54,246 – a simple reminder that Americans were not alone in the fight to save Korea.

Images of soldiers and scenes etched into the wall came from thousands of photos taken by soldiers, showing faces, war scenes and equipment from all of the armed services. There are nurses, chaplains, airfield construction workers, supply depots, radio and communications officers, reporters and even the canine corps. Two of the etchings show veterans from the Cincinnati area, who were shocked to discover themselves depicted on the wall during their Honor Flight visits.

Four Honor Flight veterans of the Korean War are chosen to lay a wreath near the flagpole that looks back at the soldiers on patrol. Since the Memorial was dedicated in 1995, there has been a live wreath laid every week by someone from Korea. The Korean people remember with grateful hearts, what was accomplished by so many Americans in this far off land.

As the visit continues, the veterans also have time to visit the Vietnam and Lincoln Memorials.

The Vietnam War Memorial is nearly 500 feet long, containing the names of more than 58,000 who died in the war. Each name is etched in black marble that is polished to a mirror finish, reflecting the faces of those who visit, uniting the war dead with the living who come to remember them.

Like the war in Vietnam, the Memorial is unique and controversial, dipping below ground level into the depths of sorrow and despair before gradually climbing back up into the sunshine. In the shadows of the Wall are the names of all the men who laid down their lives to build a human wall of resistance between freedom and communism. The black granite wall bends sharply at its lowest

Lt. Matt Allen pays his respects at the Vietnam wall.

point, showing the strain and pressure that led to the eventual collapse of the American effort to save South Vietnam.

The path alongside the Wall is crowded with letters, photos, flowers and mementoes left by friends and family members near the names of their lost soldiers. As visitors find the name they are looking for, many make a tracing of it on paper to take home. The entire Wall cuts into the earth like a wound, symbolically following America's gradual journey deeper into the war, then its gradual climb back out of Southeast Asia.

"The Wall," as it is commonly known, was dedicated in 1982. The designer, Maya Ying Lin, was a 20-year-old student at Yale University, when her design was chosen. Although criticized at first as too symbolic and simple, it has become timeless and popular, and is now the most visited Memorial in Washington.

In 1993, a sculpture depicting three women nurses helping a wounded soldier was added in a grove of trees across from the Wall, partly in answer to those who wanted a more representational tribute to the War in Vietnam. Like the Korean War Memorial a short walk away, it tells a powerful and emotional story of sacrifice, dedication and sadness.

Some veterans on the Honor Flight have had sons who fought in Vietnam. And that makes the Wall one of the more touching and moving stops on the tour. "All those names," a veteran in a wheelchair says, gazing on the Wall as he fights against tears. "All those names."

The Lincoln Memorial fittingly overlooks both the Korean War Memorial and the Vietnam Wall. As he sits in repose, gazing out across the National Mall at those recent monuments and the World War II Memorial in the distance, President Lincoln

The Lincoln Memorial is another stop on the Honor Flight tour of Washington, D.C. The brooding president who led the nation through the Civil War has a commanding view over the Korean and Vietnam Memorials.

seems to watch over the nation he held together by faith and willpower. Here is a face that has seen crushing sadness, but his expression is still loving and hopeful, watching, waiting patiently to see if all the sacrifice – all the lives lost at Shiloh, Belleau Wood, Okinawa, Normandy, the Chosin Reservoir, Khe Sanh and Fallujah – were worth it. Does America remember? Does a grateful nation honor those who answered the call? Have we learned the steep price of freedom that must be paid so that this exceptional "nation under God shall not perish from the earth?"

Lincoln is remembered for many things as our nation's 16th president. He signed the Emancipation Proclamation to abolish slavery, and was assassinated before he could finish his second term. He was also one of our greatest war presidents, who led the Union in battle against the Confederacy and bonded together a country torn apart by its devastating Civil War. It was Lincoln who kept hiring and firing generals until he found one who could win, Ulysses S. Grant; it was Lincoln who started the healing even before the war was over with his graceful and eloquent Gettysburg Address, honoring all of the Americans who died in that July 1863 battle that claimed more than fifty thousand lives.

The entire speech is displayed on his Memorial. Some of the speech is especially appropriate to all the memorials visited by Honor Flight veterans:

"We cannot dedicate – we cannot consecrate – we cannot hallow – this ground. The brave men, living and dead, who struggled here, have consecrated it, far above our poor power to add or detract. The world will little note, nor long remember what we say here, but it can never forget what they did here. It is for us the living, rather, to be dedicated here to the unfinished work which they who fought here have thus far so nobly advanced. It is rather for us to be here dedicated to the great task remaining before us – that from these honored dead we take increased devotion to that cause for which they gave the last full measure of devotion – that we here highly resolve that these dead shall not have died in vain – that this nation, under God, shall have a new birth of freedom – and that government of the people, by the people, for the people, shall not perish from the earth."

Lincoln was killed only weeks after the Civil War ended in 1865. Two years later, Congress formed the Lincoln Memorial Association. But it took until 1901 for the Memorial site to be chosen and another ten years before President William Howard Taft approved $2 million to build the Memorial. It was finally completed in May 1922.

The inside of the marble temple is 99 feet tall, with Lincoln seated in a chair. The statue itself was originally designed to be ten feet tall, but designer Daniel Chester French realized that the statue would be dwarfed inside the large building, so the statue was almost doubled to nineteen feet.

Over the years, the Lincoln Memorial has become a gathering place for protests and political rallies. Martin Luther King's famous "I Have a Dream" speech was delivered from its steps, where

a marker indicates the spot where he stood in 1963.

Some of the most beautiful views of Washington can be seen from Lincoln plaza, across the Reflecting Pool to the World War II Memorial, the National Mall, the Washington Monument and the Capitol.

At 5 p.m. the exhausting and emotional day is winding down, but most of the veterans are still going strong. As the buses take them to a buffet dinner, the excitement and camaraderie of the day creates a lively buzz of conversation and laughter around the dinner tables. Over fried chicken, roast beef, ribs and lots of desserts, men who were strangers as the day began make friends and memories they will keep forever.

"Today meant so much," they say. A guardian and her father agree: "What struck me was so much reaction from the people who were around us – in the airport, at the monuments. They were not part of the people on our trip. They were just coming up and telling the veterans 'Thank you.' Some of the young people were so nice, saying 'Thank you for your service, sir.'"

Every veteran has heard the spoken thanks from a grateful nation. All of them have finally had a chance to see the monuments that were dedicated to their service and sacrifice. They've felt the appreciation and respect from strangers wherever they went. Many who haven't been farther than the neighborhood grocery store in years have come to the nation's capital to be treated like conquering heroes.

After dinner, at 7 p.m., the buses return to the airport for the flight home. As soon as they arrive at their gate, the Honor Flight veterans are greeted by the USO with music and 1940s-era swing dancers. A few of the vets get up and join in, some climbing out of their wheelchairs to hug the USO greeters. Spirits are high. They seem to have shed sixty years in one long day. The magic has happened again.

On the flight home, it's time for Mail Call – another echo of their days in the service when they eagerly waited for a letter from their family or a girlfriend. This time the letters are from family members and students, who have written to every veteran on the trip. They express admiration; thanks; gratitude; respect; appreciation.

It's nearly 10 p.m. by the time the flight lands back home, as all the veterans and guardians make their way to the arrival gate. It's been a 16-hour day for most, even longer for some. Everyone is anxious to get home to their families and their beds. But their Honor Flight has one more surprise in store.

The Honor Flight Ground Crew has prepared a welcome home rally that looks like the homecoming for a world champion team – which is exactly what these veterans are. There are color guards, bagpipers, pinup girls, reenactors, military personnel, wives, children, grandchildren and well-wishers who don't know anyone on the Honor Flight but know they want to be there to applaud the returning veterans.

The entire airport arrival area is jammed and overflowing with a cheering crowd. Signs say,

"Welcome Back Grandpa – You are our Hero!" And, "We love you Dad, Welcome Home!"

The rock-star welcome is a surging sea of smiles, tears and hugs. It takes twenty minutes to wade through all the handshakes, kisses and misty-eyed applause. The men are choked with emotion, overwhelmed. They can't believe it. Nobody can. "All this for us?" they ask again in wonder. The love, honor and respect for these conquering warriors energizes the crowd like an electric current, pulsing in red, white and blue flashes of pride.

Tired backs straighten. Old men stand tall again. Drooping chins lift up. Shoulders are squared away. They stare in disbelief, searching the crowd for their wives, children and grandchildren. They are greeted with hugs and wave after wave of applause.

A group of pretty young women, dressed and made up for a big date – pinup girls – welcomes the vets with kisses that leave dark lipstick impressions. A Korean War veteran dives in like a man at a buffet of beauty, "stealing" kiss after kiss, laughing and smiling hugely. The years fall away. The ladies love him again.

Here, finally, is the victory parade they never had, an outpouring of gratitude for a job well done. As the veterans melt away into the crowd, throwing their arms around their families, the cheers go on and on.

While they make their way to their cars, their Honor Flight day has come to an end. But the memories will last forever.

Popular places in Arlington include:

The Kennedy Memorial is the resting place for the assassinated President John F. Kennedy and his wife and son, who are honored by an eternal flame and a small plaza. The president's brother and attorney general, Robert Kennedy, is buried on a slope nearby.

President William Howard Taft's Grave is marked with a large monument. He's the only president from Ohio buried in Arlington.

The Space Shuttle *Challenger* Memorial gives tribute to seven astronauts who died in that horrible disaster on January 28, 1986, when a rocket booster exploded after liftoff, 73 seconds into the flight. Engraved on the Memorial are the haunting words of John Gillespie Magee Jr.'s poem *High Flight*.

Oh! I have slipped the surly bonds of Earth

And danced the skies on laughter-silvered wings;

Sunward I've climbed, and joined the tumbling mirth

Of sun-split clouds, — and done a hundred things

You have not dreamed of — wheeled and soared and swung

High in the sunlit silence. Hov'ring there,

I've chased the shouting wind along, and flung

My eager craft through footless halls of air. . . .

Up, up the long, delirious burning blue

I've topped the wind-swept heights with easy grace

Where never lark, or ever eagle flew —

And, while with silent, lifting mind I've trod

The high untrespassed sanctity of space,

Put out my hand, and touched the face of God.

Medal of Honor winner Audie Murphy had a film career after the war. Visitors to Arlington often leave tokens of respect on headstones.

The USS Maine Memorial, built from the ship's mast that was salvaged from its sunken wreckage, is inscribed with names that tell an inspiring story of the American people: Suke Chingi, Michael Flaherty, Gustav Holm, Joseph Schoen, Tomekichi Nagamine, James O'Connor. Their families came from Germany, Ireland, the Philippines, Japan, France, Africa – but they fought side-by-side as Americans. They served a nation that was unlike any place on earth; a country where men named Tomekichi, Schoen, Flaherty and Gustav died together to defend each other and a common dream of freedom. When the USS Maine exploded on February 15, 1898 in Havana Harbor, 264 sailors and Marines lost their lives; 160 are buried at the Memorial. All of them are remembered at Arlington.

The Sentinels at the Tomb of the Unknown

The Sentinels at the Tomb of the Unknown Soldier are volunteers selected from the best of the elite 3rd U.S. Infantry ("The Old Guard, Company E"), headquartered at Fort Myer, Virginia. Sentinels are selected after two weeks of training and interviews. They must be in superb physical condition with an unblemished military record. Each must memorize seven pages of the Arlington National Cemetery History and all of it must be recited verbatim in order to do the guard duty "walk." Night walks are one hour. Daytime walks are 30 minutes in summer and one hour in winter.

In the second phase of training, Sentinels must memorize the location of 300 veterans' graves and more history of Arlington. They learn to keep their uniforms and weapons immaculate for inspection. Guard changing and the manual of arms must be memorized along with all Changing of the Guard procedures.

After several months, Sentinels are tested to serve as Tomb guards. They must correctly answer 95 out of 100 random questions. Those who pass are awarded the silver Tomb Guard Identification Badge, which has been given to only about 600 soldiers since it was created in 1958. The badge is an upside-down laurel wreath surrounding a depiction of the front face of the Tomb. Peace, Victory and Valor are portrayed in Greek figures and the words "Honor Guard" are at the bottom of the badge.

Once a Sentinel passes probation, he gets a permanent badge that may be worn on his uniform for the rest of his military career. When Tomb service begins they join three relief groups, each composed of a relief commander and six Sentinels. The groups are divided by height (5'10" to 6'4") so guards look similar. They work one day on, one day off; second day on, one day off; third day on, four days off.

Changing of the Guard at the Tomb of the Unknown Soldier

"I was fighting tears all day."

"Yesterday, December 7, 1941 — a date which will live in infamy — the United States of America was suddenly and deliberately attacked by naval and air forces of the Empire of Japan. As Commander-in-Chief of the Army and Navy, I have directed that all measures be taken for our defense. With confidence in our armed forces — with the unbounded determination of our people — we will gain the inevitable triumph, so help us God."

— President Franklin D. Roosevelt, Dec. 8, 1941

CHAPTER THREE
Legacy of Sacrifice

Special things happen on every Honor Flight. Moments are captured in memories like snapshots, to be shared with friends and family.

Maybe it's the ancient warrior bond, a brothers-in-arms kinship of a common experience that can't even be imagined by anyone who wasn't there. Maybe it's the dramatic statues and monuments that somehow bring back the deafening thunder and choking smoke of distant battles, resurrecting memories that were packed away 60 years ago in an attic trunk, along with the olive-drab Garrison Cap, medals and uniform. Or maybe it's the awareness that the years are slipping away too fast, like sand through their fingers, and they will soon join their friends who fell in battle.

The magic always begins with stories. Some would shame the most thrilling war movies made in Hollywood.

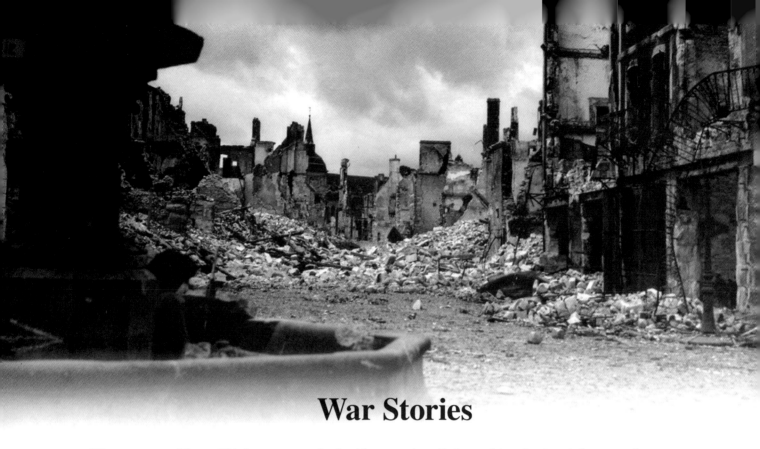

War Stories

There was an Honor Flight veteran who had been quiet all day, taking in the sights, pausing thoughtfully at the monuments, occasionally wiping away a tear. He kept to himself and held his memories as tight as a clenched fist. At dinner, as more than a hundred veterans, guardians and volunteers filled their plates at the buffet and sat down to eat, someone asked him about his war experience.

Nearby tables were loud with laughter and conversation. But when he answered, his table became as quiet as a graveyard.

"I was at Normandy on D-Day," he said softly.

A shadow passed over the group. Everything stopped, as the men sitting with him laid down their silverware and leaned in to listen.

"I saw a lot of men die that day. So many. So many friends. There were bodies in the surf, boys who couldn't make it to shore…" He bowed his head and covered his face with hands that were gnarled and scarred from hard work. They were the hands of a tough man who didn't cry. But his shoulders shook and the tears flowed. He was back there again on the shell-cratered beach, watching American boys being cut down by machineguns, blown up by artillery or pulled under the water by their own heavy equipment as they charged off their landing crafts into a hurricane of death.

The veterans at the table reached out and put reassuring hands on his back. Most were too choked up to say anything. The few who could speak said, "Let it out," and "It all comes back." They squeezed his shoulders and stepped in to rescue his dignity by changing the subject, giving him space to recover himself. As he wiped his eyes, the look on his face showed the inner scars of battle. For a few moments, in the presence of other veterans who would understand, he had traveled back in time to that blood-soaked beach, reliving an experience that words could never describe.

Sometimes an Honor Flight takes a veteran much further than anyone could imagine.

And sometimes an Honor Flight can magically erase the distance of time and space and bring people together unexpectedly.

Honor Flight Board Member Ed Finke saw that happen at Arlington National Cemetery, as he and the veterans watched the Changing of the Guard at the Tomb of the Unknown Soldier. A woman approached the group. In a thick French accent, she asked who they were. When they said they were veterans of World War II, her eyes brimmed with tears.

She asked if any had served in France. Several stepped forward as the rest gathered to listen. "Yes," the veterans of the war in Europe said, "we fought through France. We liberated Paris."

As they shared their memories, she asked if any remembered a small village where she lived as a little girl during the war.

"I fought the Germans in that village," one of the vets said, stepping forward.

She described the small farm where she lived with her grandparents.

"I remember that," the veteran said. "I stayed in your barn one night."

The woman from France with veteran Lindy Brigano.

Overcome by emotion, she kissed every veteran and vowed that she would never forget the American G.I.s who saved her life, her family and her country.

For a few magic moments, the calendar had been rolled back. Those veterans were back in France, a world away – getting the heroes' welcome they deserved. The grainy old black-and-white newsreels were rewound and they were showered with kisses and flowers again.

If every veteran has a library of stories to tell, each Honor Flight is a new book on the shelf, with each veteran contributing his own chapter.

Ezra Rohr was a country boy who went to town the day Pearl Harbor was attacked. "They were lined up for half a block to enlist. Farm boys, grocery boys, what have you. Anything they were doing they just quit and went in the service. I tried three different times to enlist and they said, 'You're too young.' I was just 16. Finally I went home and wrote my mother's name on the paper and took it back to another recruiter and he took me.

"The job I had was on a 105 Howitzer. There were five or six of us and a truck driver. We might ride two or three days to set up in a certain place. Four guns would set up and shoot, maybe for two days, maybe for an hour. I was shooting shells in the air and killing people over there. Then we'd get the gun and the boys loaded up, and take off again.

"The worst time I had was late in 1945 when we came up on these concentration camps. We were cleaning them up. It was the worst time I ever had. Those people were in horrible shape. Melted, dehydrated, dying. We had to get them out and put them in a truck and take them to where they could be buried. That was the worst. Killing somebody – I didn't care about that. But this…"

"When they said, 'Ezra, you're going home,' I said…" He paused to swallow and choke back tears. "…'Thank you!' I was ready to go. I'd done my bit. I was ready to come home."

Dr. Henry Heimlich

Dr. Henry Heimlich, who lives in Cincinnati, is known all over the world as the inventor of the Heimlich Maneuver that has saved countless lives of people who would have otherwise choked to death. He is respected and admired in the medical world as the inventor of a chest-draining valve that saved countless lives at field hospitals in Vietnam, as well as in hospitals at home. But on his Honor Flight, he was simply a veteran – along with all the rest.

"After the attack on Pearl Harbor on December 7, 1941, the government required medical-school students to join the military to ensure that there would be medical personnel in the field," he wrote in his biography, *Heimlich's Maneuvers*. "Because I had always loved the water, I chose to join the U.S. Navy Reserve as an unpaid ensign."

After graduating from medical school, he was called up in 1944, then told to report to the Chief of Naval Operations in Washington, D.C. in early 1945. "They could say very little about my assignment, although they did let me know it was dangerous."

He was told it was part of a secret project, strictly voluntary. He could tell his family only that he was going to China. "I was given five huge mail pouches and a letter marked 'Secret.' In the pouches were mail, rifles and ammunition. In addition I was loaded down with a half dozen .45 cal. pistols hanging from straps over my shoulders and in holsters on my belt. The pilot didn't want me to board the small plane because it was too much weight."

But the pilot was overruled, and off he went, eventually landing in the remote Gobi Desert, where the U.S. had set up camps to monitor weather patterns that could forecast conditions for fleets in the Pacific.

He was assigned to maintain a hospital behind Japanese lines in Inner Mongolia. "Set squarely on the edge of the Gobi Desert, Camp Four was the most remote American-backed clandestine military-training base in China." It was protected from the Japanese by a 100,000-man army of the Nationalist Chinese. "The sea-lover in me had joined the Navy to sail the high seas, and here I was about to head to just about the driest place on earth."

Dr. Heimlich survived fevers and dysentery as he treated plagues and diseases that hadn't been seen in the West since the Dark Ages. After the Japanese surrendered in August 1945, he was finally sent home in April 1946 – under orders to transport a prisoner who had killed nine men on his ship.

"I look back on my time serving as a military doctor in China as one of the most challenging and rewarding times of my life," he wrote. "But as my wartime service drew to a close and I was back with my parents in New York City, it was time to move on. And so I began to fulfill my lifelong dream of becoming an accomplished surgeon."

Not every veteran has stories that sound like John Wayne storming machine gun nests on Iwo Jima or Robert Mitchum leading the charge through a hail of bullets on Omaha Beach at Normandy. Even among those who survived combat, the stories seldom sound like Hollywood, because Hollywood seldom sounds like real combat.

And for every veteran who outdid Hollywood and carried an M-1 or BAR into battles in Europe and the Pacific, there were many more who supported them by driving trucks, directing traffic, filing reports, unloading crates, shipping food, weapons and ammunition, making battle plans at headquarters, training recruits and caring for the wounded.

Estimates of what the military calls the "tooth to tail" ratio in World War II vary. Some say four out of ten in combat, with the remaining six in support. Others say seven or eight support troops in uniform for each combat soldier on the front lines.

U.S. Marine invasion of Saipan

All of them served. And how they served was seldom their choice.

Ralph Ross served in the Army. "I remember the news when Pearl Harbor was attacked. That was real exciting. We had two children, so I was classified 3A, and I was not drafted. Later, when I had three children, I was drafted, and it was a relief. I was uncomfortable. All of my friends and the guys I worked with were drafted and I had some guilt about it, so when I was drafted it was a great relief.

"I was assigned to train 18-year-olds who were coming in. I was 25, so I was like the old man to them. I had to teach them what this man's Army was all about."

Dorothy Racke was a U.S. Army Nurse sent overseas. "My parents didn't want me to go because my brother was already overseas and they didn't want to lose two kids. Finally I convinced them, though." She remembers the wounded. "I really had sympathy for all of them. They didn't have any family around."

Dr. Robert Krone served in the U.S. Army Medical Administration Corps. Holding his original Army-issue officers' uniform hat and wearing an Honor Flight T-shirt, he was interviewed in 2012 by Jennifer Otten, producer and videographer for an Honor Flight video.

"I was collecting stamps and had the radio on. I remember clearly the moment it was announced," Dr. Krone recalled of the attack on Pearl Harbor. Before he knew it he was in Basic Training, rated as a Battalion Surgical Assistant.

"I would sit on a foot locker up at the front lines, examining and triaging. We might put a bandage on one guy and send him back into combat, or send another one the other way. They were losing too many doctors and I guess they figured we were expendable." He made it home. "I was lucky."

Charles Frank Smedley joined the Army just in time for the Korean War. "I was a typical young man, trying to make a buck and stay out of trouble, and I decided to join the service. It looked like it had better opportunities. I was made a platoon sergeant in Basic Training. That was a laugh."

Firefight in the Pacific

He was shipped to the Pusan Perimeter, a 20-square mile peninsula that was the last toehold for the U.S. Army. "That's when they hit us real hard. I was wounded in a heavy mortar attack. We were standing too close together, I guess. It hit in the midst of us and the only one they didn't kill was me. I made it back to the field hospital.

"I had shrapnel through my face and through my mouth, because I always had my mouth open anyway. It got me through my shoulder. A field radio took the biggest part of the shrapnel.

"I never was a religious person, but I thought, 'Well, I sure don't have anything to lose by saying a prayer.' When you're in a firefight, saying a prayer like 'Thou shalt not kill' sounded a little silly. But I guess it worked because I'm still here."

These men and women and so many like them never talked about what they did in the war because they felt like "I just did my share." They would tell you that the real heroes were the ones who were in combat. And even the ones who were in combat, who were wounded or saw things that they can never forget, are just as modest. The real heroes, they insist, are the ones who did not come home.

The World War II Memorial and the Korean War Memorial are not dedicated only to the men who died in combat, or even to the ones who fought while others served in support. The greatest emotional power of the memorials comes from the gold stars that represent the lives that were lost in World War II, or the realistic statues of ghostly Korean War soldiers who carry their weapons on patrol.

The memorials are for all veterans who "quit whatever it was they were doing" and answered their nation's call to serve. They didn't ask where they would go or what they would do. Our nation should not ask either. All who served deserve our gratitude and respect. They all deserve a chance to see the memorials that were built to honor their victory for freedom.

And their reactions are worth whatever it takes to make sure they do.

"I never expected that 65 years later I would go on an Honor Flight to Washington," said Ralph Ross, fighting tears. "When we were discharged it was nothing at all. They just said, 'You're on your own, young fella. Go. You're out. Here's your money.' To be treated now with such honor. To stop and think and appreciate who we are."

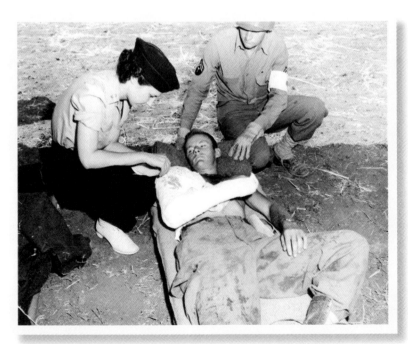

U.S. Army nurse tends to a wounded soldier

"Even now I can't believe it," Dorothy Racke said of her Honor Flight. "I can't believe this happened to me. What did I do to deserve it? It was amazing. Breathtaking."

"I felt like Caesar taking over Rome," said Charles Frank Smedley. "It was a tear-jerker to me. It's kind of hard to explain, but it was really something. It was an experience I will never forget."

Landing at Normandy;

General Eisenhower encourages the troops ahead of the invasion;

Pushing through France.

World War II

'Never in the field of human conflict, has so much, been owed by so many, to so few.' — British Prime Minister Winston Churchill

Close your eyes and put your finger on a spinning globe, and no matter where it lands will be a place that was swept up in the manmade hurricane of World War II. It was not one war, but hundreds of wars – a worldwide contagious epidemic of killing; a stark, black-and-white battle of good vs. evil; a fight-to-the-death between freedom and totalitarian tyranny.

More than fifty nations were directly involved. To each, it was their war. Battles were fought in deserts, jungles, cities and on beaches, in bone-chilling cold and scorching heat, across every imaginable landscape, over and under the sea, and in the skies. Huge naval and air battles spanned the oceans of the world, turning the Atlantic and Pacific oceans into battlefields and graveyards. China, Eastern Europe, Great Britain, France, Russia, Africa, Italy, Southeast Asia, the Pacific Islands, Holland, Australia, the Philippines – hardly a nation was spared.

But to the soldiers, airmen, sailors and Marines who fought for the USA, and for all the families who prayed for their safe return in Cincinnati and across America, World War II was two wars: The European Theater war against Germany, and the Pacific Theater war against Japan.

The War in Europe began and ended with Adolph Hitler. And his story began with World War I. As that "War to End All Wars" came to a close in 1918 with the crushing defeat of Germany, the seeds of the next war were planted in the rubble, and watered by the Treaty of Versailles. The treaty took one-sixth of Germany's territory and made its people pay crippling reparations that destroyed their economy. Inflation bled away the value of their currency until a wheelbarrow of cash was needed to buy a loaf of bread.

As a worldwide Great Depression destroyed faith in government for millions who were homeless, jobless and starving, the door was opened for the rise of totalitarian dictators in Japan, Italy and Germany. Stalin showed them how it was done in Russia, where his collectivism killed millions.

Adolph Hitler was a decorated veteran of World War I who believed his country had been betrayed by it leaders. He called the Treaty of Versailles a "disgrace," striking a chord of resentment in the German people. He rose to power in 1933 by harvesting Germany's poisoned crops of anger, humiliation and bitterness, as he promised to restore "The Fatherland's" glory, territory, military might and national pride. Unable to win a majority of support, he bullied, lied and muscled his way to power in typical totalitarian fashion.

Standing against Hitler was war-weary Great Britain, which had lost a generation of its young men in the trenches of World War I and had no appetite for more conflict. British Prime Minister Neville Chamberlain personified that pacifist reluctance, and Hitler took advantage of Chamberlain's foolish appeasement by taking back territory and invading Czechoslovakia in March of 1939. As Chamberlain naively proclaimed "Peace in our time," Hitler sent his tanks, infantry and Stuka dive-bombers into action, making a mockery of Chamberlain's negotiations at Munich. "The men I met in Munich will not enter into a new world war," Hitler predicted.

He was right about Chamberlain, but fatally wrong about the next British Prime Minister. Winston Churchill warned, "Britain and France had to choose between war and dishonor. They chose dishonor. They will have war."

When Hitler launched a blitzkrieg ("lightning war") invasion of Poland in September of 1939, Great Britain and Europe went to war. World War II had begun. "Today we rule Germany, tomorrow, the world," Hitler said.

In the U.S., President Franklin D. Roosevelt struggled to arm and support Great Britain against the wishes of an isolationist Congress. It took the surprise attack by Japan at Pearl Harbor on December 7, 1941, to get the U.S. to declare war against Japan and join the battle for Europe.

Meanwhile, Churchill held on by a thread, pleading for U.S. help as the Battle of Britain raged over London and an invasion was expected by the Nazis any day. He rallied the British to a valiant defense with his vow, "We shall not flag or fail. We shall go on to the end. We shall fight in France, we shall fight on the seas and the oceans, we shall fight with growing confidence and growing strength in the air, we shall defend our island, whatever the cost may be. We shall fight on the beaches, we shall fight on the landing grounds, we shall fight in the fields and in the streets, we shall fight in the hills; we shall never surrender."

The European War began for the U.S. in late 1942 in North Africa, with Operation Torch, an allied attack by Britain and the U.S. under command of U.S. Gen. Dwight Eisenhower. The objective was to crush Field Marshall Erwin Rommel's Germans in the Italian Army in a vise. Italy's fascist dictator Benito Mussolini had invaded Egypt in 1940, then joined Germany in the Axis Powers alliance.

After pushing the Germans and Italians out of North Africa, U.S. forces invaded Sicily in 1943 and fought their way north through Italy, town by town, house by house, even room by room. Mussolini was captured and executed in September that year.

German tanks and weapons were often superior early in the war. But the muscle of America's "arsenal of democracy" was overwhelming. The German Panzer and Tiger tanks had better armor and bigger guns, but for each of them, Detroit could build dozens of fast and maneuverable Sherman

Crosley Radio circa 1940s

tanks, and supply unlimited ammunition, men and fuel to keep them fighting. More than 53,000 Sherman M4 tanks were built for the war, including several thousand from Lima Locomotive Works in Lima, Ohio.

Among the war efforts from Cincinnati: Crosley Broadcasting was recruited to build transmitters and antennas to send broadcasts in dozens of languages all over the world, to "tell the truth about the war." Hitler called it "the Cincinnati liars." Cincinnati Milling Machine Co. (later Cincinnati Milacron) built machine tools for making weapons and machined all of the big guns for the U.S. Navy. Wright Cyclone aircraft engines for B-17 bombers and other military aircraft were built in Cincinnati. Union Terminal train station became one of the nation's busiest departure points for troops in the Midwest.

Cincinnati Milling Machine

Kentucky contributed 100,000 Jeeps built in Louisville, along with artificial rubber, ordinance, coal to fire the boilers of Navy and three Prisoner of War camps, at Fort Knox and in rural southwestern Kentucky.

Indiana made Allison aircraft engines, Studebaker trucks, Lilly's blood plasma, proximity fuses, cartridge cases, and one of the great fighter airplanes of the war: about one thousand P-47 Thunderbolts were built at a Republic Aviation factory in Evansville.

The sturdy, powerful P-47 was a good example of how Allied weapons steadily improved, and so did the U.S. commanders, tactics and fighting spirit. When one of Germany's top Luftwaffe officers was asked by Air Marshall Herman Goering what he needed most to win the air battle, his answer was "British Spitfire fighters." Yet even the Spitfire was overtaken by the greatest fighter aircraft of the war, the North American P-51 Mustang.

Rommel told friends that when he reported that American-made fighter-bombers "had shot up my tanks with 40mm shells," he was told, "That's completely impossible. The Americans only know how to make razor blades." He said he replied, "We could do with some of those razor blades."

As the Germans were pushed relentlessly back through Italy into France, the Allies launched the D-Day invasion of Normandy on June 6, 1944 – the biggest invasion force in the history of warfare. Supreme Commander Gen. Eisenhower became President after the war.

"United in this determination and with unshakable faith in the cause for which we fight, we will, with God's help, go forward to our greatest victory," he said on the eve of the battle.

The invasion was costly, bloody, horrific and decisive. The Battle of the Bulge and brutal warfare through France and Germany remained, but the Nazis ran out of fuel, options and weapons, as the Allies beat them to rubble with constant bombing of cities and factories, and hammered them into submission with relentless attacks by tanks and infantry on the ground.

Hitler's disastrous misjudgments, stupidity, rage and arrogance had squandered Germany's might in a catastrophic invasion of Russia. His madman ravings and paranoid meddling lost key battles and purged some of Germany's best military leaders. As America won the air war, Generals Omar Bradley, George Patton and British Gen. Bernard Montgomery won a string of hard-fought victories through France and into Germany, through smoking cities, ruined towns and cratered villages.

As the Russians closed in from the East, the U.S. and British closed the vise from the West. Hitler took his own life in a bunker on April 30, 1945. Eight days later, Germany surrendered and the war in Europe was over.

The Pacific War begins and ends in the air, with falling bombs as bookends to some of the most vicious, horrific combat in history. Between those bookends is a library of the world's greatest naval battles and heroic ground combat against a fanatical, suicidal enemy. The atomic bombs that ended the war on two days in August 1945 had been delivered at a cost of more than 100,000 American lives, by ships that blasted their way through the Pacific, and by Marines and soldiers who hacked and slogged their way through fetid swamps, jungles, islands and blood-soaked beaches.

When Japan invaded China in 1931, its military dictators were emboldened as the rest of the world looked the other way. For America, the war began on a sunny Sunday morning, as most of the U.S. Pacific Fleet sat at anchor in Pearl Harbor, Hawaii. While sailors and Marines were just waking up, Japanese fighters and bombers attacked with bombs, torpedoes and machine guns, and sank the most powerful battleships and cruisers of the U.S. Navy in a devastating ambush that killed 2,403 Americans. The Battleship Arizona still weeps oil from its shallow grave on the floor of the Harbor.

Admiral William "Bull" Halsey said, "Before we're through with them, the Japanese language will be spoken only in hell."

America finally struck back with the Doolittle Raid on Tokyo five months later. Sixteen B-25s took off from the USS Hornet aircraft carrier, bombed Tokyo and then had to crash land in China or ditch in the sea. Their bombs didn't slow Japan's war juggernaut, but shook its leaders and people with a red-flag warning: The sleeping American giant was wide awake and there would be hell to pay.

The Philippines fell with Gen. Douglas MacArthur's retreat in May 1942 – another setback as the Bataan Death March showed the world the evil cruelty of Japan toward captured prisoners. The Battle of the Coral Sea that same month was a draw – a tactical loss for the U.S. but a strategic loss for Japan, which was forced to abort its invasion of Australia.

Japan responded to the Doolittle Raid by sending a huge army to punish the Chinese for helping the Raiders escape capture. More than 250,000 Chinese were killed as the Japanese used biological weapons to spread cholera, typhoid and plague. Stung by the Doolittle insult, the Japanese high command also attacked Midway Island, to strengthen its "ring of iron" defense and threaten the U.S. mainland.

In the Battle of Midway, four American aircraft carriers that survived Pearl Harbor led a task force that sank the pride of Japan's fleet and shot down its best pilots. It was a huge U.S. victory. Japan never recovered from the loss of its best ships and pilots. But the war was far from over. The worst fighting was still to come.

New Guinea and the Solomon Islands followed – as Marines hit the beaches to take back islands one at a time. The names of those island battles are legendary to Pacific veterans: Peleliu, Tarawa, Rabaul, Saipan, Manilla, the Marianas. But three stand out for their ferocity and significance to the war.

Guadalcanal began on August 7, 1942, when 10,000 Marines landed to face 2,000 Japanese and take control of an airfield the Japanese were building that was critical to control of the Pacific. Over the next six months, Japan sent wave after wave of reinforcements. A sea battle raged back and forth as U.S. Navy destroyers and cruisers intercepted Japanese troop ships and their escorts. So many ships were sunk, the waters around Guadalcanal became known as "Ironbottom Sound," a crowded cemetery of ripped hulls and lost sailors.

In battles such as Bloody Ridge, the Marines repulsed wave after wave of attacks. When Japan finally evacuated on February 7, 1943, it had lost 31,000 sailors and soldiers; U.S. losses were 7,100. The U.S. lost 29 ships; Japan lost 38, including two battleships and six heavy cruisers.

Henderson Airfield on Guadalcanal became a devastating weapon in the U.S. arsenal. The survivors of Guadalcanal summed it up:

"And when he gets to Heaven to St. Peter he will tell:
'One more Marine reporting, Sir — I've served my time in Hell.'"

The Battle of Leyte Gulf is known as the biggest naval battle in history. In late October 1944, the largest battleships ever built fought to the death off the Philippine Island of Leyte. When the smoke cleared and the last sinking ships groaned, sizzled and burst as they sank to the bottom, the Japanese Navy was shattered. They had lost 300 planes, four carriers, ten cruisers, eleven destroyers and three huge battleships. The U.S. Navy lost 200 planes, three small carriers, two destroyers and one destroyer escort.

Iwo Jima was made famous for the flag-raising at the top of Mount Suribachi. But veterans of that hellish battle know that 21 days of combat continued after that photo was taken. Half of the Marines in the staged picture did not survive.

By early 1945, new B-29 bombers were flying non-stop missions over Japan, dropping incendiaries that razed entire cities. But attrition was high because fighters could not escort the long-range bombers. A new base closer to Japan was needed. Iwo Jima was chosen – a five-mile Island with two airstrips that had been turned into a massive, fortified bunker by the Japanese.

The biggest bombardment of the war by a fleet of 400 ships pulverized the island, but the Japanese huddled in underground bunkers, waiting in ambush for the Marines to land. Over the next 36 days, 6,821 Americans were killed in action and 18,000 were wounded. The casualty ratio was as bad as the D-Day invasion at Normandy. Twenty-seven Medals of Honor were awarded for heroism at Iwo Jima. By the time the last enemies were flushed out with flame-throwers, tanks, grenades and satchel charges, only 200 among the 21,000 Japanese had surrendered.

"Among the men who fought on Iwo Jima, uncommon valor was a common virtue," said Pacific Fleet Admiral Chester W. Nimitz.

As the U.S. found at Iwo Jima and later at Okinawa, surrender was not an option for Japan. They would fight to the death, soldiers and civilians, with 2,800 kamikaze attacks that sank 34 U.S. ships, and an insanely fanatical defense of every inch of Japanese land. The Japanese lost 77,000 at Okinawa. U.S. losses were more than 14,000 killed and 65,000 casualties.

After Okinawa and Iwo Jima, U.S. military planners prepared for an invasion of Japan. They expected to face 5,000 aircraft, 375,000 troops and countless militias and suicide volunteers. Unlike Germany, Japan had held tanks, weapons, ammunition and soldiers in reserve. It was estimated that taking Japan would cost 250,000 American lives.

There would be no surrender. Fire-bombing by a squadron of 300 B-29s on Tokyo wiped out sixteen square miles of the city, killed 100,000 civilians and left millions homeless. That was repeated in city after city. Still, Japan's defiant leaders refused to even answer demands for surrender.

On August 6, 1945, a B-29 named "Enola Gay" took off from Tinian, an island taken by U.S. Marines, and dropped the first atomic bomb, "Little Boy," on Hiroshima. The blast instantly superheated the ground to five thousand degrees, set off apocalyptic shockwaves and turned the city into a firestorm inferno. When the smoke cleared, Hiroshima was flattened to a field of rubble four feet deep; 70,000 were killed in the blast and by radiation poisoning. On August 9, another bomb, "Fat Man," was dropped on Nagasaki by the B-29 "Bockscar." More than 50,000 were killed.

Fat Man

President Truman warned Japan to surrender or, "They will face a rain of ruin from the air, the like of which has never been seen on earth."

Still, Japan refused to answer. Finally, after Emperor Hirohito broke a tie vote, Japan surrendered on August 15. The war that had ravaged the world like a titanic tornado of steel and blood was finally over. Hundreds of thousands of U.S. – and Japanese – lives were spared.

Germany was a professional, disciplined, well-armed enemy with a madman leader whose warped mind conceived of a master race and a "final solution" that slaughtered more than 6 million Jews and other "undesirables" in a string of horrific death camps.

Japan was a well-armed industrial giant with a dark ages culture that waged war with primitive cruelty and uncivilized, suicidal determination.

They were both hated and feared. But they were stopped, defeated and forced to surrender by young Americans who volunteered to invade hell, if they had to, to conquer evil.

World War II rearranged the spinning globe – it ended colonial empires, advanced the speed of technology by light years, redrew that world map, and gave birth to the Cold War from the ashes of Europe and Japan. It unleashed the atomic age.

"I realize the tragic significance of the atomic bomb," President Truman said after Nagasaki. "It is an awful responsibility which has come to us. We thank God that it has come to us, instead of to our enemies; and we pray that He may guide us to use it in His ways and for His purposes."

Unfortunately, America's enemies had already infiltrated the Manhattan Project that built the bomb. Soon Russia, then China, had their own atomic bombs. Two totalitarian tyrannies had survived the war, and now were nuclear superpowers along with the U.S.

The battle against evil was not finished. It is still being waged on different battlefields of ideology, oppression, fanaticism and terrorism. But no generation in the history of the world has been more heroic than the World War II veterans, who took on the world's most evil empires in hand-to-hand combat and rescued the free world from tyranny.

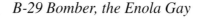

B-29 Bomber, the Enola Gay

"When I looked around, there were five planes on fire."

Lt. (jg) Ken Glass
USS Hornet

A flaming comet of steel, fuel, flesh and high explosives was headed directly at the 872-foot deck of the USS Hornet, hurtling at more than 200 miles per hour. The 38-ton carrier's engines were churning the sea, swinging the bow into the wind to launch its planes when the single kamikaze bomber came out of a clear blue sky with no warning, and dove straight for the ship.

The Hornet's five-inch cannons, 40 mm guns and 20 mm guns frantically fired at the aircraft, creating a wall of flak and lead. Sailors ran for cover, expecting a direct hit that had been fatal to so many other ships. "Without orders from anyone, the petty officer in charge of the aft 20 mm starboard battery opened fire and did enough damage to the plane to cause him to miss the flight deck," an eyewitness said twenty years after the war. Admiral Roy Lee Johnson, who was executive officer on the Hornet at the time, said, "It was a great exhibition not only of initiative but also of courage and coolness under a very difficult situation."

It was also another narrow escape for the USS Hornet CV-12, which was attacked by enemy aircraft fifty-nine times, but never hit. A previous ship with the same name, USS Hornet CV-8, was not so lucky. It was sunk, in part, by a Japanese bomber that crashed into its deck.

"Kamikaze Attack on the Hornet" became one of many famous paintings from World War II. It was painted by Comdr. Dwight Shepler, one of dozens of artists who were assigned to serve aboard ships in combat and record history as it happened.

"That actually was a painting of a scene done almost immediately after it happened," says Ken Glass, who served aboard the Hornet. "I'm sure it was at Okinawa."

For twenty-five years, Glass taught classes as a professor and administrator in the School of Education at Miami University in Oxford, Ohio, north of Cincinnati. Few of his students probably knew that he was also a member of a special society that met regularly at Cincinnati restaurants for breakfast. He was a leader of the Hornet Club, the men who served aboard one of the U.S. Navy's most legendary ships.

Along with Cincinnati-area Hornet crew members Don Brandt, Bud Newkirk, Dick Fitton and Ray Brockman, Glass planned reunions and stayed close to others who had served on Hornet aircraft carriers. In 1998, Glass and Harold Buell of Florida co-authored a book for Hornet crew members who were spread all over the USA: *The Hornets and Their Heroic Men*.

The first Hornet was a sloop of war in the War of 1812. Under command of Capt. James Lawrence, it destroyed a British Brig, the Peacock.

Hornet CV-8, christened in 1939, launched the Doolittle Raid that bombed Tokyo in 1942, then fought in the Battle of Midway, where her entire torpedo-bomber squadron was lost in an attack on the Japanese Navy, except for one survivor who spent the rest of the battle bobbing in a life-jacket, watching U.S. Navy dive bombers sink four Japanese aircraft carriers.

The Hornet CV-8 was sunk at the Battle of Santa Cruz later that year, when she was hit repeatedly by torpedoes from Japanese planes and a dive-bomber that crashed into her signal bridge. As the Hornet struggled valiantly to stay afloat, it was being towed when it was hit again by two more torpedoes and the order was given to abandon ship. Still, the Hornet refused to go under. As the fleet had to retreat, U.S. destroyers launched nine more torpedoes into her hull to keep her from falling into enemy hands. By the next morning, she was gone.

As the sinking of the heroic ship was reported back home, another aircraft carrier that was about to be launched was renamed the Hornet CV-12.

Lieutenant (jg) Glass served on Hornet CV-12 as a pilot in Torpedo Squadron 2, from March 1944 to September 1944, flying thirty-three combat missions and earning four battle stars, a Presidential Unit Citation, seven air medals and a Distinguished Flying Cross.

USS Hornet was in service through WWII, Korea and Vietnam

He was once rescued by a destroyer when his TBF-Avenger torpedo bomber crashed into the sea on takeoff. "At that time our captain thought it was better not to give us much deck space, to get planes off faster. But if your engine coughed once or twice, you were going to go for a swim. And that's what happened."

As his plane struggled to stay in the air, shipmates told him later, he was so close to the surface his airplane kicked up a rooster-tail of water. He tried everything, working the flaps, trying to climb. "I was able to keep it in the air two or three miles. But that was it."

The Avenger was huge for a single-engine airplane, the largest carrier-based plane in World War II with a cockpit standing sixteen feet off the carrier deck. It became one of the first effective ground-support planes, with bombs, rockets, torpedoes and machine guns, as tree-skimming pilots learned to skip bombs into enemy bunkers and caves. It had stubby wings, a long canopy, a rear rotating gun turret and a beer-belly where the torpedoes and bombs were released, making it look a bit like a pregnant goldfish with wings. But it couldn't swim.

"It sank in thirty seconds," Glass recalls. "I was carrying a two-thousand pound mine, and it was just too much weight. My radioman got out right away, but my gunner had a problem." He went back to help, and the gunner struggled free just as the plane sank in water almost a mile deep. "By the time he got out, I had our raft out and hardly got my feet wet."

He was picked up by a destroyer, the USS Monaghan, which later sank in a Pacific typhoon.

Glass took part in the Marianas Turkey Shoot, the greatest carrier battle of the war, and one of the most lopsided outcomes. The Japanese lost 480 planes to the U.S. loss of only twenty-nine.

"We hit Peleliu twice. I was in on one of the first raids on the Philippines. On my last mission my regular wing man's plane was down, and another guy volunteered so I had a new wingman. I led a flight of nine planes. The flak was really heavy over Manilla and they shot him right off my wing. I saw two chutes, but the third guy went in with the plane. I never heard what happened to any of them. They could have been captured and killed. The Japanese were doing a lot of that.

"I was in on one mission over Truk. That was pretty bad, too. When I looked around, there were five planes on fire. One submarine picked up twenty-six pilots. You would go back and land with a lot of flak in your plane. But our fighter cover was so good, we hardly ever saw a Japanese fighter."

Like most veterans, he felt obligated to live a full, successful, good life, as a tribute to his friends who never came home.

On one mission, he was ordered to deliver a secret message to tiny Green Island, 600 miles from the carrier. "I'd never been on such a long flight, nothing like 600 miles over open ocean. The most I had flown was twenty-five or thirty miles. I was a little concerned I wouldn't find the island. When I found it and circled to come in for landing, I remember all I could see was the corrugated steel runway. But when I landed there were F4U Corsairs under every tree. I delivered the message and got back to the carrier right at dark."

Making a landing on the pitching deck of a carrier was harrowing enough – compared to "landing on one city block during a hurricane and an earthquake." It was much worse at night.

The TBM Avenger was primarily designed as a ship-killer, and Glass made the most of his plane.

"On one of our missions to Peleliu, the same day my roommate was killed, I got separated and found myself looking down at a Japanese destroyer. He was really making headway. I had three bombs aboard and a load of rockets. One of my bombs hit on one side, the other hit on the other side. But it brought the destroyer to a halt in the water. Then I really raked it with rockets and machine guns. One of our destroyers caught up with it later and finished it off."

The USS Hornet fought throughout the Pacific, including the First Battle of the Philippine Sea, Iwo Jima and the Marianas, Okinawa and Leyte Gulf. In early 1945, the Hornet CV-12 launched the first full-scale air attack on Tokyo, keeping a promise by the earlier Hornet CV-8 almost three years earlier, when the Doolittle Raiders vowed, "We will be back."

The Hornet CV-12 was also caught in the great typhoon of June 1945, which battered the ship with gusts to 135 mph and towering seas that crushed the takeoff deck like a collapsing roof. "Her forward deck was folded down like a snap-brim hat as she limped into Leyte Gulf," Glass and Buell wrote in their book.

The ship's combat record lists 1,430 enemy planes destroyed in the air and on the ground, and the sinking of one cruiser, one carrier, ten destroyers, forty-two cargo ships and an assist on sinking of the huge Yamato, which was the biggest battleship ever built. A Presidential Unit Citation was awarded "For extraordinary heroism in action."

Decommissioned in 1947, Hornet CV-12 was overhauled and renamed the Hornet CVS-12 in 1967. It fought in Vietnam at the Gulf of Tonkin, and picked up astronauts from Apollo 11 and Apollo 12. It was retired in 1970. In 1990, Glass and hundreds of former crew members in the USS Hornet Club held a reunion in Bremerton, Washington, the shipyard that had become the home of the mothballed Hornet. They were given permission to board the old ship and relive memories of their adventures, victories and lost shipmates.

The USS Hornet, known as one of the most distinguished ships in U.S. Navy history, now sits at anchor in San Francisco Bay, as a museum in Alameda, California. Tourists can walk its teak decks, visit the bridge and stand where sailors manned guns to shoot down kamikaze attacks.

Before he retired from the Naval Reserve in 1972, Glass says, "I flew everything the Navy had with a prop on it." He came home to teach and work at Miami University in small-town Oxford, where he raised five sons who all graduated from Miami. In 1995, Ken and his wife, Rose, were named Parents of the Year by the Miami University students. In 1993, he was named Hornet Man of the Year. Two years later he was inducted into the Ohio Veterans Hall of Fame.

He is also an Honored Veteran at the Tri-State Warbird Museum in Cincinnati. And he flew again with World War II veterans on one of the first Honor Flights, an experience he described as "wonderful."

The Hornets are still getting together, sharing war stories and friendship, expanded now to include all veterans. "I only knew these guys two, maybe two-and-a-half years at most during the war," Glass said. "But they're lifetime buddies. When you're in combat you depend on each other and become friends for life. I don't know how many are left in my squadron, but as long as we're living we have kept together. We had that common bond, facing combat together."

And like most veterans, he felt obligated to live a full, successful, good life, as a tribute to his friends who never came home.

"Absolutely," he says. "My roommate was Soupy Campbell. He was shot down and killed in combat. Indeed, I can remember every one of the guys who was killed. One of them played tackle for Notre Dame before he joined our squadron. One day on takeoff, he hit the island structure, spun off into the water and they were all killed on the plane."

"I've always said the Navy was the best thing that ever happened to me. I had two years of college when I went in but I wasn't doing much. My high school record was not something to brag about. But when I got home I went back to school and finished my masters, then my doctorate at Michigan State. I got all A's. My experience in the Navy changed everything. When you get out you realized you just do the best you can.

"Here I was this kid growing up on a farm, a little old farm boy from the little old town of Dundee, Iowa. When I look back at that, it's just incredible that I did as well as I did. It's been a great life."

The TBM Avenger could take incredible punishment.

"Suddenly this periscope came up and started coming across the water."

Lt. Don Brandt
Hellcat Pilot

When fighter pilots aboard the USS Hornet were briefed about how they could ditch in the sea and be rescued by a submarine, they laughed. "When they told us you grab onto the periscope, we just roared," said Don Brandt, the pilot of an F6F Hellcat in Air Group Two.

It was not so funny a couple of days later in June of 1944, as he was bleeding in a bobbing raft, being shot at by the Japanese, desperately trying to snag a periscope so he could be towed out to sea and avoid being captured on Guam.

"I was on a strafing run when I saw puffs of flak. All of a sudden there was this huge explosion and I was sixty feet above my wingman," he remembered. The crew of a TBF Avenger torpedo bomber he was escorting looked up and spotted his crippled airplane.

"They said, 'You're on fire, you're on fire, bail out.' I opened the canopy, nosed it over and pushed out as fast as I could get out. I gave a final push and fell right out. All I had to do then was pull the ripcord."

When he hit the sea he was uncomfortably close to the enemy-held beach. "I got tangled up in my chute. I broke my ribs and lost my backpack, my raft, everything. All I had was my Mae West (life jacket). But that was enough."

As he bobbed in the ocean, "I sort of felt a little helpless, out there in the middle of nowhere. I was sure they were firing at me in the water, but they couldn't see me very good. After two and a half hours, a dive bomber pilot I knew from the Hornet came by and dropped me a raft. Now I had this bright yellow raft to shoot at.

"The day before, a guy named Duff from our squadron went down. Instead of swimming away from shore, he swam toward the shore and they cut his head off. I went the other way as fast as I could."

After more hours in the raft, "Suddenly this periscope came up and started coming across the water. I had one of my hands all shot up, and the sub has to come by at a pretty good clip so they can maneuver and stay off the coral. I missed it three times. On the fourth try, I got a rope around it and they pulled me out to sea for an hour.

"It was harder than you'd think," he said. "Those periscopes are pretty big and it was all greased up and I only had one hand to work with. The skipper was really ticked off when I finally got aboard, until he found out I only had one hand to work with. Then he said I was lucky to grab it at all."

When the sub towed him far enough beyond the range of enemy guns, it surfaced and hauled him aboard. As he was helped down a ladder through the conning tower, he spotted a familiar face – a classmate from Hughes High School in Cincinnati. "I said, 'Hi, Elmer,' and he said, 'Hi, Don.'

"The skipper said, 'You two guys know each other?' I said, 'Yeah, we went to Hughes High School together.' He said, 'I don't believe it.'"

His classmate was Elmer Bavey. They became good friends after the war back home in Cincinnati. They attended a reunion together for submarine sailors and were golf buddies.

'Thank God that President Truman had the guts to drop the two bombs. I don't think anybody out there in the South Pacific who was part of invasion force would have survived.'

Brandt was on the Stingray for a month, then was transferred back to the Hornet, passed from ship to ship at sea on a "preacher's buoy" – a contraption of lines and pulleys, with a suspended canvas bag. "They shoot a line over and put you in a sack and send you over. It was worse than a parachute jump. I saw it and said, 'Oh, God almighty.' I did that five times."

When he got back aboard the Hornet, he flew a combat mission the next day.

"You will never believe it, but the day I got shot down was my 13th mission on the 13th of June. We were flying at 13,000 feet."

U.S. Navy Hellcats on patrol

Brandt flew his Hellcat in the battles of Iwo Jima, Saipan, Truk and "a whole bunch of 'em." He logged 36 missions on two tours of duty and was awarded five air medals, the Distinguished Flying Cross and a Purple Heart.

When he came home to Cincinnati, he finished college at the University of Cincinnati, became a civil engineer, got married, and went into the construction business. He eventually started his own company building homes and developing land in the booming subdivisions of Anderson Township.

He became a regular member of the Hornet's Club, which was still meeting once a month in 2015, with attendance of 70 to 80 veterans, at the Twin Towers Senior Living Community in Cincinnati. "After our 1995 reunion we enjoyed the meetings so much we just decided to keep them going. It's the compatibility, people who went through the same kind of deals."

About 50 years after the war he went to a reunion at Pensacola, Florida and someone asked him if he wanted to meet the guy who dropped him a raft after he bailed out at Guam. "I said 'Wonderful, I'd like to meet him.' And there he was, the radioman-gunner who dropped me the raft. I asked, 'Are you the guy who dropped me the raft?' He said, 'Yes sir, I was.' I told him, 'You damn near hit me in the head with that thing.' He just about died laughing."

Brandt went back for a second tour of duty in 1945 and was sent to Saipan as a lieutenant, to prepare for the invasion of Japan in the newest Navy fighter-bomber, the F4U Corsair. "The F6F Hellcat and F4U Corsair were both wonderful planes, but the F4U outshone everything."

From his airfield, he saw B-29s take off from the nearby island of Tinian, on missions to bomb Japan. "We watched the Enola Gay and Bockscar take off. They dropped the bombs that ended the war. Thank God that President Truman had the guts to drop the two bombs. I don't think anybody out there in the South Pacific who was part of invasion force would have survived."

Brandt took one of the first Honor Flights and loved it. "It was wonderful, well planned, everyone was well taken care. It was just a great experience."

Like many veterans, he has vivid memories of the most exciting time in his life, and they're not all bad. "Do I miss it? Well, it's pretty hard to miss something that could only occur the way it did. There is no way to replace the things that happened to you. How could you possibly replace something like that? But watching whole bunches of planes taking off from carriers at dawn... Yeah. That was once in a lifetime."

As for his friends who did not come home, "You don't want to do too much thinking about it. If you keep dwelling on something like that, it will get to you. A couple of them were very close."

"The cloying odor of the newly dead, as well as the stench of rotting flesh, were with us all the time when we were on the attack."

Lt. Arthur Spiegel
USMC

Art Spiegel is remembered by Cincinnati for lots of things. He was the federal judge who sentenced Cincinnati Reds star Pete Rose to prison. He was a boxing champ at the University of Cincinnati in 1941 and 1942. He was a painter, a shade-tree mechanic and owner of a single-engine airplane he loved to fly. He also owned a donkey that he kept in his backyard and rode through his neighborhood.

But before he was Judge Arthur Spiegel, he was a lieutenant in the First Marine Division in the Pacific, who sweated, bled and suffered with other Marines at Okinawa, Peleliu and Guadalcanal.

Lt. Arthur Spiegel in the Pacific

"There were large snakes, typhus-carrying rats and mosquitos that carried malaria and elephantiasis, or filariasis," he wrote about patrols in New Guinea in his memoir, *Spiegel*. "No matter how hot it was we had to keep ourselves covered as much as possible, with our trousers tucked in our socks and our sleeves rolled down to our hands, to avoid exposure, particularly to the scrub typhus organisms, which were deadly."

During his jungle-war service, he had dysentery, malaria and ringworm from his feet to his waist. During a battle on Cape Gloucester, New Britain, Lt. Spiegel swam into the surf to flank Japanese soldiers who were shooting a pinned-down Marine. When his sand-clogged .45 pistol wouldn't fire, he threw hand grenades into the enemy position, grabbed the Marine and pulled him to safety, back to his own lines. "The Japanese with the machinegun continued to fire, and I could see the bullets striking the edge of the trench above my head," he wrote. "I later learned that the Japanese who had been shooting at me was an officer and had been mortally wounded by my hand grenades, but kept firing the machinegun at us until he died."

Like many American Marines, soldiers and sailors, Spiegel was probably saved when the U.S. bombed Hiroshima and Nagasaki with atom bombs. He was home on leave at the time, but assumed he would soon be sent back. "All of us felt, in those days, that the war would last another 18 months, and even if we were able to break the resistance of the Japanese Armed forces on the main islands of Japan, there were still two large Japanese armies on the Chinese mainland that would have to be defeated. We knew that the Japanese had fought with ferocity at Peleliu and Iwo Jima and Okinawa, and they would be twice as tenacious fighting in their homeland. None of us had any illusions about what was going to happen when we invaded the Japanese mainland."

After serving as a forward observer and artillery spotter on the ground, Spiegel began flying as a spotter in small, unarmed light planes. At Okinawa, he flew missions 12 hours a day, and sometimes at night. The single-engine Piper he flew in had only an 18-inch piece of steel under each seat to protect the pilot and spotter. They flew low and slow, often targeted by ground fire, sometimes in the path of their own incoming artillery shells.

The son of a judge and grandson of a Cincinnati mayor saw the brutality of war from the air and hacked his way through tangled vines in stinking, snake infested, poisonous jungles. "The veneer of civilization is pretty thin," he wrote, "and just how thin becomes apparent during a war. We did things and endured conditions that no sane person would expect.

"On Cape Gloucester one afternoon after we had taken our objective for the day and were clearing our fields of fire with machetes, a concealed Japanese sniper shot several of our men and pinned others down nearby. A couple of Marines circled behind him and killed him. They cut off his head and brought it back, glasses and all, and jammed it down on the end of his rifle, which they then stuck in the ground in full view of the enemy. There were no second thoughts. Time and again we would be sharing foxholes with dead enemy. The cloying odor of the newly dead, as well as the stench of rotting flesh, were with us all the time when we were on the attack."

He wrote a letter home from Guadalcanal on Christmas, in 1944. "The 'States,' as we call them over here, are like a large mongrel dog. Full of the best breeds, wise in the ways of the world and capable of taking care of himself when pressed. The Smiths, the O'Learies, the Kuyscuskis, the Cohens and the Higgins. Backyards full of rusty tin cans, rumble of trains, yelling of newsboys, cigarette ads, half-baked Congressmen, symphony orchestras, sweating in the bleachers at a baseball game, and freezing in the stands at a football game, going to the movies, then somewhere to dance and eat, hell from the old man for this or that, patter of rain against the window pane… These are America – a hodge-podge of disconnected emotions, a panorama of different colors, conglomeration of ideas, a state of mind, something so great and intangible that it cannot be specifically described but only felt."

Arthur Spiegel was remembered for many things when he died on the last day of 2014 at age 94. Among the men he served with, he was remembered as a Marine.

"We could see the water coming in, spraying through the old rivets. But we didn't want to break the surface, or the destroyer would find us."

Cmdr. Walter Kraus
Submariner, U.S. Navy

The USS S-36 was a relic from World War I, so antiquated it had no name, just a number. Launched in 1919, it was ancient in submarine years when World War II broke out on December 7, 1941.

"My worst experience was on S-36," said Cmdr. Walter Kraus, who served aboard several submarines during a 30-year Navy career that spanned World War II, Korea and Vietnam.

"Even though it was the beginning of the war, we were an old riveted boat, with no ventilation and no water. Everybody had a stainless steel bucket with your name on it, and we could put in a half-inch of water each day to brush your teeth, then save enough to splash some water on your face and under your arms, then throw it in the bilge."

There were no stills on the old boat to make fresh water. "We had to make it from our exhaust systems, which would only make about three or four gallons an hour. And we needed that for watering the batteries. It was hell. There was no air conditioning, and everything was pneumatic, there were no hydraulics."

On December 8, while patrolling in the waters off the Philippines, the crew got word on the radio that Pearl Harbor had been attacked, and they were at war with Japan. The next day, their boat started leaking air. Then the electrical steering failed, followed by exhaust-valve leaks. The war was only a few days old and the S-36 was already in trouble.

"On our second patrol we were depth charged and pretty heavily damaged. We lost our gyroscope and much of the electrical system. We went through hell for eight or nine days, then headed to Borneo for repairs."

Kraus, a machinist's mate second class, will never forget what it was like as the 217-foot sub lost control and began to sink to the bottom, hunted by a Japanese destroyer that lurked on the surface.

"After we were depth-charged, we couldn't run the pneumatic pumps because they were making such a noise. We didn't have any saddle tanks like the newer submarines, only ballast tanks, so we had no bow buoyancy. The commanding officer took over, and let me tell you we had a new respect for him after that for the way he was able to control that boat. We were dropping down close to three hundred feet, and the test depth was two hundred. We could see the water coming in, spraying through the old rivets."

As the commander flooded and vented one end, then the other, to slowly approach the surface, "All the water came back through the engine room. We were like a yo-yo for an about an hour. But we didn't want to break the surface, or the destroyer would find us."

As it turned out, the obsolete sub became a lifesaver. Unlike new subs, "It vented inward. That made it really uncomfortable and hot, but saved us, because on the new boats those bubbles would have given us away."

The enemy destroyer finally gave up, but the troubles were not over for S-36.

"Then we had a fire in the aft battery. The smoke raised hell with us. We got the fire out, but what do you do with all the smoke inside the boat? There was no ventilation and we couldn't surface, so we just had to live with that."

"When we were finally able to open a hatch, that was quite a relief."

Kraus joined the Navy long before most veterans of World War II, and finished his career in Vietnam on the Naval Forces staff of Admiral Elmo Zumwalt.

"I graduated from high school in Cincinnati in 1938. I lost my job and I was looking around for work when I went by the recruiting office on Eighth and Walnut, above the old Post Office. A recruiter said, 'Hey, why don't you join the Navy? C'mon up.' They sat me down and gave me the exam. I did so well they came to my house and wanted me to join the Navy. But my mother wouldn't sign the papers and I wasn't 18 yet. She said, 'After you turn 18 you can do what you want, but I'm not going to be involved in sending you.' So as soon as I turned 18, I joined up. I was taken on January 4, 1939."

He served briefly aboard a destroyer, the USS Shaw, which later was destroyed in dry dock during the attack on Pearl Harbor. He volunteered for submarine training, which included escaping from a chamber under 100 feet of water. He learned, "When you're really deep, you have to keep your mouth open so the air can escape or your lungs will explode."

His first submarine was the S-36 in 1940. He remembers it well.

After being heavily damaged by depth charges on January 15, 1942, the S-36 was limping along through the Makasar Strait off Indonesia. Kraus oiled red hot bearings and smoking engines with salad oil to keep the sub going. Then on January 18, the sub ran aground on a reef.

The boat was taking on water and began filling with chlorine gas from the submerged batteries. The crew fought to save S-36 for 24 hours, but finally abandoned ship and was picked up by a Dutch freighter. All of the crew members got off safely, although 36 would eventually die on other submarines during the war.

Kraus was transferred to the much newer 303-foot USS Snapper (SS-185). "When I went aboard it I thought I died and went to heaven." He also served on the USS Pickerel, "But the Snapper saw the most action. We were looking for 'em. We used to say there were only two types of ships: Submarines and targets. Even the S-36 sank a five thousand-ton freighter, which is why we got depth charged."

The Snapper delivered twenty-three tons of food to troops that were trapped by the Japanese on Corregidor, and rescued about two dozen who were spared the brutality of the Bataan Death March.

"We sank seven ships altogether. But we were plagued with torpedoes that really raised hell with us. Some fired prematurely. The magnetic exploders were no damn good. Some would be a dud, and others would launch to just 150 feet and explode. That was worse than a damn depth charge. Others would hit the side of the ship and not explode at all. Two of our submarines were sunk by their own torpedoes. We lost fifty-two submarines during the war."

But the Snapper lost just one crewman while Kraus was aboard. "We were trying to pick up a pilot. Subs picked up 504 airmen who were shot down, including President George Bush. We were going to pick up this guy in a raft. He was paddling toward us and the lookout said, 'Plane, plane,' and the commander said, 'Dive, dive.'

"The plane hit us with what must have been a 40mm. It wounded the captain and a sailor named McKee was hit in the head. When we were down to about eighty-five feet, the plane dropped his bombs. It was like a depth charge, boy it really blasted us. We tried to keep McKee alive, but he died about an hour later and we had to bury him at sea. We never knew what happened to the pilot."

After achieving the rank of commander, Kraus retired from the Navy after a career that started on a leaking World War I relic and wound up in helicopters and jets over Saigon and Da Nang. He lives in the suburb of Crescent Springs in Northern Kentucky.

He took an Honor Flight in 2010. "It was great. I enjoyed it very much. I had been to Washington before, but not to see the World War II Memorial. Those plaques they put in really tell the story."

His advice to visitors: "Start on the starboard side of the monument and go all around and it tells you the entire story from the military point of view."

Korea and 38th Paralle

China

North Korea

★ Pyongyang

38th Parallel

- -

Seoul ★

South Korea

The Korean War: Freedom is Not Free

They called it "The Forgotten War" for many reasons. Americans were exhausted, sick of war, still grieving for lost sons, brothers and husbands. But the veterans of Korea took the brunt of the nation's disgust with a limited war that fell short of victory with an embarrassing truce. It was humiliating for the nation that vanquished Germany and Japan to settle for a draw with lowly North Korea – like watching a world champion prizefighter throw in the towel in a bar fight against a puny store clerk.

But the men who are still stung by America's cold indifference and short memory have not forgotten what they endured. They fought human waves from Communist China and the best weapons, training and pilots Stalin could send from the Soviet Union. They can't forget the bone-aching cold, the desolate alien landscape, the fanatical tide of enemy soldiers, the barbarically cruel prison camps and the thousands of men who died there.

The combat in Korea was no less brutal than Guadalcanal and Iwo Jima. But the wound that never healed was not from bullets and bombs. It was from watching the same nation that gave everything to win World War II, turn its back on Korea, sending Americans to fight with worn out weapons and threadbare support.

Just as World War II was born in the ashes of World War I, the dragon's teeth of the Korean War were planted by World War II, when the Soviet Union and the U.S. agreed to divide the former Japanese colony into two zones of occupation. A civil war broke out between North and South Korea, as North Korean leader Kim Il Sung undermined national elections and prepared an invasion.

The buildup was obvious, but the U.S. was caught by surprise. Sung was given the greenlight from Stalin to invade South Korea, on the promise that it would be over so quickly, the U.S. and the United Nations would be helpless to stop it. American troops had pulled out. Stalin saw Korea as an easy pawn on the Cold War chessboard.

On June 25, 1950, the North Korean People's Army (NKPA) of 135,000 crossed the 38th Parallel dividing North and South, and captured the South Korean Capital of Seoul in three days. The U.S.-backed Republic of Korea Army (ROKA) of 95,000 was poorly armed and had no airpower. By the end of June, the South's army was reduced to twenty thousand troops, scrambling in disorganized retreat.

The U.S. Army sent troops from the occupying force in Japan. But they were outnumbered and poorly equipped, with cast-offs from World War II. The U.S. war machine was worn out after four years of all-out war, and there was no appetite to replace it. Korea was a rude interruption of the post-war victory celebration.

Under Gen. Douglas MacArthur, the U.S. sent reinforcements piecemeal, to buy time at great cost in lives and weapons. As the Communist NKPA army defeated and routed U.S. troops early in the war at Osan and Taijon, American support and morale at home evaporated.

As they were being pushed into the sea, the U.S. 8th Army made a valiant stand on the southeastern tip of the Korean peninsula at Pusan. The United Nations sent troops from twenty-nine countries, including Australia, the United Kingdom, Canada, France, Turkey, Greece, Thailand and New Zealand.

The 8th Army, with reinforcements from the First Marine Division, held its ground at Pusan and began to push the NKPA Army north. General MacArthur launched a daring invasion in the middle of the Peninsula, landing X Corps at the western port of Inchon, cutting the NKPA Army in half and retaking the offensive. Seoul was recaptured and all but thirty thousand of the NKPA Army in the south was destroyed.

On October 19, 1950, the U.S. and U.N. forces captured the capital of North Korea, Pyongyang. ROKA units pushed to within sixty-five miles of the Russian border, as U.S. forces pushed closer to the border of China. Both Communist nations warned they would not allow a U.S. ally on their borders. But the warnings were dismissed.

On November 25, China joined the war with a massive offensive. Soviet MiG-15s provided air-cover, with pilots sent by Stalin.

"We face an entirely new war," MacArthur reported to President Truman on November 28.

The "new war" was like an X-ray that revealed a Cold War cancer Americans would battle throughout coming decades. It was the first shooting war between communists and the West.

It was the first limited war, without a clear call to victory. It was the first war in which the nuclear superpowers – the U.S. and the USSR – fought through surrogates on the map of Korea. President Truman was scorned for calling it a "police action," but his extreme understatement had a purpose: He was trying to avoid escalating Korea into World War III against Stalin and Red China.

Stalin had the same fear, and prohibited Soviet pilots from flying over South Korea where they could be captured and provoke a direct attack on the USSR by the U.S. Meanwhile, Truman, MacArthur and the Air Force pilots who fought them in F-85 fighter-jets knew that Soviet pilots were flying those MiGs, but kept the secret.

Truman believed Stalin was testing America's resolve, hoping to knock over Asian nations like dominoes as he diverted attention from his primary goal in Europe.

Personal friction and poor leadership by MacArthur and Truman also turned Americans against the war. MacArthur arrogantly ignored Truman's commands by threatening to attack China, and Truman was forced to fire him – proving that generals who play politics are as dangerous as politicians who play war.

Americans were dismayed and disillusioned to see their pipe-smoking World War II hero in the Pacific "relieved" in disgrace. MacArthur came home to wage a maudlin, personal war against Truman. He did not fade away gracefully.

Perhaps the most important lesson from the Korean War was the way it exposed the Achilles heel of a free democratic republic: popular opinion.

The threat of an atomic World War III made all-out war unthinkable – and Americans quickly turned against the painful "play not to lose" alternative. But totalitarian dictators such as Stalin and Mao Tse-Tung didn't care about popular opinion, military morale or massive human losses. They soon realized they could outlast an enemy they could not outfight. America's enemies have often learned that lesson better than we have.

None of that fine print was in the enlistment papers signed by the soldiers, sailors, Marines and airmen who fought at Pork Chop Hill, the Chosin Reservoir and the Pusan Perimeter. They battled, died and bled for their country just like the veterans of World War II – and many were veterans of World War II, whose homecomings were cut short by call-ups to Korea.

An armistice was signed at Panmunjon on July 27, 1953. The truce is still in effect, as both sides patrol and stand ready across a Demilitarized Zone of trenches, tunnels, barbed wire and locked and loaded weapons.

The Pentagon lists 33,651 Americans killed in combat in the Korean War. They are not forgotten.

"It was so cold, if you stopped moving long enough you would freeze to death."

Sgt. Harry Falck
Korean War POW

They thought it was over. "We were all packed up, ready to go home. Then all hell broke loose."

It was early November 1950. Sgt. Harry Falck was leading a twelve-man patrol about five miles south of the Yalu River, which divides North Korea from China. He had landed in Korea in September and joined the battle as U.S. and South Korean troops fought their way out of the Pusan Perimeter at the southern tip of South Korea.

"They were pushing troops in like nobody's business. Once we broke out, we kept on pushing north and the North Koreans kept falling back. Combat was rugged."

As the North Koreans retreated all the way to the Chinese border, Red China warned that they would not allow the U.S. or its South Korean ally on their border. Gen. Douglas MacArthur ignored the warnings and assured leaders in Washington that the Chinese would stay out of the war.

"We got as far north as five miles from the Yalu River," Falck said. "We were told to stop, that we were going home. All we had to do was patrol the area. There was not much fighting."

Then the Red Chinese invaded on November 2. "We saw people coming across the river as soon as it got dark. During World War II, the Japanese had used Chinese prison labor to cut down trees and drive pilings into the lowest parts of the river. They filled them with rocks and dirt and made bridges that were one or two feet under the water. You couldn't see them from the air.

"So when we radioed and reported that the Chinese were coming across the river, they told us, 'There are no bridges there.' I cussed out that colonel and told him, 'If you don't believe it, come here and see it yourself.' Our officers thought the war was done. They weren't paying attention."

Falck's K Company of the 8th Cavalry Division was swamped by a tidal wave of Chinese troops who were blowing bugles, throwing grenades and firing machine guns from every direction. "They came from this way and that way and every way. To the day I die I will never forget the killing of those poor kids, just piling them up. We fought 'till we ran out of ammunition. "

As his patrol retreated south, he didn't know they were already surrounded. "We were walking through rice paddies and we passed a group, it looked like thousands of South Koreans, so we stood aside to let them pass. All of a sudden someone stuck a pitchfork at me. They had sickles, rifles, spears, anything they could find. I said, 'I guess this is it,' and they took our rifles."

For Falck, who grew up in the Cincinnati suburb of Madeira, the shooting war was over and the long, dark hell of being a prisoner of war was about to begin.

He joined lines of prisoners that stretched for miles. "We had to take care of our own. If someone got weak he would say, 'I'm a burden, just leave me.' And we'd say, 'Forget it.' We dragged them along. Then someone would run off and you'd hear a pop! Goodbye. That was it. We had to just leave them. That was hard to do. Just unreal."

The POWs were marched for five days through brutal cold to the Pyoktang Prison Camp. Stragglers were shot. For the next three years he was shuffled from camp to camp, and starved from almost two hundred pounds down to barely a hundred pounds when he was finally released in 1953. He and other prisoners had to survive on a few handfuls of rice, corn and soybeans, and an occasional unlucky stray dog.

He wore the same uniform for a year. "It was so cold if you stopped moving long enough you would freeze to death."

Each day, they were sent on work details to gather wood, fetch supplies or dig graves. Or they would be herded into an open field to listen to communist indoctrination from English-speaking Chinese who had been educated in the U.S.

"They'd say, 'Comrades, why are you fighting a war for the capitalists who send you to kill innocent people in a peace-loving nation while they stay home getting rich?' Our response was, 'Why are you fighting for Korea? Why don't you stay home?'"

If one man spoke up, they all stood with him, but that meant being labeled as 'reactionaries' who would be punished. "Even though you were living in misery and filth, you had to write home that you were well treated and had good food. It was propaganda."

When Falck 'accidentally' struck a guard while wrestling with another prisoner, he was buried alive in a vertical grave so narrow he had no room to sit or scratch bites from bugs that crawled over him in the pitch dark. They kept him there for three days.

When the war ended and he was finally set free in September of 1953, "We all stripped off our Chinese uniforms in the ambulance. We were stark naked when we came to the hospital, and there was a whole line of nurses waiting for us. Our faces were so red."

Several days of interrogation followed. "They wanted to know who stayed, who died, did you see any Russians. I knew of twenty-one prisoners who switched sides."

He came home a walking stick-figure. When his family asked if it was true that he had been well fed, he replied, "Just look at me."

He was married and went to work as a bank security guard. Years later, Falck was honored as Grand Marshal of his local Memorial Day parade, and seldom missed gatherings on Veterans Day, where he was in the most exclusive veterans' club: former POWs who survived captivity, torture, frostbite and merciless hunger.

At one of the gatherings, one of the former POW's wives joked that, "These guys will eat anything." Falck laughed. He had stared into the gaunt face of starvation and survived. "I'm no hero," he would insist. "What I am is just a survivor."

The landing at Inchon was a turning point in the Korean War

"When they signed the armistice, the feeling I remember was joy. I was very happy."

Seamen Joe Santoro
Korean War, U.S. Navy

Hub and Joe were as close as crossed fingers. They worked together every day, making bumpers for Chryslers at the Sharonville Autolite plant. They raised their kids together – an even dozen, six each. They vacationed together, spent family-time together and grew old together with their wives, two couples living life through babies, graduations, celebrations and setbacks, sickness and health, for better and for worse.

They even served in the Korean War together, although neither knew it until they came home and met each other at the bumper factory.

"We were lifelong friends," said Joe Santoro. "We got married within a year of each other, and we were in each other's weddings. We'd needle each other about high school. He was Elder and I was Roger Bacon. We all called him Hub. His name was Howard Paff. He was in the Army, I was in the Navy. He never talked about it and I never asked, but I think he saw combat."

In April of 2015, they took an Honor Flight – together, of course – and loved it. They were inseparable, a friendship welded by more than sixty years of shared jokes, good times, family vacations and common experience in work and war. Four months after their Honor Flight, Hub died of cancer. And Joe misses him a lot.

Santoro was stationed on the USS Fort Marion, a landing ship dock that was used for amphibious assaults by Marines. At battle stations, he operated a 40 mm anti-aircraft canon. "It was ideal for shooting aircraft out of the air. It had twin cannons, and two of us operated it, targeting by line of sight. The only contact we had with planes was when they towed a drone for practice. Other than that, nothing at all."

He considers himself very lucky. He was in the Navy from 1951 to 1955, some of the worst years of the war, but most of the time he was stationed in San Diego. "By the time we got to Korea, they had just signed the armistice. It was signed a week before we got there. I was pretty elated by it. The feeling I remember was joy. I was very happy."

The USS Fort Marion was put to work mainly as a transport to haul dredging equipment from Japan to Korea, to improve South Korea's shallow, debris cluttered harbors and allow more heavy shipping.

But he says it was an amazing experience. "This may sound funny, but what I remember most was all the traveling we did in the Pacific area. We went to the Philippines, we were in Hong Kong and we spent a lot of time in Japan, where we were stationed after San Diego."

His assignment was to take care of storerooms and take inventory of supplies. "I was a Seaman. I couldn't seem to pass a typing test," he joked.

"I don't think too many Americans know about the Korean War. When they think about that part of the world, they think more about Vietnam. But it was something that had to be done, I suppose. I don't know if I totally agree with all the wars we get into, protecting other people when we're not being invaded. I often wonder if we were really under any kind of threat. We were in Korea to help the Koreans."

He's heard about the term "The Forgotten War," and doesn't much like it. "A lot of men were killed over there, so it's hard to say it was a forgotten war."

He understands why war-weary Americans mostly ignored the sacrifices by veterans of the Korean War. "I've always thought I was treated pretty well. I never had any problems. We didn't get the welcome home a lot of vets had after World War II. But when people found out what we had been doing over there, they were respectful."

As they toured the monuments in Washington on their Honor Flight, Joe and Hub were most impressed by the Korean War Memorial. "It was very, very interesting the way it was – with people coming out of a jungle area, that was very impressive. I thought to myself I hope we never do that again."

And when they got home and landed in Cincinnati, they were amazed to be greeted by a huge crowd. "I was just overwhelmed with all the people there. There must have been a thousand. All my family was there, Hub's whole family was there.

"We've had a lot of good times over the years," he said, remembering his buddy. And the Honor Flight was among their best. "Don't miss it if you have an opportunity to go. My son was my guardian. And now he wants his three boys to see the memorials. Everyone should see them."

Santoro now lives in Mason, Ohio after years in nearby Sharonville. And when he goes to Veterans Day ceremonies, he always remembers Hub. "I like to wear my Korean War hat and my Honor Flight shirt. A lot of people see it and talk to me about it."

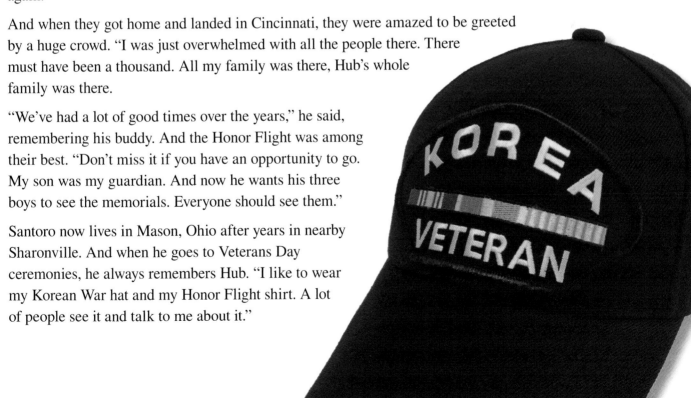

Vietnam: Tragic Sacrifice
For an Ungrateful Nation

It was a war that was born in doubt and ended in bitter regret. As if given a second chance to pass the Cold War test of limited warfare, America repeated the mistakes of Korea and added political malpractice to make Vietnam worse.

Vietnam still raises unanswered questions, such as: How could the legacy of courage from the World War II generation be so quickly trampled in the anti-war protests and draft-dodging peace marches of the next generation? How could the nation that defeated fascists in Germany, Italy and Japan decline so fast into stalemate in Korea and defeat in Vietnam?

America turned its war-weary back on Korea, but it turned violently against Vietnam. The result was a divided country, generational hostility, abiding distrust of political leaders, loss of faith among our allies, an increasingly biased political media and loss of confidence in American power.

There was no truce that divided the nation between freedom and totalitarian communism like the barbed-wire border at Korea's 38th Parallel. Vietnam was a total loss, a deep wound in the nation's spirit that couldn't be whitewashed with doubletalk about "de-escalation" and "peace with honor."

As the last Americans scrambled aboard helicopters on the roof of the U.S. Embassy in Saigon in 1975, we left behind the tragic sacrifice of 58,000 American lives. Our friends and allies who fought by our side in South Vietnam were betrayed, left to the mercy of North Vietnam's invading army (NVA), which made a cruel mockery of the peace agreement signed two years earlier. The war that began with the first support for South Vietnam by President Eisenhower in 1954, was America's first loss, and the wounds, especially among the veterans who sacrificed so much for an ungrateful, feckless, poorly led nation, are still not healed.

Just like Korea, Vietnam was destabilized by the collapse of colonialism after World War II; another Asian nation that became a battleground in the struggle between the free world and communists in China and the Soviet Union. Korea and Vietnam were divided by lines on a map – Communist north and democratic south – and shared many parallels.

As Communist North Vietnam attacked the South, it was Korea redux – a fresh line in the sand between the superpowers. The Domino Theory that originated in Korea applied again: If one nation falls, the rest follow. "Wars of national liberation" were certainly the plot by the USSR and China, as both supplied massive artillery, aircraft, weapons, training and other materiel, just as they had in Korea.

In 1961, President John Kennedy called Vietnam "the cornerstone of the free world in Southeast

Asia." He sent advisers, then 9,000 troops in 1962 as his own advisers told him the army of South Vietnam (ARVN) was losing.

When Kennedy was killed in 1963, Vice President Lyndon Johnson became President. He had visited Saigon in 1961. Almost immediately he sent 16,000 troops in 1963 and 23,000 in 1964. But Johnson saw the war as a distraction from his extravagant Great Society domestic programs. Once again, America was slipping into an undeclared, limited war in Asia with no clear plan for victory, uncertain public support, unclear goals and an undecided strategy.

The North escalated with massive waves of NVA regulars, sent to aid the Viet Cong insurgents in the South via the Ho Chi Minh Trail. As President Johnson considered bombing North Vietnam, the Destroyer USS Maddox was attacked by Vietnamese torpedo boats in the Gulf of Tonkin. Congress rushed to pass the Gulf of Tonkin Resolution to escalate, and the bombing of North Vietnam began.

By the end of 1966, more bombs had been dropped on North Vietnam than on Japan during World War II, but with little effect. The arms and supplies came from Russia and China. Bombing the North to cripple its war effort was like bombing a beehive to stop a termite infestation. North Vietnam's weapons were people and patience. They had both in abundance. The Communists had learned well from the Korean War that free democratic republics quickly tire of protracted, limited war by attrition.

As President Johnson sent 100,000 more troops in 1965 and again in 1966, the draft became a target of violent protests and civil disobedience. The media brought the war into American living rooms for the first time, with reports that scathingly undermined public support. The names of battles became household headlines: Ia Drang, Khe Sanh, the Iron Triangle, Quang Tri, the Mekong Delta, Haiphong, Hanoi, Bien Ho, Da Nang, Hue, Hamburger Hill…

In 1967, 35,000 protesters marched against the war at the Pentagon, chanting "Hey, hey, LBJ, how many kids did you kill today?" The credibility of the military was damaged by false optimism and inflated body counts. Media coverage openly turned against the war. Sensing America's weakness, the Viet Cong launched a massive attack in 1967, simultaneously hitting hundreds of cities and U.S. air bases. The Tet Offensive was a military disaster for the North, which lost 37,000 troops compared to 2,500 Americans killed. But the media reported it as a shattering defeat for the U.S.

In 1968, President Johnson conceded that he had lost the war politically. He announced plans to "de-escalate" and shocked the nation by refusing to run for re-election. The peak of 550,000 American troops in Vietnam would slowly dwindle, but the fighting increased in ferocity as the North saw America flinch. In the following weeks, 3,700 Americans were killed and 18,000 were wounded.

That same year, President Richard Nixon was elected on his promise to end the war. As troops were pulled out, those left behind felt abandoned and betrayed by windsock politicians waging a pointless war. Troop morale cratered, with drug abuse, race conflict and "fragging" murders of officers.

Between 1965 and 1973, more than 300,000 young men were dishonorably discharged for desertion, while another 500,000 dodged the draft. Protests climaxed when National Guard soldiers fired on students at Ohio's Kent State University and killed four students. Even today, more baby-boomers know how many were killed at Kent State than how many of their classmates died in Vietnam.

President Nixon bombed North Vietnam's Capital, Hanoi, to the peace table and forced an agreement on January 27, 1973, the same year the draft was abolished. The last military units left three months later. The Communists ignored the agreement and invaded the South. The demoralized South Vietnamese army that had often fought valiantly, in spite of corrupt political leaders, collapsed in two months. President Nixon asked Congress for help to rescue our allies who were targeted for murder and brutal "re-education" camps, but the U.S. Congress that had supported and escalated the war refused.

Thousands of South Vietnamese refugees perished at sea as they fled the country in boats, barges and anything that would float – a tragic testimony to the dishonorable indifference of America's politicians.

The media and protesters were so effective in undermining support for the war, that they also destroyed support for the troops who fought, often through no choice of their own. The veterans' courageous service to America was literally and figuratively spat upon by anti-war protesters and treated with shrugs and suspicion by many of their own generation.

It was a sad and discouraging end for the legacy of courage from the World War II generation. The hangover of "another Vietnam" lingered until the 1991 Gulf War victory, and it's still a reliquary of anti-American resentment on the left.

Now, 40 years after the war ended, Vietnam veterans are joining veterans of World War II and the Korean War on Honor Flights to finally get the thanks and appreciation they always deserved.

"We were all out there looking for each other. When we did encounter each other, we tried to eradicate them."

Pfc. Gary Flesch
Vietnam

"The first thing I remember is stepping off the plane and having the air sucked right out of me with all the heat and humidity."

It was 1970. While some of his friends enjoyed the "Summer of Love" with drugs, rock concerts and protest marches, Gary Flesch landed in Vietnam carrying a duffle bag of anger. A few months later, he brought home a head wound and more anger than he could carry.

"I had the feeling we weren't over there to win. And as a draftee I had that anger then that I was there while others were dodging their duties and commitments. Put all together, there wasn't any great sense of accomplishing anything over there."

As he got off the plane, he was told to pick up his equipment and get ready for a drive to headquarters at Long Binh Post near Saigon. "We were going through a shooting gallery – the perfect place for an ambush. That was the first word we had. Welcoming news."

After arriving safely at headquarters, he was assigned to the 4th Infantry Division in the Central Highlands, at An Khe. "We were told to go out and find the Viet Cong and engage them. So we would throw on a rucksack and hump the boonies. Most missions were about two weeks, hiking through the jungle, looking for Viet Cong. And they were doing the same. We were all out there looking for each other. When we did encounter each other, we tried to eradicate them."

At the time, de-escalation of the war was just beginning – which only intensified attacks by the VC and North Vietnamese Army, who saw that the weakening U.S. had no appetite for the war and could be defeated. As the U.S. pulled troops out, North Vietnam poured on the attacks.

"On one day we had pitched camp, and I heard some rifle fire. I remember just standing out there in the camp, with something whistling right by us. It's true that bullets whistle. It must have been right by my ear, because I heard the whistling. Out of the corner of my eye I saw a figure jump out of the brush a few meters ahead of me. He just jumped out and opened fire."

That was the only time he saw the enemy face to face.

"A few days later, we were in another location and heard a thump, thump, and someone yelled 'Incoming!' They were firing mortar rounds at us. I didn't know much about mortars, but one of the guys had humped a big tube and shells, so I ran over to help him and get off some rounds. I was dropping rounds in there while the others adjusted for direction and elevation. I would yell 'Round hanging!' and drop it, and we were returning mortar fire.

"As soon as you drop it in, you have to bend over, to make sure you don't get your ears damaged. As I was bent over, I opened my eyes and saw purple gushes coming out of my forehead. My arm was burning too. A fragment had gone down my arm and creased my left front temple area."

Flesch had been hit by shrapnel from an incoming mortar round.

"They called in a dust-off (helicopter) to pick up the wounded. With a few others, I was the only one hit in the head. I didn't lose consciousness. We were all just kind of joking about how we got to go back to the rear. Those other guys were patched up and sent back out. But they held me in the field hospital. They told me the head wound had creased my skull and was putting pressure against my brain."

When he was told he needed surgery immediately, "I said nah, nah, send me back out, you're not doing any head surgery on me."

But it was not his choice to make. "They said, 'We're not asking, we're telling you.'" He was put on a gurney and rolled into a hallway to await surgery. "I was terrified the whole time over there, and now that I had this head wound I was scared even further."

A nurse found him there and said, "You're scared, aren't you."

"Damn right," he replied.

"Would you like me to stay and hold your hand?"

"Yeah, I would."

He never forgot her. "I was just 19. She rubbed my hand a bit and gave me a little bit of soothing and comfort. Just the idea that someone was kind to me, that human contact… I will never forget that nurse."

He was sent home and discharged four months early. "Still, to this day, that's one of the happiest days in my life. I had a lot of difficulty accepting the draft. At that time it seemed like everybody was going to Canada or becoming a conscientious objector. Throughout the years it was a source of great anger and resentment for me."

Gary Flesch at the
Vietnam Nurses Memorial

He wasn't alone. The troops sent to Vietnam while others were being pulled out wondered what was going on. Why were Americans being sent to die in a war that the nation and its leaders no longer wanted to fight? If America was pulling out, why were more troops being sent?

"There were morale problems over there. We had the feeling that the South Vietnamese weren't pulling their weight. We were fighting their war for them, and it was discouraging."

'It owned me and it was kicking my can. That was it. No more.'

Coming home was also discouraging. "There was a feeling of estrangement. People didn't try to contact me or welcome me. No one said, 'Thanks, that must have been tough,' or, 'You really did a great job.' There was no positive input of any kind."

As the nation turned against the war, many protesters inexcusably turned against the men who fought it, often by no choice of their own. "They sure did. We were the face of the politics of the time. We caught the brunt of it. I remember one time I was home on leave in uniform, walking in downtown Cincinnati when a carload of guys went by screaming all kinds of profanity at me."

He withdrew into alcohol and his own world, diagnosed with traumatic brain injury and PTSD. "I was anti-social. I became an alcoholic. I only spent time with heavy drinkers. That was my only real connection with anybody. Just heavy anti-social behavior. My way of coping with Vietnam when I was there was just "ef"-it, it doesn't matter. It served me well over there to deny life's value. But when I got back to the states it stuck with me, and you can't transition to happy, productive civilian life if that attitude lingers. I had trouble attaching values to anything. Relationships, friendships. I was always angry. Just leave me alone, get the hell away from me. I don't need friends, I don't need anybody.

"I shut everybody out. I was emotionally dead for decades, other than bad emotions."

Then something amazing happened.

"After the war I floated around, tried college and didn't do well. I hated myself for it, for drinking and not being able to commit to a job or school. My dad raised us to give it the best you can. So finally I went to VA counseling. At first, they didn't quite know what to do. But the Cincinnati VA Hospital is incredible. They have made great strides in care, customer service and appreciation of veterans. I finally got help."

He quit smoking and got sober. "When I was drafted I was owned by the Army. I swore to myself I would never be owned and abused again. Then one day it hit me: That's exactly what this alcohol was doing to me. It owned me and it was kicking my can. That was it. No more."

He got a job as a Veterans Services Employment Counselor for the state of Ohio – helping other veterans find and keep good jobs.

Then something else amazing happened.

A friend recruited him for an Honor Flight, and he was one of the first Vietnam veterans to get aboard when the flights were opened up to all veterans age 65 and older. He had no idea how that flight in May 2015 would change his life.

"It was a tremendous purge of emotions that I had learned to live with. So much came out, that needed to come out. When we got to the Nurses Memorial, I broke down. I cried and cried. Dee Daniels (the guardian who convinced him to go) helped me a lot. We talked. That was therapeutic. I can't overstate that. All of these folks cared enough to put all this together because I was a veteran, whereas for the past forty-five years people had criticized and blamed me because I was a veteran. I was finally being thanked.

"There were a lot of grade school field trips in Washington that day. I was one of the veterans in a wheelchair, and the kids came up and said thank you, thank you, all day long. I thought, 'Oh my gosh. Teachers and parents are telling them these are veterans and they fought to protect us. That's the saving grace. I try to find the good in everything. And after how the public treated Vietnam vets, I think this country learned that that's not how you treat people who go out and fight a war for you. I think our country appreciates veterans a little bit more, out of that mistake."

Gary Flesch still has a hole in his skull from mortar shrapnel. He gets headaches and has an exaggerated startle response to unexpected noises or bumps. He had a stroke recently, but has recovered well.

"Each battle serves as experience and backbone for the next one. It provides the tools to fight the next one. I found the same was true with my stroke."

He's not angry anymore. He's happy and deeply grateful that he was able to finally lay it down at the Vietnam Wall and the Nurses Memorial.

"When we got home the entire airport was just packed. It was truly the parade and welcome home that we never had. People were saying 'Thank you, welcome home,' and shaking hands. The bagpipe band… I cried throughout to the end of it. I couldn't believe it. Forty-five years I waited for that and needed it. What a healing."

"It was hell – total confusion, total initial shock, then absolute focus on survival."

Specialist 5th Class, Tom Adkins

Artillery Combat Leader, Vietnam

"An interesting thing about Vietnam that a lot of people don't understand is that we did not fear the sky like they feared the sky," said Tom Adkins, who was a Spec. 5, Field Artillery, at Artillery Hill near Chu Lai in 1970. "We owned the air."

There were no North Vietnamese helicopter gunships flying around, and the enemy had nothing like "Puff the Magic Dragon," a converted slow-flying cargo plane that was armed with devastating firepower from Gatling-style mini-guns. The AC-47, also known as "Spooky," could pour a river of neon-red lead onto a target at eighteen thousand rounds a minute.

U.S. troops also had the biggest guns in the sector where Adkins was stationed, which was so close they could see North Vietnam. He worked in a Fire Direction Center, as the ranking non-commissioned officer who checked all the data for artillery, often in close support of U.S. soldiers and Marines in battle. "The idea was to verify your shooting accuracy. When you shoot you would have a set of eyes in the area to tell you if you are short or long, then you adjust by twenty-five or fifty meters at a time, depending on how close they were in combat."

They fired 105 mm howitzers, which were light enough to be carried by helicopters, but heavy enough to inflict terrible damage on the enemy. "When I first got to Vietnam we had 155s," Adkins recalled of the bigger guns that were airlifted to nearby firebases. When they fired at night, "I slept about six inches off the ground until I got used to them."

When the infantry called in artillery, Adkins would take their coordinates and calculate the trajectories and powder-bag amounts to put the shells precisely on target, to shield the soldiers with a wall of high explosives and shrapnel. "We would shoot different types of fuses, depending on if you wanted it to burst above ground or in the ground, sometimes with white phosphorous, some pure shrapnel. At night we would fire the first round for illumination, to tell our guys where the fire was coming from and let the enemy know they better dig in because all hell was about to break loose."

His unit, the Third of the 16th attached to the Americal Division, was designated Artillery Combat. When Viet Cong and North Vietnamese soldiers attacked their position on Artillery Hill, they found out why.

"It would start with a mortar attack, then wave after wave of Viet Cong or North Vietnamese, taking over the area. We didn't have much or a perimeter defense out there in the boonies. We were pretty much at their mercy."

Asked what it was like, he replied like so many combat veterans before him.

He paused. Then offered a single word: "Hell."

He paused again, remembering. Then continued. "It was hell – total confusion, total initial shock, then absolute focus on survival."

During one of those battles, his close friend Bruce Thomas of Morehead, Kentucky, was killed. "A single shot took him out on September 21, 1970. It was like reality. Not only could it happen, it did happen."

He saw other friends and soldiers killed. But that was his worst day of loss.

"Just taking all of those incoming mortar rounds up on Artillery Hill, just trying to survive. It was just wave after wave. When the gunships got there, everything took care of itself."

There was no more welcome sight to troops under assault than the arrival of the Air Cavalry flying UH-1 Huey Helicopter gunships, or a Spooky AC-47 orbiting overhead while pouring fire on the enemy.

Adkins was 24 when he was drafted. He had a wife and a college degree and was working as an adult parole officer in Cincinnati. He was no fan of the war, and his first impressions when he landed at Cam Ranh Bay did not help. "It was hot and it was humid and it smelled like hell when I stepped off the airplane. The ground was just sort of saturated. I had experienced hot hot and cold cold at Fort Sill in Oklahoma, but neither of those extremes fit my description of stepping off that plane. It just caught you in the lungs."

Morale was not good. The war was supposedly "winding down," but the North Vietnamese were launching a new wave of attacks. "There was a class system that I recognized almost the instant I got to Vietnam. First came the officers, then the NCOs, E6 and above, then there were us peons, privates through E-5s."

He came home at the end of February 1971. "You went over there with a stamped one-year sentence."

Nobody threw a parade. While Korean War veterans were forgotten and ignored, Vietnam veterans were sometimes greeted with hostility and insults.

"I came home and changed into my civilian clothes and went back to work as a parole officer. You can't go through that type of situation and not change. I was

Tom Adkins makes a rubbing of his friend's name at the Vietnam Wall.

more withdrawn because of my experience. My wife saw that with greater detail than anyone else, even other family members."

When he came home, he and his wife lived in a trailer. "When it would thunderstorm, the top of the trailer would rumble as though it was incoming mortar fire. More than once I would find myself on the floor, not really understanding where I was. Just the sounds. Many times the sounds were more devastating over there than the reality of the situation.

"I'm sure I put a mask on and put it behind me. I didn't expect anything. No tickertape parade. None of that was necessary and none of it was anticipated, by me or many of the others."

He had a 30-year career in criminal justice and human resources, raised three kids and lived with his wife in Anderson Township, where he became trustee for American Legion Post 484 in Mount Washington.

Then in August of 2013 he took an Honor Flight. He was 68. His guardian for the day was his son, Aaron, who was 48. "It was a learning experience for both of us," Adkins said.

He was especially interested in the Korean War. "I had not given it much attention. The numbers killed in action were just staggering. The brutal weather conditions."

Being at the Korean War Memorial with Korean War veterans made a deep impression. "It gave me a respect that I otherwise would not have."

His son felt the same way about being with his father at the Vietnam Wall, where Tom Adkins traced the name of the friend he lost on Artillery Hill, Bruce Thomas.

Aaron Adkins wrote to Honor Flight Tri-State, "I can't thank you enough for everything you did for both me and my dad yesterday! That was one of the most special days in both of our lives. I haven't spent that much time with him one-on-one since I was a kid."

Aaron described how the day brought them closer than they had ever been. "We spent a lot of time talking, I spent a lot of time listening and learning."

Tom Adkins said simply, "That was a great bonding day."

And although he never expected a parade or thanks, he was overwhelmed by the rally at the airport when they landed in Cincinnati. "There had to be six hundred people at the airport, just to welcome us back. All these people – they couldn't all be family members. I have no idea where they came from. That was the overwhelming moment."

There are many interesting things that a lot of people still don't understand about the Vietnam War and the veterans like Tom Adkins who did their duty and fought there. But thanks to an Honor Flight, one veteran's son now understands it a whole lot better.

In Your Honor

Unselfishly, you left your fathers and mothers,
You left behind your sisters and brothers.
Leaving your beloved children and wives,
You put on hold your dreams – your lives.

On foreign soil, you found yourself planted,
To fight for those whose freedom was granted.
Without your sacrifice, their cause would be lost
But you carried onward, no matter the cost.

Many horrors you had endured and seen.
Many faces had haunted your dreams.
You cheered as your enemies littered the ground.
You cried as your brothers fell all around.

When it was over, you all came back home,
Some were left with memories to face all alone.
Some found themselves in the company of friends
As their crosses cast shadows across the land.

Those who survived were forever scarred,
Emotionally, physically, permanently marred.
Those who did not now sleep eternally,
'Neath the ground they had given their lives to keep free.

With a hand upon my heart, I feel
The pride and respect; my reverence is revealed.
In the tears that now stream down my upturned face
As our flag waves above you, in her glory and grace.

Freedom was the gift that you unselfishly gave.
Pain and death was the price that you ultimately paid.
Every day I give my utmost admiration
To those who have fought to defend our nation.

Author Unknown

James Garvey, left, of Deer Park was among those chosen to travel to Washington, D.C., war memorials. PROVIDED

Thank you for the trip of my life

On April 16 I was chosen to travel to Washington, D.C., with over 70 other WWII and Korean War veterans, and an equal number of guardians, to see our war memorials.

I would like to thank all the donors and volunteers who make Honor Flight Tri-State happen, especially Cheryl Popp and Ed Finke.

After the sendoff from CVG, the ladies of the USO greeted us in D.C. that morning and saw us off in the evening – thank you, ladies! I received a kiss on the cheek that morning and wore it all day. I was advised to wash it off before I got home (what happens in D.C. stays in D.C.!).

We were welcomed home late at night by about 100 Tristaters, many with school-aged children. They are the best.

The next morning when I was telling my wife about my day, I started crying. I couldn't help it. It was the first time my wife of 62 years ever saw me cry. Thanks to all for a memorable day!

James Garvey, Deer Park ■

"Here in the presence of Washington and Lincoln, one the Eighteenth Century father and the other the Nineteenth Century preserver of our nation, we honor those Twentieth Century Americans who took up the struggle during the Second World War and made the sacrifices to perpetuate the gift our forefathers entrusted to us: A nation conceived in liberty and justice."

— From the World War II Memorial

CHAPTER FOUR
Legacy of Gratitude

"Thank you."

Those two simple words capture the spirit and the essence of Honor Flight Tri-State. All of the volunteers, the hours of planning, the generous donations, family celebrations, spontaneous handshakes, airport greetings and the spectacular monuments in Washington come from the same spirit of deep gratitude for their sacrifice and service.

It's all a way of saying thank you.

But that's not the end of it. After the long day is over, when the "Welcome Home" signs have been folded up and the confetti has been swept away and everyone has returned home, the notes and letters from veterans start filling the Honor Flight mailbox. As if postmarked from an earlier time when handwritten thank-you notes were basic courtesy, the letters express joy, wonder, appreciation and poignant gratitude.

Honor Flight began with an idea: To thank our veterans before it was too late. This book about Honor Flight Tri-State started with another idea: to share the veterans' own words of appreciation for a special day in Washington.

Peggy Mack wrote about her trip with her father, Frank Mack: Frank and I both want to thank you for the Honor Flight. Probably the most fantastic day Frank has had in his 89 years! Our son took the day off and met the group at the Columbus Airport, and they were both thrilled. Everything about the trip was first class and the welcome back was terrific. Every day my father thinks of more little tidbits to talk about, and he says what a thrill it was to be in D.C. There is no way he could have gone any other way. This experience will last him his lifetime. Thank you, again, to all of you, for a day that will not be forgotten.

Frank Schleper wrote: As one of the World War II vets from your trip to Washington on May 10, I would like to say thank you on behalf of all the vets for an unforgettable day. Our war memorial was an unforgettable sight and the trip past Arlington brought back memories of all the G.I.'s who marched over hills but never made it, or the planes that did not return, or the ships and subs that are on eternal patrol. All of your staff and guardians did such a great job to make our day one I will never forget.

May 20, 2015

Dear Honor Flight Volunteers,

Please know that you and your 5/19/15 Honor Flight repaired a forty-five year hole in the soul of this wounded-in-combat, drafted Vietnam veteran. Your love for America and her veterans shone brightly through a well-organized and perfectly executed outing. The pain-purge and healing facilitated by the Honor Flight volunteers and program are nothing short of miraculous.
I thank you for everything you did for me and my fellow veterans. The Honor Flight is truly America at her best.

With deep appreciation and best wishes,

Gary Flesch

Specialist fourth class, infantry soldier
Fourth Infantry Division
An Khe, Vietnam, 1970

Paul Freeland wrote about his experience on an Honor Flight in August

2013: It is difficult to know where to begin, so let me start by expressing my deepest appreciation to all of the people who made my Honor Flight a most memorable day. It was an experience which, honestly, words cannot adequately describe. It was a very emotionally moving time and I cannot count the number of times I literally had tears running down my cheeks. Each time I wondered "How can it get any better?" you found ways to outdo yourselves.

It began with the orientation and sincere words from the staff, followed by the flight on a plane decorated in red, white and blue streamers. The warm welcome we received at Reagan National Airport, followed by a military salute to the buses as we departed, was another thoughtful touch. The military monuments and memorials speak for themselves, but laying of the wreath at the Tomb of the Unknown Soldier was a special moment. And then when we returned to the airport in Washington, D.C., and saw those school children holding the banner which read, "FREE HUGS," I lost it again. The jewel in the crown was the Welcome Home reception at CVG. I couldn't believe that many people would turn out, especially at the late hour, to express their appreciation.

Another thing which impressed me the entire trip was that all of the volunteers, both locally and in Washington, seemed to be genuinely happy to be participating in the event and couldn't do enough for us.

Thank you for the special day which I will cherish for the rest of my life!

May God richly bless you as you continue to provide this special recognition to veterans.

Guardian John Whittlaker wrote after escorting his father: I am back in

Alabama now and caught up on things. I now have time to reflect on our Honor Flight. As my thoughts have returned to the day, I wanted to thank you for the honor I had to accompany such a great group of heroes.

I heard so many moving stories, but one in particular will remain with me forever. It was at the restaurant and my father was seated on my left and this other guy on my right. As we talked, I asked him where he had served during the war. He told me many of his experiences in the CBR (China, Burma, India) Theater. He came back to San Francisco and married a girl he had met earlier. He and his new bride came to his hometown of Cincinnati and had their only child, a son, who was tragically murdered in Cleveland. Two years later to the day his wife died of a broken heart.

Then he turned and looked me straight in the eye, with tears in his eyes, and said, "This is the best day of my life." This man was in his 90s and no doubt doesn't have many years left. I felt so honored to be a small part of his "best day," and I want to thank you for allowing me to be with my father and the rest of these heroes.

Howard Gregory wrote about his son being with him on the trip: I just participated in the Honor Flight on August 16, and I want to express my feelings to you and your associates, who organize and carry out this program.

It is a memorable experience and, for me, very emotional. To be on such an outing with the other veterans, none of whom I knew previously but with whom I shared a common experience years ago, was warming. And to have my son along as a guardian was icing on the cake.

All of this because you folks who not only arrange, organize and carry out this program, but who do so with such enthusiasm, care and friendliness – I could not have asked for more. Please accept this modest donation to help fund another flight.

Chris Burkart wrote: I can't begin to express my appreciation for such an awesome trip. I was so impressed with how organized and smooth everything went. The care you and your crew showed these very special people we call veterans was beautiful!

I count myself especially blessed to have attended as my father's guardian. He was overwhelmed by the adulation and commented that no one had ever saluted him before. What a wonderful gift for an amazing man! Your organization is filled with such generous and selfless people, and it was such an honor to be with you for the day. I am forever grateful and may God bless you.

Mrs. Pryor wrote of her husband's trip: I want to express my thanks and admiration for your Honor Flight. My husband, John, had the time of his life. He just bubbled! He could not get over his admiration for your whole organization. He leads a very sedentary life and this was a true highlight.

Debbie Lips, daughter of William Merz, wrote about her Honor Flight day: Thank you for giving us the opportunity to share Washington, D.C. together. Thank you so very much for organizing this honor for our Tri-State veterans. My dad and I had a wonderful time and created a very special memory for him and me! The trip really affirmed our pride in the USA and the human race. The medics, chaperones and board members who volunteered their time and talents were amazing.

Everyone was so kind and giving. We were extremely impressed with how well planned and organized the trip was. You all created a fantastic, beautiful trip for dad (probably the last one he will ever take), and made a sweet memory for me that I will never forget.

Rahe Roehring wrote a short note on patriotic stationery: Thanks for a great trip on August 16. One of the best days of my life.

He was buried in his Honor Flight T-shirt …

Fred Burke wrote: To the gang at Honor Flight Tri-State: What a wonderful time my daughter and I had on May 21. Everything was top notch. Your group did a wonderful job and the weather was perfect. I had my family over and my display was on the table for them to see. I was so proud to show all of the goodies I received. The notes from the kids got to me a bit. Words cannot express my thanks!

I am always pleased to spend time with my daughter and this was a most wonderful time for her. She was so pleased to see her dad and all of the THANKS that came my way. Thanks, thanks and thanks again – and may God bless your group.

Mr. Hayes: Words cannot describe my Honor Flight. I'm still two feet off of the ground!

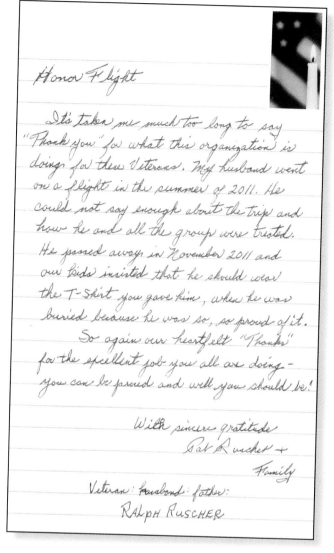

Honor Flight

It's taken me much too long to say "Thank you" for what this organization is doing for these Veterans. My husband went on a flight in the summer of 2011. He could not say enough about the trip and how he and all the group were treated. He passed away in November 2011 and our kids insisted that he should wear the T-Shirt you gave him, when he was buried because he was so, so proud of it. So again our heartfelt "Thanks" for the excellent job you all are doing – you can be proud and well you should be!

With sincere gratitude
Pat Ruscher + Family

Veteran: husband: father:
RALPH RUSCHER

Nicholas Lashutka of Ohio Children's Hospital Association was a guardian for his grandfather: I hope this letter finds you well. This is a thank-you letter to Honor Flight Tri-State. I cannot think of a more deserving cause to honor our veterans of World War II and Korea, the men and women who made extreme sacrifices to allow our great country to be the home of the free because of the brave.

On Tuesday, I had the privilege of traveling as a guardian with my 92-year-old grandfather, who is a Navy veteran from the Pacific Theater of World War II, to Washington, D.C. with the Honor Flight. It was an unbelievable experience for him and the other seventy veterans of World War II and Korea, as well as for me and the other family members and guardians.

My grandfather is a hero to me and my family. To see him with his World War II colleagues, being honored for their service throughout the day by a grateful nation – from the time we left Greater Cincinnati Airport to when we returned to see more than four hundred people cheering and celebrating the veterans that evening – was an experience I will never forget.

Thank you for making this trip a reality for my family.

Edward Luguillon: It has been more than sixty years since I served in Korea. The only welcome home I ever received was an Army band playing a few songs, as the ship docked in California. I want to thank Honor Flight Tri-State, and all the volunteers in that group, for the most enjoyable day.

The welcome home greeters at the Cincinnati airport, and in Washington, D.C. made this a most enjoyable day. Our group was treated as if our group alone had won the war!

Earl Whirle: To Ed Finke, Donna Hasselbeck, Cheryl and Tom Popp and everyone that made this the remarkable trip that it was:

I have been sitting here for four days trying to write a letter to all of you that might let you know how proud I felt being honored on this flight.

First, let me tell you I know a lot of people put a lot of time making this the success it was. There were too many things that happened right to have just been hashed together. Now, I will say that no one ever called me a child killer, so I never had that stigma hanging over my head. But I never had people standing in line to shake my hand, either. But on the Honor Flight, they were singing and clapping their hands for me! Believe me, it made my eyes water up, a real tear jerker, and I was discharged more than sixty years ago.

In my eighty years I have become suspicious of anyone wanting to do something for me. Thank you for showing me there are a lot of good people still in this world.

Honor Flight Forever.

6/25/10

DEAR CHERYL,
JUST WANTED TO SAY THANKS AGAIN FOR MAKING
JUNE 23, 2010 ONE OF THE MOST MEMORABLE
DAYS OF MY LIFE.
YOU, YOUR STAFF, AND THE GUARDIANS, ARE
REALLY SPECIAL PEOPLE.

THE WHOLE DAY WAS GREAT, BUT I THINK THE
HIGHLITE FOR ME WAS HAVING COMPLETE STRANGERS
AT THE WWII MONUMENT APPROACH ME TO SAY
"THANKS" AND ASK TO HAVE THEIR PICTURE TAKEN
WITH ME.
AS I TOLD MY FAMILY, YOU REALLY HAD TO BE
THERE TO APPRECIATE THAT SPECIAL MOMENT.

THANKS AGAIN TO YOU AND ALL THE HONOR FLIGHT
PEOPLE. GOD BLESS YOU AS YOU CONTINUE TO DO
YOUR GREAT WORK.
                    LOVE YOU ALL!
                    Charlie Carraher

August 24, 2013

Dear Cheryl & Tom,

Mom & I had the best day of our lives together on the Honor Flight! It is all thanks to you — your Big Picture and Smallest Details vision.

It's not so much the memorials that make the Honor Flight so wonderful, as the countless kindnesses, courtesies and respect blanketed upon the veterans from the moment they get to the airport. They are treated like the heroes that they truly are!

Thank you for the care & compassion shown to my Mom every step on & off the bus. Thank you for the special stop at the women's military memorial.

We were all smiles, all day — a day of absolute perfection!

Mom & I remain aglow in our million memories of our Honor Flight experience!

Sincerely
Donna Hartman

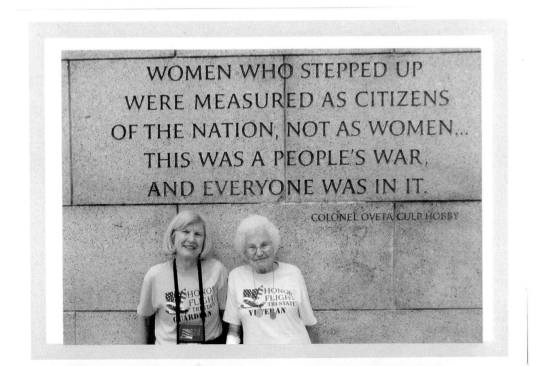

WOMEN WHO STEPPED UP
WERE MEASURED AS CITIZENS
OF THE NATION, NOT AS WOMEN...
THIS WAS A PEOPLE'S WAR,
AND EVERYONE WAS IN IT.

COLONEL OVETA CULP HOBBY

To all at Honor Flight Tri-State,

October 12, 2010 was to be my parent's 64th anniversary, but my mother died in April. My father through a series of events, was given a trip of his lifetime. On this day, that was to be his first anniversary without the love of his life.

My gratitude to you all cannot be expressed in words, but this is my (feeble) attempt. I am 56 years old and have listened to Marine WWII stories all of my life. I mean a lot of stories !

The first song I learned all the words to was, "from the hall of Montezuma." Odd to think of a 3 year old singing this song completely oblivious to what it meant, and I'm sure mispronouncing the words Tripoli, Montezuma and United States Marines etc.

My father has been an active member of his American Legion for 60 plus years, so of course, I was in parades with him holding flags and singing the song. As I aged, my thoughts of freedom, and my pride that my father was actually part of what I now experience living in a free America has grown year after year.

My father has always been and will always be my hero in many areas of my life. The trip that was given to him, especially this year, was an experience neither my father or I will ever forget. Even though, I was not with him in Washington, D.C. to see the memorials, I feel I was there, every step of the way. My father has never shown much emotion, so much gratitude, so much humility (of course that this big bad tough Marine never complains, just endures, only gives, never takes, always there for everyone else happily). I even heard it in his voice on the phone when he called to let me know he was home. It was an unforgettable trip. As he said and repeated," there were strangers clapping, saluting and thanking me."

He was absolutely overwhelmed!! The organization of the trip sounds flawless and the care of my father by his guardian, Erich, will never be forgotten by him, or myself (admittedly as a daughter who is also a nurse, I was anxious about letting him go without me). Erich not only pushed him in a wheelchair at each memorial, and all the activities you provided, he and his father, also a guardian, took my father back to his hotel at the airport since it was late and the shuttle was no longer running.

I hope you see a bit of what I mean, about how important and wonderful and perfect and how unforgettable, and how safe and enjoyable… how new story producing (ha ha) and truly how life changing an experience this was for my father and myself. I thank you all for everything, especially for showing my hero father a day he will never ever forget nor will I.

Sincerely,

Debbie King

P.S. There is so much more to say to your organization as I reread this, but I've cried myself silly writing it. Please know how grateful I am to you for rolling out the red carpet for my hero –

Lawrence Czumbal, WWII veteran of Iwo Jima, Tavawa, Waynaskawki.

Thank you, thank you, thank you, and his guardian even gave him a picture book the next week.

12-07-09

'My name is Jan Roos and my son, Cpl. Timothy Roos, was killed in Iraq in 2006. He was a Marine doing what he loved! We have benefits in his memory and we would like to donate to your organization To ensure that all of the Veterans get to see their monument! Thank you

May your holidays
be filled with
heart-warming moments!

The Roos Family

EDGAR L. WILLIG

May 3, '12

Dear Cheryl :—
Thank You, Thank You, for a Wonderful Day on the Great Honor Flight.
You are a great Director. I know you did so much to see that everything went so smooth May our dear Lord bless you and give you strength to continue on doing this great work for God and our country. God bless you.
Love and Prayers
Edgar Willig

Thank You for the hard work

Y'all HAVE done be save us!

We all really appreciate it!

Thank you for a Million times!

I got your email address from the business card you gave my dad, Herman Royer. I can't thank you and the folks responsible for Honor Flight enough for recognizing our WWII veterans.   As a Viet Nam veteran and retired US Government Civil Servant myself, I'm proud of the contributions made by all veterans, but Honor Flight has made it so much more.

My Dad is a very proud man, and seldom shows his emotions; but the reception he and the other vets received at Baltimore has humbled him beyond belief.   Each time he tells that part of the story about his trip, he chokes up and gets tears in his eyes (and blames it on "stupid" sinuses). He then gets himself under control again, and shares the experiences of his day in DC. If the pride and joy in serving his country and telling of all he got to see on this trip, were a "fossil" fuels, our country would never need a single barrel of foreign oil again.

SO ...... Again, Thank you and Honor Flight Tri-State, for giving my Dad this wonderful opportunity.

God Bless you, God Bless our Service Personnel, and GOD BLESS AMERICA!

Diana Irwin

Hi:

I have been wanting to do this for close to a year I was on an
Honor Flight. Last October.

After getting back affter spending two years over seas in the
Navy on a LCT, 65 years later I had the High Light of my life,
this was because it was People like You and ALL thers who made
this possible.

To see so many people see us off and be there when we got back
shows me we are not forgotten.

When we got back to the Air Port and to walk up those steps to
se so many people brought tears to my eyes like many of the others.
Veterans

We got Hugs, Handshacks and letters, and letters from students.

I got five and sent them letters thanking them and recieved
ten or twevle back from others

When I meet other Veterans I tell them to get on an Honor Flight
and if they need the address I gine it to them.

Thank all of you from the botton of my heart for giving me a day
in my life I shall never forget.

                                      Bless you all and
                                        thanks again.

                                        Andy Mack

PS: If possible I would like to know when some flights are
    leaving as I will try and be there. At 90 years old I don't
    get around like I used to.

Peace

Found in Henry's handwritten notes:

"First Commandment: Love the Lord your God
with all your heart and with all your soul and
with all your mind."

"May you always be happy wherever you
are—
When the going gets tough pray for courage to
carry on. God will take care of you."

6-28-2010

Dear Honor Flight Staff,

It was a great honor to be able to go with you to Washington on June 23, 2010. My brother, Harry Kirby, and I had the opportunity to take this wonderful trip together and it was a trip of a lifetime. It means so much to me that you allowed Harry to accompany me. I had never even flown in an airplane before and never dreamed that I would get to see the memorials in Washington.

Being greeted at the airport by all the military people was such a touching experience that I will always remember and cherish. I never felt that I deserved recognition for my part in WWII but it sure is nice to have people thank me for it. What you are doing for us veterans is an incredible thing. Thank you and may God bless you.

Donald M. Kirby

May 26, 2015

Mrs. Cheryl Popp-Director
Honor Flight Tri-State Headquarters
8627 Calumet Way
Cincinnati, OH 45249

RE: Honor Flight, May 19, 2015

Dear Mrs. Popp:

I'd like to thank everyone associated with the Honor Flight Tri-State for giving veterans the opportunity to visit their respective Memorials in Washington D.C. on May 19th. From the very beginning of our experience and the return that evening, I was completely in awe of the entire day. The entire day was far above any expectations I may have had.

Words cannot express enough gratitude to all who were involved in this endeavor. When my wife and daughter came to pick myself and Gary Homer up at the airport that evening, we had no idea of the intensity of our welcoming home.

I have always been proud to be an American and a Marine, but never more so than upon arrival home that evening. Seeing the multitude of people there awaiting our arrival to THANK and WELCOME us home was overwhelming. Also, the letters from several students were very emotional. I will continue to share this experience with others.

THANK YOU again Honor Flight and Guardians for honoring our country's veterans in this manner. In a world where many can only see the negative side of current events….my trip was proof of the greatness of people and our country.

Warmest Regards,

John (Jack) Strauss

Dear veteran, my name is Jesse and I'm from Wyoming middle school. I want to thank you for risking your life to keep our coun free. It's a great honor to be writing to you. I can't express eno of how much of an honor it is to have you to serve our country. I do think that most people understand how you guys risk your lives to us free. Without you guys fighting america might have been called ge. Thank you for serving us. and have fun on the honor flight!

JOHN F. STEELE   May 21, 2015

Dear Ms. Popp,

This is to congratulate and thank you along with your many associates who planned and hosted our Honor Flight this past Tuesday, May 19.

It was a trip to remember for all time. It was well organized and provided good opportunity for us, veterans and our guardians to see the outstanding war memorials.

Each of you who hosted the trip went out of your way to insure that we had good occasion to view and appreciate the message that every memorial conveyed. You fed us well, made us comfortable, showered us with attention and praise.

I never have had so many people of all ages thank me for my service to our great country. The welcome ceremonies were out of this world.

Please accept my thanks for an experience which I will cherish for my remaining years.

Very best wishes,
John Steele

Please accept the enclosed check.

Dear Veteran,
Thank you so much for serving in World War II. I cannot even start to understand how hard it must've been to leave your family, not knowing if you would come back. You are worthy of more adoration than the world could possibly give.
Thank you so much,
Sincerely,
Colin

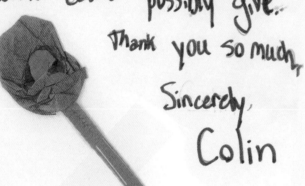

Thank you for Saving our country.

May 21st 2015

Honor Flight

I was deeply Honored to be a part of the Honor Flight. My expectations were far exceeded.
Your careful planning is much appreciated in making this a great trip. My thanks to you and all your staff. Special thanks to Ed Finke and Lisa for their kind letters. My guardians, Jim Gephardt, also sends his thanks.
Sincerely
Martin Bonte

P.S.
I am enclosing a check to cover the cost for another Veteran to have this great experience.

Dear Veteran,
You have done so much for our country. You have been braver than I ever could have been, and ever will be. I cannot thank you enough, because without you, our country would not be here. You sacrificed your time to make sure all of us were safe, and may God bless you.

From Sophia D.

6-8-15

To Honor Flight Tri State
Staff Headquarters
8627 Calumet Way
Cincinnati, Ohio 45249

To Cheryl Popp & All The Staff,

I was one of the participants that on Tues May 19, 1915 had the honor & pleasure of traveling to Washington D.C on the Honor Flight. Next to getting married this was one of the high lights of my life. My guardian was my son Gary who really enjoyed this most memorable & exciting trip.

I'm so thankful that you let me go on the trip having spent my time in the Merchant Marines that I was eligible to make the trip. I'm 90 yrs old & thankful I'm still in fairly good health.

I have been around the block a few times & I know that this trip didn't just happen but has taken place by much planing, experience & a lot of dedicated volunteers. Everything was first class and all areas covered.

I really enjoyed visiting the various monum-ents & sights. Perhaps the most impressive & memorable part of the trip was the changing of the guard at the Tomb of the Unknown Soldier.

It was a very humbling experience for me especially the many children coming up to me, shaking my hand & thanking me for my service time.

The flights to & from Washington D.C were just first class including the accomodations. Thankful also for the beautiful day weather wise & the fire trucks that were out shooting a stream of water over the plane before take off.

"over"

When we arrived late Tue evening back at the airport I was really humbled & blown away by all the people who came out to pay their respects, honor & welcome us home. Also the Bag Pipe Players, The Drum & Bugle Corp, The Honor Guard were outstanding.

The food was excellent including the box lunch at the Air Force Memorial, the late afternoon meal & the snacks on the plane.

I'm also thankful to our bus driver who drove us around safely to the various monuments locations. Also the packet of information given to us including the collection of 16 Easton post cards, the Honor Flight memorial.com & other information including the letters written by school children thanking us for our service.

This note falls so short of the way I could and wanted to express myself & thr the deep heart felt feelings of thankfulness & sincerety. Keep up the good work. Gods Richest Blessings. With "His" Love.

Troy E. Clemonz

P.S. A great big Thank You to the many people that have given money & especially to the fund raisers that made our trip possible.

August 24, 2013

Dear Cheryl Popp and the Honor Flight Tri-State Team.

On behalf of myself and my guardian (Bob) we wish to thank you all from the bottom of our heart to the most Wonderful day of my life. What a tribute to us Veterans. I was so Glad to be on that trip. I can't thank you all enough - So many people stopping us and taking pictures. All the young people so interested and taking time to ask questions and pictures. I am so glad to live in this great Country - What a welcome home. I couldn't believe it. I do hope I know when the next honor flight will be, so I can be there to welcome the Veterns home. I am so glad I joined USAF in 1952 toward the end of Korean war and to serve my country for three years in the medical field, which gave me a vocation that I worked in till Sept 1. 2012 - We must keep our country safe. I pray always for the men and women in uniform. Again thank you for the greatest day of my life - all you do to make this event possible. My our Lord Jesus Christ bless you all always.

Sincerly
A/2c Sophie J Hathorn
United States Air Force

I want to thank you for the fantastic job that you and all those associated with the Honors Flight Program did for all of us veterans. I was accompanied by my daughter, Chris Burkart, who gave me this trip as a Christmas gift. I had no idea that I would enjoy it so very much. One of the veterans was an old grade school friend of mine - what a pleasant surprise that was!

I appreciate all of the efforts by you, your husband, Tom, and Sam Keller to make us comfortable and to give us the "royal treatment". I, for one, felt like a king.

May God bless you and yours in your work - it is appreciated very, very much.

Sincerely,

John

John J. Jones

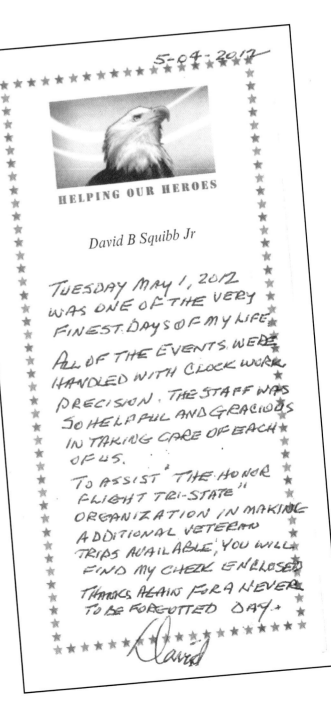

Dear Mrs Popp:
I want to thank you and all of your crew for a great time. It went from start to finish. I never herd one gripe. Every body was very nice. The reception at the end was a real shocker and surprise. On one of those colonal group I run into a fellow I hadn't seen in 70 years. Thanks again from my two daughters that were happy to be there.
Regards
John (Jack) Siles

HELPING OUR HEROES

5-04-2012

David B Squibb Jr

TUESDAY MAY 1, 2012 WAS ONE OF THE VERY FINEST DAYS OF MY LIFE. ALL OF THE EVENTS WERE HANDLED WITH CLOCK WORK PRECISION. THE STAFF WAS SO HELPFUL AND GRACIOUS IN TAKING CARE OF EACH OF US.
TO ASSIST "THE HONOR FLIGHT TRI-STATE" ORGANIZATION IN MAKING ADDITIONAL VETERAN TRIPS AVAILABLE, YOU WILL FIND MY CHECK ENCLOSED. THANKS AGAIN FOR A NEVER TO BE FORGOTTED DAY.
David

May 20, 2010

To all involved in the Honor Flight—
THANK YOU! THANK YOU!!!
The experience of attending this trip
to Washington strengthened my belief
that our country will survive in
these serious times that will come.
It was overwhelmed by the warm
reactions of those who met us
in the WWII Memorial. (Folks
came up to me, hugged me,
shook my hand. I felt humbled
and was deeply impressed.
May the Lord bless you in
your efforts — Your staff, your
Guardians were so accomodating!
We veterans appreciated that
you and the people we met
really cared!
                        Sincerely, Charles L. Geraci
                        (Division 2, US Army)

Dear Soldier,

Thank you so much for helping to protect our country! I was very
lucky to be born into such a selfless country. The men + women
who layed down their lifes, left their families, and helped make the
world a better place, are true heros! Your courage is truly
astonishing to me, + makes me feel proud to live in the
land of the free, + the home of brave!

        I hope you're proud of everything you've sacrificed
for our country; I know that I'm very proud of you! Thank you
again for everything you've done for our country!

From,
Caitlin

05-23-10

Dear Chyrl Popp,

I am sending you this note to try in some small way to thank you and your staff for the wonderful experience of Honor Flight. I have never enjoyed myself so much as I did on this trip.

You and your staff of Guardians are to be commended in the highest way for your unselfish special care that you extended to we veterans.

Everything was so well planed and took place very smoothly. (1&2)

I probably would never have gotten to take a trip like this were it not for you.

There are not enough "Thank U's" in the book for me to express my gratitude.

So its "off I go into the dreams of my Honor Flight experience. Thank You Cheryl & thank you Guardians for a service well done.

Sincerely
Lawrence "Larry" Tepe

Honor Flight Tri-State
Headquarters
8627 Calumet Way
Cincinnati, OH 45249

Attn: Cheryl Popp   7/20/10

Dear Ms Popp,
I am Sorry For the delay in Sending my Sincerest Thanks to you and all who were responsible For a Wonderful and emotional trip to Washington and the WWII memorial. It was Impressive to learn From all those who greeted us, that So many People really cared about us and what We gave For our country. Many of us have Suffered From injuries and went on with our duties as Citizens, husbands, Fathers, With no real thought to what we had done.

Pg 2: Cherys Popp
This recognition, the Honor Flight, Was imotional, in the Fact that Some of us Felt important For the First time as WWII Vets.

May God Bless You all!

Sincerely,
Wayne D. Weber
Wayne D. Weber

Dear Veteran,
Thank you so much for your service, cuz I respect what you did. You have to be the toughest guys out there. Hope all is good today. You deserve the best from everyone.

Sincerely,
Kathy Chilinski

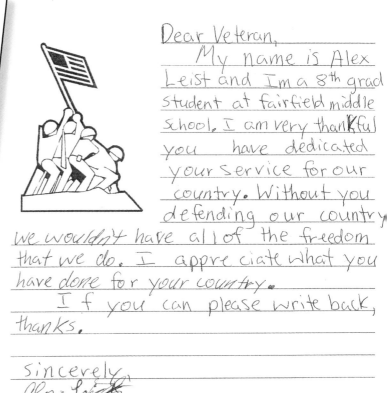

Dear Veteran,
My name is Alex Leist and I'm a 8th grade student at fairfield middle school. I am very thankful you have dedicated your service for our country. Without you defending our country we wouldn't have all of the freedom that we do. I appreciate what you have done for your country.
If you can please write back, thanks.

Sincerely,
Alex Leist

To the Honor Flight Tri-State Team,

It has taken me several days to be able to sit down to write this note. I just didn't know where to begin to thank you all for the incredible experience we had on Tuesday.

From the beginning to end we felt like we were treated like royalty. I don't know if there were any glitches that day, but from our perspective the whole day flowed seamlessly like a well-oiled machine.

The trip was life enhancing, emotionally charged all day, a once in a lifetime experience. The opportunity to visit all of the memorials in one day was tremendous. Words can't begin to describe the fabulous experience. We had heard from others about the trip, but it exceeded our every expectation ! It was a " Kleenex" day.

One of the things that struck us most was the reception we received everywhere we went. Starting at CVG, the love, caring, and dedication was evident. The thought of the group that met us in DC, all of the tourists that greeted us at the various memorials, and finally the overwhelming reception we encountered upon our return to Cincinnati still brings tears to our eyes when we think about it.

The changing of the guard ceremony at the Tomb of the Unknown was one of our favorite parts of the day. Knowing the background and the history of it, and the dedication of the men and women who served in this capacity is very inspiring.

Mail call was the icing on the cake. Your letters, and the ones from the children make us feel there is still hope for our country.

The fact that my husband, Joe and I were able to go on the same Honor Flight, made it especially poignant since we met in the service. He was a submarine officer and I was a Navy nurse. We recently celebrated our 48th anniversary.

An extra thank you from me for the chance to see the Women's Memorial.

Donna said our homework was to recruit other veterans to go on the Honor Flight. So far, we have 9 that are interested. Living in a retirement community makes connecting with veterans very easy.

All in all it was a wonderful experience. Thank you again for all you do.

Warm Regards,
Nancy Vaughan

October 13, 2010

Mrs. Cheryl A. Popp, Director
Honor Flight Tri-State
Headquarters
8627 Calumet Way
Cincinnati, Ohio 45230

Dear Mrs. Popp,

Yesterday, at the age of eighty-six years, eight months and fourteen days, I was in the group of World War II Veterans who made the flight to Washington D.C. to see first hand the World War II Memorial, and to visit other beautiful and meaningful memorials and points of interest! The day itself was beautiful! The flight was as smooth as silk; the lunch on the bus was wonderful; the Guardians were kind and generous with their time and assistance; and the plans and directions were clear and much appreciated! Your presence, guidance and friendly touch throughout the day were a special gift. Thanks to you and all who participated and shared in making it a great day!

I would be remiss if I failed to mention the delicious meal of abundant and appealing food choices at the Golden Corral Restaurant. When I finished my meal and chatted with fellow veterans at the tables, I thought of my father who used to say, "I have had an elegant sufficiency of numerous delicacies! Any more would be an unsophisticated superfluity!" In other words I had a great meal which I thoroughly enjoyed and am indebted to the Golden Corral for its thoughtfulness and generosity! Thanks to them and to Honor Flight Tri-State!

Tuesday, October 12, 2010 is a day of information, inspiration and forming new friendships which I shall always remember and cherish! Thanks to you, to generous donors and to all others who volunteered for this great occasion! May God bless you all richly for your thoughtful, generous sharing!

Sincerely,

C. Edwin Pellett, Pastor Emeritus
Sharonville United Methodist Church
Sharonville, Ohio

Dear Veteran,

Thank you. Thank you for protecting our country, for fighting for our freedom. Because of you, we are still the U.S.A. We can make our own decisions. Thank you for fighting for us. Thank you for freedom.

Sincerely,
Ken at Wyoming Middle School

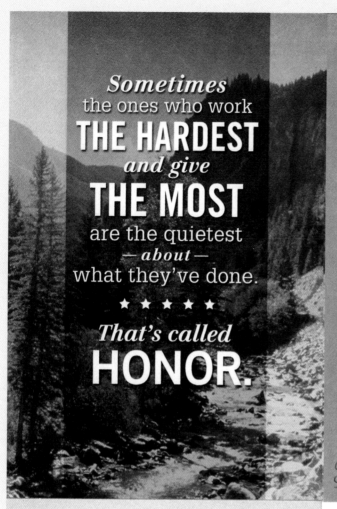

Sometimes the ones who work **THE HARDEST** and give **THE MOST** are the quietest —about— what they've done.

★ ★ ★ ★ ★

That's called HONOR.

HONOR... INSPIRE... PRIDE: THAT'S HONOR FLIGHT TRI-STATE, GOD BLESS ALL OF YOU!!

They INSPIRE the rest of us.
That's called **PRIDE.**

★ ★ ★ ★ ★

THANKS FOR ALL YOU ARE AND ALL YOU DO.

Rebecca M. Weigold (on behalf of Charles H. Mitchell)

like to see you make a reality-type documentary of the entire process of putting an Honor Flight together — from application process, to Donna's prayers of them, to matching vets/guardians, to all the preparation your staff/crew/volunteers and guardians make, the ceremony that officiates the guardians, the send-off, highlights of the trip, and the return celebration — complete with interviews of the directors (the Popps) and Donna and all others, including some vets and guardians, →

Dear Good Folks of Honor Flight Tri-State,
Words cannot express my deepest respect and gratitude for your efforts and your mission. On August 20, my father - Charles H. Mitchell (U.S.A.A.C. WWII) - was honored to take the Honor Flight, thanks to your generosity. We were in awe at the send-off ceremony and filled with patriotic jubilation at the return celebration. He was thrilled to come home to see my mother (who lives in a nursing home) waiting to greet him along with my brother and me. The whole day was a real treat for him and so special. We still talk to him about it today and suspect we will for a long time. Thank you for recognizing our veterans this way; It's awe-inspiring, respectful, humbling, and solemn. Thanks to Donna for pairing him with Andy Turner as his guardian. They were perfect together. Andy related to us that he chose to be a guardian in honor of his grandfather who had served in WWII. Turns out both his grandfather and my dad were Southern Baptist ministers. Andy said he knew Divine Intervention was involved. In fact, Donna had told me she spreads out the applications of both vets and guardians and prays over them for God's guidance in matching them up. My dad and Andy are proof that he does. I would very much

and reactions of family and the public. It is a documentary the public must see. I know 2 were offered for sale but I am suggesting something extremely detailed covering start to finish the entire process. Please consider it. Again, thank you for this, for my dad, the vets, for us all. You restore a sense of pride and patriotism and honor

Sunrise
every artist has a story

and love for our country in all of us through your mission and your efforts which we so desperately need to feel again. God bless Honor Flight Tri-State! America bless God, and God bless America!

Rebecca Weigold
Proud daughter of Charles
Mitchell, USAAC WWII

Charles Mitchell and Guardian
Andy Turner (top right)

Charles and wife Gwen (left)

Honoring our heroes while we still can

Nathan Bachrach and Ed Finke
Simply Money

We always enjoy sharing our thoughts with you about the issues affecting your financial life, but occasionally there is good reason to step away to discuss important events in our community. One such event took place Tuesday: Honor Flight Tri-State kicked off its 2013 season by taking 72 World War II and Korean War veterans on an all-expense paid trip to view their memorials in Washington, D.C.

Honor Flight Tri-State (HFT) is an all-volunteer organization, and it exists for one reason: to take as many of these deserving veterans on a trip of a lifetime to honor and thank them for a job well done. They gave so much and asked so little, this is the least we, as a community, can do for them. Almost 700 WWII heroes pass away every day, and in many cases, this is the only chance they will have to see the memorials dedicated to their bravery and sacrifices.

The day starts with a powerful and poignant departure ceremony at CVG that includes the Hamilton County Sherriff's Patrol Bag Pipers. Once the flight touches down at Reagan National Airport, exuberant crowds welcome the Vets as the heroes that they are. It's then off to visit the Marines' Iwo Jima Memorial at Arlington National Cemetery, followed by the Changing of the Guard at the Tomb of the Unknowns.

In the afternoon, a tour of the WWII Memorial, the Korean War Memorial and the Vietnam Memorial round out the day. There are wreath-laying ceremonies at the World War II and Korean Memorials in remembrance of their 500,000 brothers and sisters in arms who died during these two wars. It's an incredibly emotional day with lots of laughter and some tears as new and old friends reminisce, and those who didn't return are remembered.

After a liesurely dinner, the Vets return to CVG, met by a large crowd of well-wishers that explode with a loud and enthusiastic welcome home! And once again, the tears and emotions start flowing. This day of honor becomes a cherished memory.

This is a cause we are very passionate about. Ed is an Army Vet and member of the HFT board. If you know a Veteran who served during World War II or Korea, please encourage him or her to sign up for this day of thanks.

Additional information is at www.honorflighttristate.org or by calling 513-277-9626

My trip to Washington DC was, to say the least- fantastic! Although I didn't realize it at the time, my participation in the Korean action was the first of our now four "no win" engagements. When our ship the USMS Marine Sergent, docked in Seattle after the armistice, we felt like conquering heroes and were met by a six piece band in clown costumes and no one else.

This Honor Flight put to rest some long-standing bad feelings about my service. The trip was so well organized from the Welcome Ceremony to the arrival back at CVG. I felt I was in a dream world. I realize I was on the "Fun Bus", but nothing was left to chance from the hand sanitizer, to the free cameras, to the best location to get pictures, and we were never in a hurry to get to the next memorial.

Our reception at CVG at the end of the trip made this day one I will never soon forget. You all brought tears to the eyes of this ol' man and I know I had to get this note off before I start to get "teary eyed" again.

Thank you for a job well done,

Sincerely,

David Adams

I am the only surviving brother. We all returned home within two weeks in December 1945.

Al Wessel

Richard A. Wessel   Albert B. Wessel   Carroll B. Wessel   Robert J. Wessel

Four sons of Mr. and Mrs. Albert B. Wessel, 969 Kirbert Avenue, Price Hill, are in the Armed Forces. Sgt. Robert J. Wessel, 25, who qualified as a combat swimming instructor, has been in England since September. He is a graduate of Elder High School and a former employee of the Heekin Can Co. Aviation Cadet Albert B. Wessel, Jr., is in training with the Army Air Forces in San Antonio, Tex. He was employed at the Wright Aeronautical Corp. at the time of enlistment in April. Sgt. Carroll B. Wessel, is now with the AAF somewhere in India. At the time of enlistment in January 1942, he was employed by the City Maintenance Department. He was also well known as a wrestler and swimming coach at YMCA. Capt. Richard A. Wessel is now on deployment in California. He was employ- Finance Co. at the time of enlistment.

Mr Roy A Hasenjaeger

I can't thank you and the Board members and Ambassadors enough for making this wonderful trip possible–

The trip was more than I expected. I had tears in my eyes more than once that day. The trip started out great that day and just got better as the day went on ending at CVG with a wonderful wonderful welcome home

Again I can't thank you and your group enough

Love,

Roy A Hasenjaeger

Dear Cheryl and all the rest of you fine folks:

I was lucky enough to go on the Honor Flight on April 14 (Tom I was on bus 2).

It was an honor to travel with the hero who were in the service. It was a treat to be with such good men. It was wonderful to be treated with respect, not to hear any grips or complaints and to be moved by the things that we saw on our trip.

In 1955 I graduated from High School at the end of May. On June 5 I joined the United States Army. From a town of 750 people (Calhoun, Ky) the Army took me places I had never dreamed of seeing and of doing things I never dreamed of doing. I left the Army in 1958 and went to work.

Except for my family nobody ever thanked me for serving until April 14, 2015. That meant I lot to me. Don't know that I deserved it all but I loved it and appreciated it.

The trip was beyond anything I expected but upon our return to Cincinnati it was hard not to lose it. The tears flowed. You chocked up. Emotions were high. It was the best reception I ever had.

The folks who went with us were great. The ground crew and everyone at the airport on both ends went out of their way to thank you and help you. You placed me with George Pritchard; he was great.

It was a great day and I just wanted to say to all of you "THANKS".

God bless,

Charles W. Abney
Charles W. Abney

FERD G. POPP

LaVerne carried the photo
of Nick (above) in her wallet
while he was overseas,
and Nick carried her
picture all through the war.

Our Wedding
Ray & Helen Zepf Volz

Lt. Alice H.

"If you can read this, thank a teacher.
If you can read this in English, thank a veteran."

— Honor Flight Tri-State T-shirt

CHAPTER FIVE
Legacy of Service

What could make dozens of people set their alarms at 4 a.m., take a day off work and show up at the airport long before the sun comes up, to pass out nametags, check passenger lists and greet Honor Flight Tri-State veterans and guardians with a smile – all without being paid?

It turns out there are as many reasons as there are volunteers.

In their own words, here is why Honor Flight ambassadors, donors, board members and volunteers work so hard to make every flight a success.

The Honor Flight My Father Never Got to See

Cheryl Popp
Honor Flight Tri-State Director

It all began with a smile on a streetcar in 1943.

Back in the days when it was safe to smile at a stranger on a streetcar, my dad smiled at a pretty blond and her friend on a streetcar. The story has been handed down and became part of our family lore. My mother, LaVerne, was going downtown on the streetcar to see a movie with her Aunt Ruth, who was only two years older than my mother. That's when they caught the eye of a handsome soldier in uniform.

Nick was riding home on leave after basic training. He thought the ladies were getting off the bus, so he jumped off the back to "bump into them," when suddenly he realized they were not getting off! He ran all the way to the next stop, hoping to catch them, and they were surprised to see him running alongside the bus, smiling and waving his arms.

When they got off at the next stop, he asked them to join him for a cup of coffee. My mother still thought he was smiling a little longer at her Aunt Ruth, but it turned out he asked my mother for a date the next day. He was shipping out in two weeks, and time was precious during the war. He once told me, "Things were different back then." Everything moved very quickly. No one knew what the future would hold for a G.I. shipping out to war.

When his leave ended, he was among the twenty percent of all American soldiers who left aboard trains from Union Terminal in Cincinnati. My mother was there to see him off. Dad was always very superstitious, and he told my mom he would kiss her goodbye and then walk to the train and never look back. That's exactly what he did – and she did not see him for two and a half years while he was stationed in the Pacific.

> ### *I just had to do more to finish the mission and take them to see their memorials. I had to work with them in my father's honor.*

They wrote letters every day and their romance blossomed. To keep busy while her boyfriend was overseas, my mother volunteered at the Red Cross, taught music and played in an accordion octet at local supper clubs. She and her friends also collected sheets and old tablecloths to be used as bandages. They tore them in long strips and then rolled them into balls to be sent to medics on the

front. She always said a silent prayer that they would help a G.I. make it home.

When my father returned in late 1945 he was ready to propose. My mother said later, "You can really get to know a person when you write letters. You learn their very intimate dreams and thoughts. It happens fast and is almost better than dating." But her mother was not convinced, and said she did not know him well enough.

LaVerne married Nick anyway. It all worked out very well. They were married sixty-five years when she passed away. It was a match made in heaven. They moved as one, finished each other's sentences and raised four kids with all the love you can imagine.

We were brought up to appreciate what little we had, to "make something of yourself," get up when you fall down, learn from your mistakes and always be responsible for what you do. My parents were always there to support us – but we were expected to "do it on your own." You always knew where you stood – even when that was in the corner. My mother took care to correct us, but we knew it wasn't over until "your father gets home." I never liked disappointing my dad.

He never talked about his military service. We knew bits and pieces, but he never really said much until I got my pilot's license. It was as if that made the grade. He was not a pilot, but had served from 1943 to 1945 in the Army Air Corps as a finance officer. His stories of paying the soldiers in cash and carrying it all around in a duffle bag always made him smile. He was discharged as Major Nicholas J. Kuhn.

He came home and took the CPA exam and went to work as an accountant. Quiet was required at all times when he was home, especially during tax season. That was not easy with six of us in a three-bedroom ranch, sharing one bathroom. You learned how to get along or else. When the baseball game started with the National Anthem, my dad always stood and put his hand over his heart. This was just what you did.

He taught us a great work ethic, love of God and country and to always "give back." Both of my parents volunteered and it became a way of life for the whole family. If anyone asked for volunteers, we just raised our hands and did what we could. That's what happened to me with Honor Flight Tri-State.

I felt like I had never done my part for my country. I had been newly married when the Vietnam War started, and my husband, Tom, was 2-A. The war ended before he was called. I never protested the war, but I never did anything to honor the vets, either. I just rolled along, enjoying the life that they had all made possible, not thinking too much about it.

When we first heard of Honor Flight from a speaker at the Cincinnati Warbirds, I raised my hand to volunteer as a guardian with the Dayton Honor Flight three times. Tom was on two of those, then another of his own.

When Honor Flight Tri-State started, many of the founding members were from the Cincinnati Warbirds and we knew them well. They asked me to join the Honor Flight board to help with fundraising. When the director took a job and moved out of town, I became the Honor Flight Tri-

State director in 2009. The fledgling hub was struggling to find vets and to pay for trips.

Everything changed for me when I got involved with the veterans. My respect for what they have accomplished touched my heart. I just had to do more to finish the mission and take them to see their memorials. I had to work with them in my father's honor.

We have assembled great board members and outstanding community support and sponsorships. I am proud to be a part of one of the most respected Honor Flight hubs in the U.S.

My biggest joy on an Honor Flight is to see how much the veterans enjoy their day. But the tears and smiles that I see are my father's. The firm handshakes and hugs are his. He did not live long enough to go on a flight, but I feel him behind me when we are on the trip. He whispers in my ear, "Well done, Cheryl, this is what you should be doing with your life. These veterans saved our nation and now you are finally thanking them. I am proud of you."

Uncle Freddy would be proud

Tom Popp
Honor Flight Board Member

I had three uncles who served in World War II and another who served in Korea. But I was closest to my Uncle Freddy. My grandfather was a builder and I tagged along behind him when I was a real little guy. Uncle Freddy was also a builder and I would go on to become a commercial and industrial electrical contractor, so I guess you could say I followed in the footsteps of his work boots.

*Ferdinand G.
"Uncle Freddy" Popp*

Uncle Freddy was a Golden Glove boxer before the war and he was built like a rock. I think that's why the Army made him a medic, because he could easily pick up and carry a man. He was a soft-talking kind of guy, but I don't think anyone would want to mess with him. I worked for him when I was 14 and 15, cutting grass on the new houses he built. I couldn't wait to turn 16 so I could work on the houses with him. But Uncle Freddy was a tough task master, and as a 145-pound, 16-year-old, I had never worked so hard in my life. I think he was quietly smiling as he watched me struggle. But whatever he asked, I got the job done.

Whenever he talked about the war, which was rare, he got very serious. He described his time in the Aleutian Islands. The Japanese had occupied Attu and Kiska. They were dug in so it was tough going. Uncle Freddy was aboard a ship and did not go ashore, but the guys came back pretty beat up. His turn came on the morning of August 15, 1943. It had been foggy for several days, and that morning the fog finally lifted and they went ashore. Much to everyone's surprise and relief, the Japanese had snuck off to their ships on the other side of the island. "So much for military intelligence," he said with obvious relief.

Uncle Freddy was then transported across the country by train to fly to England for Operation Overlord, the invasion of Normandy. He said they trained constantly, but at least it kept the boredom at bay. Then on D-Day, he went ashore, luckily in the second wave. He said the first wave was horrific. He and a friend kept a German map to mark all the places they went and noted where they were in big battles. I still have and treasure that map.

When I became a pilot and bought my first airplane, he opened up about something that was jarred loose when I started talking about aviation. One time in Europe he had come across a downed plane. He didn't remember what it was, just an American single-engine fighter. It had crashed straight in with its nose stuck in the ground. But the image that Uncle Freddy could never forget was that the pilot was decapitated and his head was about forty feet away on the ground in front of the plane. He looked me straight in the eye and said: "Be careful, Tom." Lesson learned.

> ## *Then on D-Day, he went ashore, luckily in the second wave. He said the first wave was horrific.*

Early in my career I worked with a lot of World War II veterans. They were the wise old guys and I was the kid. I learned the electrical trade and business from them. I can never repay them for all that they taught me about life. But they were pretty quiet about their war duty. I always wondered what it was like during the war.

Now, thanks to Honor Flight, I have a chance to hear those stories.

My wife, Cheryl, and I have been involved with Honor Flight since 2006. We heard a speaker from the Dayton Honor Flight ask for guardians, and Cheryl and I signed up. Pretty soon we were helping the Honor Flight Tri-State hub get off the ground.

We receive many thank-you letters from the veterans and their guardians, reminding us that their generation actually wrote letters and felt obligated to send thank-you notes. Many have said that they could not have wanted for a thing, and that their every wish came true on their flight. When they say it was "gratifying, seamless, and marvelous" and "came off without a hitch," that's my proud piece of the Honor Flight puzzle.

As I learned in business, it's important to see the operation from all points of view – "management by walking around." For Honor Flight Tri-State, our method is CANI: Constant And Never ending Improvement. After every flight, we assemble and de-brief by going through a four-page checklist. Every item is discussed and critiqued to improve the next flight. That becomes a "flight plan" that gives every member of the team specific duties.

Planning starts each January with flight dates. We negotiate and sign contracts for the airplanes and buses as early as possible, to lock in dates and prices. Then we contact the Army for access to Arlington National Cemetery. Until a few years ago, bringing three tour buses to the Tomb of the

Unknown Soldier was not allowed. But Pentagon officials finally realized that our veterans would not be able to pay their respects to their fallen brothers-in-arms without bus access.

In January we also do an inventory of our merchandise: nametag lanyards, veteran and guardian shirts, ground crew and ambassador T-shirts, challenge coins, hats, scarves, umbrellas, picture post cards, note cards and souvenir books that help raise money for Honor Flight Tri-State.

We verify insurance, dinner reservations, buses, planes and Arlington access two months before the flight. We continually take applications for veterans and guardians. Donna Hasselbeck calls to notify them for a flight. Larry Cole, Donna's husband, is our medical director who reviews medical forms to verify a doctor's signature and make sure each veteran is capable of making the flight.

About four weeks before each flight, Donna sends out "yellow sheets" – short medical forms carried by the medic on each bus, in case of emergencies. Another important yellow sheet that must be signed is the "covenant not to sue," to protect Honor Flight Tri-State.

My job is to keep track of the many lists that organize Honor Flights, to assign everyone to buses, get them nametags, check them through TSA at the airport and make sure nobody is left behind. By the time I'm finished, I have twenty lists. Then we pray there are no cancelations, and get to work printing and assembling nametags.

On the morning of an Honor Flight, Cheryl and I arrive at the airport by 5:15, to be greeted by Honor Flight ground crews who are welcoming the veterans with smiles, directions and Honor Flight T-shirts.

A few years ago, Cheviot Fire Chief Bob Klein introduced me to Steve Watt, coordinator of the Hamilton County Sherriff's bagpipers. Steve told me he wanted the bagpipers to be there for every Honor Flight send-off, and they have played for every flight since, adding a thrill of respect and honor. When the TSA Color Guard joins up with the bagpipes and drums to post the colors, that gets everyone's attention.

If we have done our job right, the rest of the day will go well. Now we just pray for good weather and a safe trip. I think Uncle Freddy would be proud of me.

The challenge coin

A challenge coin was first used during World War I. According to the legend, a British flying squadron commander had given his pilots a coin depicting their battle colors and symbol. One of their pilots was shot down over French territory and his captors thought he was a spy. They were about to execute him when they found the coin in his pocket, and someone recognized it from the British squadron, saving the pilot's life.

During World War II, challenge coins were given to flying squadrons. Today they are widely handed out and traded as a symbol of respect between men.

In many Air Force officers' clubs they are almost a necessity. If an officer taps his coin on the bar, that's a challenge to everyone to show their coins or buy a round of drinks.

Toward the end of the day on each Honor Flight, we give each veteran a coin, with individual thanks for serving our country. It's our way of saying we're honored to be with them to share their experiences and stories. At dinner we offer challenge coins for sale to family members and guardians. Many of the veterans give their coins to the children and grandchildren, to be passed on through the years.

I knew it was going to be spectacular

Donna Hasselbeck-Cole and Medic Larry Cole

Donna Hasselbeck

Honor Flight Board Member

My husband, Larry, had been a paramedic on Honor Flight Tri-State trips for several years. He came home with amazing stories about his adventures and asked me over and over to be a guardian. I was hesitant because I didn't know if I could do it. When one of our family friends asked Larry for a guardian to go with, Larry suggested me. I had no expectations, and didn't know if I would like it.

About halfway through that first flight I knew without a doubt that it was going to be spectacular. It's hard to describe what if feels like. Shame on me, I had never really thought about what it meant to be a veteran and what they had done for our country. That Honor Flight opened my eyes to being part of the American family.

What these veterans had done for my way of life hit me, and now I wonder why it took me so long to figure it out. Honor Flight has changed everything for me. I was cruising through life doing nothing to make a difference. But after my Honor Flight I told Larry that I wanted to do more. I kept asking, "What can I do to help?" It turned out they needed someone to call the veterans to schedule them. I knew I could do it.

It is a big job, but it connects me to each veteran and guardian. After I receive all of the paperwork, the calling begins. To fill a flight of 149 seats, five times a year, takes a lot of phone calls.

Everyone laughs about how I seem to know all of the veterans before the trip. I have spent hours on the phone with them, listening, scheduling and answering questions. The thing that touches me most is that after waiting months or years to be called, they often say, "I'm not sure I deserve it."

My reply is, "Did you wear the uniform of the United States Armed Forces?"

They say, "Yes ma'am, I did."

"Then you are qualified to go." The graciousness and humility of this generation never ceases to amaze me. They don't think they're worthy of all of the fuss, as one veteran put it.

They often say, 'I'm not sure I deserve it.'

My family laughs about how often I walk up to a total stranger after noticing a military hat, and ask him to go on an Honor Flight. I keep applications in my purse to recruit at the grocery, the mall, at church, at a baseball game – anywhere I spot a veteran.

I have made a ton of new friends and I look at the veterans as my buddies. The joy I see on their faces makes all of the work worthwhile. They wash away fatigue with their tears of happiness. When a grown man breaks down in tears, you know you have made an emotional connection. Their generation has so much to teach us and we are so lucky to be able to spend the day with them before it is too late.

*Donna Hasselbeck-Cole
with LT. Matt Allen*

When the world loses a veteran the light in the world becomes a little dimmer. The widow of one veteran called me to ask for another Honor Flight shirt, so she could bury him in a new shirt and keep the one he wore as a family treasure.

A guardian who went on a flight with his Vietnam veteran father told me, "Dad would still be lost if it were not for his Honor Flight." Their flight mended their broken relationship and he heard about his father's war experiences for the first time.

I didn't know I was looking for something when Honor Flight found me. We are making a difference and I love it! I am touched beyond measure.

We laughed, we cried, we prayed

Sam Keller
Honor Flight Board Member

October 17, 2007 was one of the most memorable days of my life. I was given the privilege of escorting forty of the most incredible men and women to our nation's Capital, as a guardian on an Honor Flight. I cannot begin to describe the range of emotions I felt on my first flight. It is a day I will never forget.

I can still see the faces of the veterans we escorted. We laughed, we cried, we prayed and, most of all, we remembered the many sacrifices made for the freedoms we enjoy today.

Many of the veterans told stories, and I would hang on their every word. As Will Rogers once said, "We cannot all be heroes. Some of us have to stand on the curb and clap as they go by."

Sam Keller

The one regret I have in life is that I never served my country in the military. But that makes Honor Flight more special to me. For at least one day, I feel like part of the special brotherhood of the veterans. My first trip convinced me to do more. Now I'm on the board and go on several trips every year.

One of the hardest parts is when we return home. We know we will not see many of them again. I still get choked up when I think of our final parade through the terminal to the waiting arms of their families, with bagpipers leading the way. It's my favorite part of the trip.

I try to shake every hand as they leave the plane.

I try to shake every hand as they leave the plane, to thank them – and every one of them thanks me. That's who they are: grateful and humble heroes.

I have had many jobs in my life and many experiences, but there is nothing like an Honor Flight. So I work to raise money and awareness of our mission to make sure we continue. This is a magical journey that I want to never end.

God speed to every Honor Flight. All across our nation, they are doing what Americans should have been doing for the past seventy years.

Sharing memories and tears of joy

Ed Finke
Honor Flight Board Member

There are lots of ways we can spend our time and money, but few rise to the level of honoring the oldest of our veterans for their sacrifice and service. As a former Army officer, to me the mission of Honor Flight Tri-State is extremely personal and emotional. These are the men and women who were the parents and relatives and neighbors of my generation. I'm sorry to say that I took them for granted, as all kids tend to do, with no real appreciation for the world they lived through and the sacrifices they made. We knew they had served, but it seemed so long ago and most never talked much about it.

Ed Finke

Once their wars were over, a weary country didn't pay a lot of attention to them. They returned without any fanfare or celebration other than with their loved ones. They didn't expect much attention and certainly didn't get it. They did, however, humbly and quietly help build this country into the great place that it is. Their Honor Flight is truly the parade they never had.

Every trip is an emotional journey for me. Sharing the day with these true heroes is one of the great honors of my life. Hearing their stories – sometimes gut-wrenching, sometimes side-splitting – I can see the years melt away. They return to a time when they were very young, yet had tremendous responsibilities thrust upon them.

> **They didn't expect much attention and certainly didn't get it. Their Honor Flight is truly the parade they never had.**

Sons and daughters who accompanied their parents have told me they'd never heard the story their dad just shared with me. It puts a tear in my eye when I think about it. This is one of the reasons Honor Flight Tri-State has such a strong pull on me.

It's hard to describe the honor and awe of watching a Vietnam vet trace his buddy's name at The Wall and tell me about the day his best friend died in the boonies; or the Korea vet who described what it was like to be at the frozen Chosin Reservoir at thirty below zero, when the Chinese troops overwhelmed them; or the bomber pilot who recounted his repeated, harrowing missions over Germany. Those memories will be with me always.

The tears in the eyes of veterans as they are cheered at the airport, or thanked by schoolkids at the monuments, or hugged by visitors from the foreign nations they saved, make every effort for Honor Flight worth it. When someone asks what it's all about, my answer is that the tears of those heroes is all the thanks I'll ever need.

Spending the day with a true hero

Jennifer Selm
Honor Flight Board Member

Once you meet the veterans as a guardian, the thrill is beyond your wildest imagination. I have been a guardian for both World War II and Korean War veterans. Both were humble; neither felt deserving of any belated recognition of their service. And both found the Honor Flight experience beyond their expectations. The same was true for me. I look forward to accompanying Vietnam veterans in the coming years.

Jennifer Selm with Roger Burdorf

I had the privilege to be the guardian for the late Honorable Judge S. Arthur Spiegel, who was a Marine in the First Division and served as an artillery spotter in the South Pacific. He was just shy of his 90th birthday when we took our Honor Flight. I had met him many years before at Blue Ash Airport, where he kept his Clipper airplane. We shared the same airport, and connected as pilots, forming a lasting friendship. I found out he was multitalented. He surprised me by painting my portrait – and it was phenomenal.

When I picked him up he was proudly wearing his red Marine Corps cap.

I was so excited to accompany him on his Honor Flight. When I picked him up at his home at "o'dark-thirty," he was proudly wearing his red Marine Corps cap. He was the only Marine on the trip. One of the most memorable moments was the welcome at the airport in D.C. by soldiers, bands, flags and warm handshakes. Both of us had tears streaming down our faces.

The next "magic moment" was the visit to the Iwo Jima Marine Memorial. To hear him name all the locations where he fought – it was by the grace of God that I was in the presence of a true hero, enjoying his company as he shared stories with fellow Veterans.

We were both exhausted on our return flight. I thought he would sleep on the flight back. No way! He was wide awake, reminiscing and chatting with his fellow veterans. At the heroes' welcome-home at CVG, his family, friends and work colleagues were all waving American flags.

Judge Spiegel embodied the true spirit of "Semper Fidelis" his entire life. He was truly a great American hero.

Honorable Judge S. Arthur Spiegel

Healing: An Army nurse and a veteran

Dee Daniels
Honor Flight Ambassador

Volunteering with Honor Flight Tri-State has been one of the best things I have ever done. It all began because of my parents, but especially my mother, 2nd Lt. Mary A. Martinez.

In my mother's later years, she began reminiscing and sharing some of her most personal thoughts from her time in the military, thoughts that were never shared with her family due to the pain and loss of her husband in Korea.

Mary Martinez

Mom completed her nursing education in 1941 and worked at Jewish Hospital. Then on July 25, 1942, she and a friend enlisted in the Army. Her brothers Bob and Eddie were already in the Army. She met my father during Basic Training at Fort Knox, Kentucky. He was being shipped out the next day, and told her he had nowhere to stay for the night. My mother hid him in an empty bed in the hospital, gave him some food and sent him on his way the next morning.

Soon she was shipped to Europe, to the 25th General Hospital. But no matter where she went, my father was always there ahead of her. She was sent to England, France, Belgium and Germany. She recalled when buzz bombs were dropping all around them, the nurses and doctors continued to care for soldiers that were injured. As the bombs dropped closer, the flaps of the tents were blown inward by the blasts. She talked about having to use her helmet as a wash basin to get cleaned up, and latrines were out in the open with no privacy.

Mom rose to Second Lieutenant and earned three battle stars in the European Theater for her duty at Normandy, the Battle of the Bulge and the Rhineland.

During the war she married my father, Major Frank Martinez – "Frankie," whom she always referred to as "the love of my life." Their married life was cut short, when my father was killed in Korea on May 13, 1952 at age 32. She never really got over his death.

Major "Frankie" Martinez

In October 2010, we took our Honor Flight together. She was 92, so I wasn't sure she could handle it. But she told me, "Come hell or high water, I'm going on that trip." When we got home she said, "Now my life is complete." She died five weeks after her flight.

After experiencing this amazing trip with my mother, it opened my eyes as to how special our veterans truly are. The following year, I found out just how important Army nurses like my mother were to soldiers wounded in war.

I met Gary Flesch in 2011 when he wandered into a little shop in Bellevue, Kentucky where I worked. We struck up a conversation. He happened to notice the Honor Flight brochures in a rack by the door, and that opened another door just a crack on our new friendship. Gary was a bit wary, but I was able to draw out enough to find out he served in the Army during the Vietnam War. I told him about Honor Flight's mission to fly our veterans to Washington, D.C. to see their memorials. He thought it was a really nice thing to do.

As I found out later, that planted a seed in Gary's mind. As time passed, he came back to the shop. Each time we talked about Honor Flight, he asked if Vietnam veterans were allowed to go yet. I had to tell him no, but I encouraged him to send in an application so that he would be at the top of the waiting list.

Then in April 2015, Honor Flight Tri-State opened to all veterans age 65 and over, which included the Vietnam era. I immediately contacted Gary to see if he was still interested. He was delighted to hear from me. I asked if he had anyone to accompany him, and offered to go with him. He said, "I would be honored to go with you."

He was so grateful to go and he was honored that I wanted to go with him. I knew it was going to be a great flight.

He said that after forty-five years of bad feelings about the war, he could finally let it go.

When our flight day came, we were both up early and couldn't wait to get to the airport. His wife, Linda, joined us at the welcome ceremony. She is a gem, but I could see that she was concerned about "her guy." I promised to take good care of him and made it a point to text her throughout the day to let her know that he was doing fine. Gary had suffered a stroke a few years back and lost the use of one arm. I knew he had other physical problems, but no more than that.

The day started off great. Gary was outgoing and engaged everyone he met. He absolutely loved the people who thanked him for his service. It was so great to see him tell them, "I did it for you." That said it all. He was especially happy to be greeted by the children at the memorials. Again, he let them know that he did it for them. He was very observant and took it all in.

Have you ever given a gift that was perfect and you couldn't wait to have the recipient open it?

That's how it felt to be with Gary. Each memorial we visited was special, but I was excited about visiting the Vietnam Wall and the Vietnam Women's Memorial that shows nurses holding a wounded soldier. After a long day, we finally arrived.

We located his high school friend's name on the Wall, made a rubbing of it and placed a bouquet in his memory. We then moved on to the Nurses Memorial, which was the most emotional moment of the day. Gary told me that he had been 19, in Vietnam for only three months when he was hit in the head during a mortar attack.

It must have been so frightening for a young man all alone. But while he waited for surgery a nurse had stopped and asked if he was okay and offered to stay with him. As he remembered it all, he broke down. He wanted to get close and place a hand on the nurses' statue. We held each other and cried and one of our medics placed a hand on Gary's back.

He said that after forty-five years of bad feelings about the war, he could finally let it go. I was overwhelmed with joy. To be a part of someone's healing, even in the smallest bit, was such a gift. I was extremely thankful to be that person for him.

Nothing could be better than my first Honor Flight with my 90-year old mother. I dedicate all my volunteer efforts to her.

But Gary was truly a blessing to be with. I believe that God puts people in our lives at a certain time, and God sent Gary to me at my shop in Bellevue, so our friendship would grow enough to take our journey together.

When we returned home to the airport that night, Gary was still going strong. He was looking for his gal, and she was looking for her guy. It was such a joy to see the love they shared. She was there just as she would have been after the war.

Mary Martinez (right) surrounded by her fellow women veterans at the World War ll Memorial.

Honor Flight healed my heart from Vietnam

Raymond L. Frey
Honor Flight Ambassador

I didn't know it at the time, but my long journey to become an ambassador for Honor Flight Tri-State actually began on my 21st birthday, in March 1966. I was a struggling junior in college looking for purpose and direction. I had already changed my college major three times. I knew I was wasting time, money and my educational opportunity by just plodding through college.

The war in Vietnam was starting to heat up. I naively decided to give up my college deferment and volunteer for the draft. I was in the Army by May and in Vietnam by the end of December. I served my twelve-month tour with the 9th Infantry Division, down south in the very muddy Mekong Delta.

I came home in January of 1968 in time, thank God, to watch the Tet Offensive on TV. I was a very different person with a much different outlook and perspective. I was not anti-war or anti-military, but I was very anti-government. President Lyndon B. Johnson (LBJ) boasted that "his boys couldn't bomb an outhouse in the North without his permission." Defense Secretary Robert McNamara counted the tonnage of bombs dropped, and Gen. William Westmoreland wanted to count bodies and fight an extended war of attrition. These were our "Best and Brightest." We had not "lost" the war yet, but I knew we were never going to win. We had lost our way. We had become the aggressors in a foreign country. The war would last another six years and cost the U.S. more than 58,000 deaths of our young soldiers, and the lives of more than 3 million Vietnamese civilians.

I understood the criticism of the war but I never did understand the criticism of the warriors. I spent the next forty years trying to get by. I never denied my service in Vietnam, but I seldom spoke of it. I married my high school sweetheart, finished college and earned an MBA. I raised two fantastic sons, maneuvered through the business world and eventually started my own business. I never looked back. I always wanted to look forward and move ahead with my life. Too many Vietnam veterans get stuck in the past.

Eventually, things began to get better for Vietnam veterans. The war ended, LBJ and Nixon were history, the Iranians freed our hostages after 444 days of captivity, President Reagan lifted the American spirit with his "Morning in America" message, and rock star Bruce Springsteen screamed "Born in the USA."

Ray Frey,
9th Infantry Division

Later in my life, I was forced to deal with some of life's lemons. My wife and I became empty nesters. My parents and slightly older brother passed away, along with friends and relatives. I had a bout with cancer. I entered a stage in life where I moved from full-time work to semi-retirement to full retirement. All of these changes gave me free time to think about my life.

I realized it was time to address my military service. After forty-five years of lying and denying all things military, my service almost became an obsession. I knew I had to address my issues. I decided I wanted to volunteer my free time to assist veterans. In my heart and mind, I wanted to thank our veterans and make sure that they felt appreciated for the job that they did for our country.

I understood the criticism of the war but I never did understand the criticism of the warriors.

I jumped in to serve the Hamilton County Veterans Treatment Court, the VA Medical Center and the Ohio Patriot Guard. These groups let me meet and deal with all of our veterans, ages 20 through 95, from World War II, Korea, Vietnam, the Cold War, Grenada, Iraq and Afghanistan. I quickly developed an affinity for the World War II veterans.

They truly are "the Greatest Generation." When they stacked arms and were discharged, they must have been given a little slip of paper that was engraved: "I'm no hero, I was just doing my job." How many times have we heard that on Honor Flights?

My desire to serve the diminishing numbers of World War II veterans led me to Honor Flight. I accompanied World War II veteran Billy Dean as his guardian in 2008. It was a life-changing trip for me. I immediately called Tom and Cheryl Popp and asked them to sign me up for whatever I could do to help. I passed Honor Flight brochures out like M&Ms at the VA, the American Legion Post and Kroger stores, wherever I saw an older veteran. I stuffed cookies and donuts in sandwich bags, grilled hot dogs, spoke at fund raisers, collected checks, parked cars, manned information booths, participated in flag ceremonies, assisted at guardian meetings, and showed up to send off and welcome home our Honor Flight veterans.

I answer Cheryl's "bat-signal" whenever she needs help. I will do anything and everything that I can to help. My greatest thrill came in April 2015. Due to a last minute cancellation, I had the honor and privilege of traveling as an "at large ambassador." I tried to meet with and speak to all of the veterans and guardians, from bus to bus, memorial to memorial, table to table.

Honor Flight gives me the greatest sense of satisfaction and accomplishment, serving the "Greatest Generation" with our Honor Flight "Band of Brothers" volunteers. The board of directors, the medics, the ground crew and all of the other ambassadors are simply top notch, honorable and dedicated volunteers. No one receives any compensation.

I urge everyone to pick a charity, a service or a group and get involved. Honor Flight has been good for my soul. It has helped to free me from negative issues I carried for many years.

The day is long, but at the end, when I see the welcome-home gathering, I'm so reenergized I could immediately turn around and redo it all over again.

Our veterans have finally been given their day, their parade and their homecoming celebration. I would go on every flight if it were possible.

A day with my dad that I will always treasure

Karen Unger
Honor Flight Ambassador

I first learned about Honor Flight Tri-State when my dad, a Korean War Air Force veteran, told me he had been accepted to go on a flight. I didn't know he had applied, but after research and several phone calls, I was thrilled to find out I could be his guardian on the August 2012 flight.

We planned and talked about our day, going over the agenda to anticipate what it would be like. Little did either of us know that it would be so extraordinary, one of the best days of our lives.

Karen Unger with her father Dick Holstegge

As we arrived at the airport there was an air of excitement. The ceremonies, the flag folding and speeches were the perfect beginning. As my dad and I walked hand in hand to the gate, I was so proud of him. The reception at the airport in Washington was unbelievable. At the memorials it was so heartwarming to see strangers thank the veterans for their service.

All those signs, balloons and cheers were phenomenal, but seeing our entire family there was very emotional.

I saw such camaraderie among the veterans. Then we arrived home to an awesome celebration. All those people with signs, balloons and cheers were phenomenal, but seeing our entire family there was very emotional.

My family sat up for hours after we got home and talked about the whole day. My dad and I have always been close, but I know this brought us closer. It was something only he and I could share. It's a day I will always treasure.

After that first flight, I became an ambassador. I knew I had to get involved and I was totally hooked. I was so impressed with how well organized everything was, the attention to detail and especially the dedication and respect shown to the veterans by the board members, medics and ambassadors. I've been a guardian on two more flights since the one with my dad.

I enjoy helping at Honor Flight events and fundraisers, and putting "mail call" envelopes together. But most rewarding for me is participating in the flights.

I love being at the airport in the morning to greet the veterans and see their excitement as I shake their hands and thank them for their service. The Welcome Home Celebrations have become spectacular, with lots of smiles, some tears and sincere gratitude. Comments such as, "This has been the best day of my life," and, "I never got this when I came home from the war," make me so proud to be a part of Honor Flight.

Although I have only been involved for a couple of years, it has been a fulfilling part of my life. Because my dad was so proud to be a veteran, I have always had a special place in my heart for them all. Unfortunately, I lost my dad in April 2014. I feel it is a tribute to him when I help our true American heroes experience a wonderful and memorable day like he and I had together.

It's a day of living history

Scott Klein
Honor Flight Ambassador

I grew up with my uncle telling the occasional story about when he was in the Navy during the war. It always sounded like the experience of a lifetime. So when I first learned about Honor Flight in 2011 from a friend who went as a guardian, it sounded like something I needed to do.

I have always been a history buff, and I'm especially interested in World War II. I like to go beyond the facts, to learn more about the people who were there. As I got to know more of the veterans, it became clear that they made this country the great nation it is today.

I sent my application in and waited for my opportunity. One April night I finally got the call. Someone had canceled and I was invited.

I went to the guardian training and met Cheryl and Tom Popp and other board members. The Saturday before the flight I contacted my assigned veteran, Donald Mann. Donald did not live too far from me and we spoke for a few minutes on the phone. On the day of the flight I arrived very early, and there were already two veterans sitting in the airport talking. One was a World War II vet, wearing his Purple Heart medal on his hat. The other was my Korean War veteran, wearing his black cowboy hat.

We got along well right away. After the emotional opening ceremony, we left the TSA area, escorted by bagpipers from the Hamilton County Sheriff's office. It was very moving, to say the least.

As our plane taxied to our runway, there was a water salute from the airport fire department. Our flight to Washington, D.C. took just over an hour so we got to know each other better. Donald was a cook on an LST and moved troops to and from the shore. He had many stories, and told me about the prisoner exchange he was part of at the end of the war.

Inscription at Korean War Memorial

As I got to know other veterans on our flight, the saying that "uncommon valor was a common virtue" was an understatement. For the most part, they don't see what they did as any more than just doing their job – and that is amazing.

One 93-year-old veteran wore her uniform. She worked in intelligence in Washington during the war, typing secret coded messages. I met another veteran who followed General Patton through four battles, including crossing the Rhine. Yet another was in the Pacific with the Marines. There were seventy veterans with hundreds of stories to tell.

He said the inscription 'Freedom is Not Free' had been on his mind all day.

I have great respect for Marines, such as my best friend, who served three tours in Vietnam. He has asked me to be his guardian when he goes on an Honor Flight. My wife's uncle, also a Marine, made the ultimate sacrifice and gave his life at Iwo Jima in 1945.

As we visited the monuments, I learned that Donald was not so different from my own father, who was a cook in the Army from 1951 to 1953, and passed away three years before our flight. The Korean Memorial was the highlight for Donald. He said the inscription that "Freedom is Not Free" had been on his mind all day. We spent a lot of time there. A Korean family stopped us and thanked Donald for fighting for their country, which brought tears to his eyes.

As we got back on the bus and headed for dinner, you would think that the day would start to wear on veterans in their 80s. But they were still going full speed.

The welcome-home crowd was the most moving part of the trip. I got to meet Donald's family. The following week, I took him my pictures from the trip. We still stay in touch.

When I got home, I signed up to become an ambassador for Honor Flight Tri-State. This is the greatest honor we can give these vets as they age, to get the proper thanks they never received, and a day they will never forget.

A day you will never forget

Stretch Hoff
Honor Flight Ambassador

If you want to say thank you to a veteran in the most significant way possible, and at the same time give yourself the gift of a day you will never forget, be an Honor Flight guardian. Never will you feel better about serving others. That's what Honor Flight has meant to me.

My veteran was totally impressed.

One of my veterans was Bob Andrews, my friend who served in Japan after the war, under MacArthur, to rejuvenate that country. Bob was overwhelmed by his experience on Honor Flight. He was totally impressed with the entire day, with how well it was organized, how he was treated, discussions with other veterans and the entire atmosphere. Five months later Bob died. It is wonderful that Honor Flight made it possible for him to spend one of his last days in such a meaningful, interesting and rewarding way. Thank you to all veterans.

A veteran found by a random snapshot

Deanna Beineke
Honor Flight Ambassador

In 2001 I retired from teaching and used my free time to revisit my family history. In my research I ran across a new project for the Library of Congress, The Veterans History Project. As the daughter of a World War II veteran, it called to me. My first interview was with my father. I had always known he served under General Patton as a tank driver, but I had no idea about any of his experiences. That interview was the first of nearly sixty that I completed over the next few years, most with World War II veterans from all branches.

Deanna Beineke with Ed McKinney

Fast forward to 2008. My husband and I went to Lunken Airport for an open house to look at some of the old airplanes. Honor Flight Tri-State had a booth there with information and applications to become guardians. I felt that same tug to "do something," and filled out an application. This wasn't just something I wanted to do; this was something I needed to do. I had seen the site for the World War II Memorial when it was just a hole in the ground. My father watched the dedication on television but never got to visit before his death in 2005.

Those emails are forwarded to another five hundred addresses, and our Welcome Home Rallies have become legendary.

So I screwed up my courage and called Cheryl Popp to plead my case to serve as a guardian. She explained about a waiting list and listened very graciously as I became emotional about why I needed to serve. A couple of months later, I was scheduled for the July 2009 flight. This was when Honor Flights flew out of Columbus and shared a plane with other passengers. Each guardian had two or three veterans, and I think we spent as much time on buses as we did at the memorials.

But oh, what a day! It didn't matter how hot it was or how much travel time we had. Those men were energized just by being together. Before we left Baltimore, I told Cheryl that my husband, Jim, wanted to serve as well, and we would do whatever we could to help. He ended up on a flight in the fall, and we were both hooked.

Cheryl took us up on our offer to help. She had few contacts in Northern Kentucky, and we had lots of them. My teaching experience and passion for Honor Flight led to speaking engagements, and our contacts helped recruit veterans south of the Ohio River. When Honor Flight Tri-State began flying out of Cincinnati, we became regulars at the airport both morning and evening for each flight. I started inviting friends to greet the veterans when each flight returned and that led to an email list of more than two hundred folks. Those emails are forwarded to another five hundred addresses, and our Welcome Home Celebrations have become legendary.

Once in a while, we find connections that defy imagination. In the spring of 2004, Jim and I and our daughter visited the Normandy beaches where my father landed with Patton, three weeks after D-Day. We visited the American Cemetery there and took random pictures of some of the markers. In June of 2015, an Honor Flight ambassador friend showed me pictures of his trip to France and the Czech Republic. I showed him my album the next day. While he was looking through it, he stopped at one of the grave-marker photos and asked to take a picture of it. His wife came over to look and told me that they had also visited the Cemetery to find out if two uncles were buried there. The directory at the visitor center listed one, but the attendant was not able to find the other. The random photo we had taken eleven years before was the uncle they couldn't find. It was one of those moments that makes your heart swell just a little.

If Honor Flight had not come into being; if we had not met fellow ambassadors Mickey and Kathy Hoffman; if we hadn't shared pictures, that healing moment would never have happened. Honor Flight is good karma.

We were immediately hooked

Mickey and Kathy Hoffman
Honor Flight Ambassador

We became involved with World War II veterans many years ago. I started attending army reunions with my father in 1977. He was a veteran of the 16th Armored Division. Mickey got involved when we married in 1985. My father passed away in 2001, but we have stayed active with the 16th Armored Division Association. We've hosted their reunion four times, and we've traveled to Europe with them four times, including a visit to Pilsen, Czech Republic, for the Liberation Festival – celebrating seventy years since they were liberated by the U.S. Army.

Mickey and Kathy Hoffman
with Charles Connor and John Jackson

Our involvement with the 16th Armored Division Association led us to Honor Flight Tri-State. We applied to be guardians and were called in July 2014 to be on the August flight. We were thrilled.

At last, the flight day had arrived. My veteran, John, was as excited about the plane ride as anything. His eyes had been bandaged on his trip home from the war, so he saw nothing. Now he was experiencing air travel with his eyes wide open.

As an African-American, he spoke of how he was treated poorly in many ways while he served his country. He was a truck driver during the D-Day invasions. And later when he drove for the Red Ball Express, he had a couple encounters with Gen. George Patton. He and others in his unit had a hard time getting back home because many did not want black soldiers traveling with them. He left the military in 1947 but did not receive his medals, including a Purple Heart, until 2013.

> ## *As an African-American, he spoke of how he was treated poorly in many ways while he served his country.*

At the World War II Memorial, a little boy from the Netherlands approached us and asked if John was a veteran. I said yes, and he asked if he could shake John's hand. I said of course, he would love that. John and the little boy were grinning ear to ear as they shook hands. John said he would never forget the trip and was so thankful.

Mickey's veteran, Charles, served in the 75th Infantry Battalion. He spoke little of his experiences. He had lost his wife a short time before his Honor Flight, and preferred to share memories of his wife and loving family. Mickey was there to listen. It was a heartwarming experience for both men. Charles was 90 and in great physical condition. He was encouraged to use a wheelchair at one point, but instead he offered to push Mickey in it.

As our great day came to an end, both of our veterans were overwhelmed by the reception at the airport. They just could not believe it. John was beaming, Charles was taking it all in and we were smiling through our tears.

We were home. Exhausted. But we couldn't stop talking about the trip. We were hooked on Honor Flight. We immediately signed up to go again and volunteered to be ambassadors.

We love what we do with Honor Flight – from setting up and taking down tents for fundraising, to wrapping Christmas gifts at the airport, to wrapping hot dogs at Lunken Airport Days. Obviously, the best part is meeting the veterans before their flight and greeting them on their return. It is such a privilege to do what we do – to serve those who served. God bless our veterans and God bless America.

Who will teach the next generations?

Jayne Bonzella
Honor Flight Ambassador

I love the Honor Flight mission to give veterans the gratitude they deserve.

I got involved while working for a company that sponsors Honor Flight, and flew as a guardian twice. My first trip was with an Army nurse who, at 89, was one of the younger veterans on our flight. She was a firecracker. We had so much fun. As Irene shared her life story, I learned that she met her husband in the first grade in rural Pennsylvania. During the war, her four brothers went overseas, and her future husband was trained as a bomber pilot.

> *I did not appreciate what these ordinary men and women did for us until I heard their stories and met them face to face.*

She was in nursing school and most of her friends enlisted in the Army to stay stateside. After the war, she married her bomber pilot and had five children. They moved twenty times for his job in the FBI, and lived happily ever after. She had many thrills on the flight, from tears to laughter. When she smiled I saw the famous "Life Magazine cover" nurse being kissed on Times Square when the war ended. She was breathless with excitement when she was asked to do a swing dance in the Washington, D.C. airport. "I haven't done that in years," she said.

On my second flight, I accompanied a Korean War veteran. He didn't say much, but pointed out the things that meant the most to him. I was moved again by the welcome the veterans received in Washington and the homecoming in the Cincinnati airport. As I pushed Harold's wheelchair through the crowds, I had to stop to wipe away my tears.

These flights left me with a feeling I can only describe as "doubt." I received a good education growing up and understood what happened in the wars. I had a few uncles who served. But I wondered why it took me until my Honor Flight at age 50 to truly understand the sacrifice that ordinary people made – and still make today – when they enter the military? I did not appreciate what these ordinary men and women did for us until I heard their stories and met them face to face. Why did I always feel so shy about thanking a vet? If I didn't teach my own children the debt we owe them, who will teach the generations to come?

I hope that someday a veteran won't be able to walk down the street without hearing "thank-you" from strangers. We owe them so much. My children have seen me approach veterans in the grocery store to thank them and encourage them to go on an Honor Flight. I express my appreciation in Facebook posts on Memorial Day and Fourth of July. And I speak out about the way veterans are treated by our government.

At my daughter's high school graduation, they asked the graduates entering the service to stand. It made me think about what those families will sacrifice as they worry about their children. Then they asked all veterans in the audience to stand – young and old. My son touched the man standing in front of him on the shoulder and said, "Thank you for your service." The veteran nodded. And I smiled. There's one kid who won't forget.

'Do you think I could go too?'

Kathy Davidson
Honor Flight Ambassador

My dad, John Sullivan, never met a stranger. He would talk to anybody on the street, but he especially loved talking to other vets. He was a lieutenant in the Second Marine Division in World War II. When I decided to become a guardian on an Honor Flight, I asked him if he wanted to go.

He said, "No, I won't know anybody or have anyone to talk to." I thought, "What? You get along with everybody." But I

*Kathy Davidson with her father
John Sullivan aboard Honor Flight*

decided I would still sign up because I knew it was something that I wanted to do.

A year went by and I totally forgot about it. Then I got a call from Honor Flight Tri-State. I was very excited, so I called my dad right away and told him I was going on the Honor Flight. It became quiet on the other end of the phone. I asked him what was wrong and he said, "Do you think I could go too?" I was kind of mad and said, "Why didn't you sign up earlier?" I was heartbroken that he wouldn't be able to go, as I knew the waiting list for the vets was long, and that it was too late.

> ## *I still keep a picture at my bedside*
> ## *of us together on that Honor Flight.*

So I called Honor Flight back and asked if there was any way he could go. They told me that another veteran had backed out two days prior and there was now an empty seat. They asked if I would like to take that seat for my father, and would I like to be his guardian. It was a dream come true, like divine intervention.

We had the best time ever. I still keep a picture at my bedside of us together on that Honor Flight. Our flight was in May 2011, and we lost him in February 2012, so if not for that flight he never would have had the chance to go.

After I took my dad, I was so impressed with the experience. It was so true and genuine. I asked how to sign up to be a volunteer and I've been volunteering ever since. It makes you feel so great, so uplifted to help them. It's all about them.

A friendship that lasted for years

John Mock with Tommy Mosley

John Mock
Honor Flight Ambassador

I consider myself a patriot, and I tend to associate with those of like mind and kindred spirit. My good friend Timothy E. Cassady is one such patriot. I admire and conscientiously emulate his love of country, his devotion to our flag and his appreciation and respect for all our veterans.

In 2013, Tim strongly suggested that I apply as a guardian. I was phoned on the day prior to the October trip. The good news was bittersweet, because my opportunity came as a result of another guardian's eleventh-hour inability to make the trip.

I met my veteran on the morning of our flight: U.S. Army Pvt. Tommie Lee Mosley. He was from Lauderdale County, Mississippi when he enlisted on August 11, 1943. The newly married 20-year-old recruit was sent to Camp Shelby, just south of Hattiesburg. His enlistment was "Code 5," which meant "for the duration of the war or other emergency, plus six months, subject to the discretion of the President or otherwise according to law." The date was easy to remember: Fifty-one years later to that day, my daughter Rebecca was born.

A remarkable display of reverence for fallen comrades.

After Basic Training, Pvt. Mosley was assigned to the Tenth Army, XXIV Corps, 7th Infantry Division, as a light and medium truck mechanic and driver. He participated in the invasions of Leyte and Okinawa in the South Pacific. He said it was painfully noisy in Okinawa. "Everybody was calling it the 'Steel Typhoon.' Metal was everywhere, you could feel it!" He hated the noise. He was a quiet man, a gentle giant with hands twice as big as mine and a heart of gold.

When the fighting and shelling was quiet, one of his favorite duties was driving the mess sergeant to the forward lines, loaded with mess kits. He talked about how appreciative the boys were to receive warm food. Following the Japanese surrender in 1945, his division was stationed in Korea, then returned home after New Year's in 1946.

Tommie divorced when he got home and moved to Cincinnati, where he worked in the maintenance department for the City of Cheviot until his retirement.

The morning of our flight, we were as giddy as a bus full of kids on their way to camp. Our excitement became more contemplative as we saw the massive human figures of the Iwo Jima statue, and visited Arlington National Cemetery, where we watched the Changing of the Guard at the Tomb of the Unknown Soldier, with military precision, dignity and respect at its finest – a remarkable display of reverence for fallen comrades.

While enjoying a boxed lunch at the Air Force Memorial, Tommie was interviewed by Cliff Radel of The Cincinnati Enquirer. Mr. Radel had tears in his eyes when speaking with Tommie about his service in Okinawa.

We were "two-thumbs-up" for most of the day, and Tommie was appreciative of the special attention he received from Sgt. Krystle Williams, USMC, who was kind enough to volunteer her entire day as an official escort for our Honor Flight group.

Tommie never shared more than a few comments about his service, but his emotions during our visit to the World War II Memorial said plenty. He spent the rest of the afternoon on the bus. We returned to the airport to much fanfare. The guardians were sometimes more emotional than the veterans, especially as they witnessed the respect and honor given to these heroes.

I met Tommie for lunch about every three months at the Chili Time Restaurant in St. Bernard. He loved their biscuits and gravy, grilled cheese sandwiches with pickles, and sweet tea. He would bring his photo journal that I made for him each time we met. Tommie's favorite subjects were his friends and co-workers in Cheviot. I came to admire his humility, and his sincere appreciation for simple, kind gestures.

My first experience with Honor Flight Tri-State instilled a desire to volunteer. Now Tim Cassady and I enjoy working together on committees and as ground crew and ambassadors at special events.

Tommie Lee Mosley passed away at the age of 93 on my thirtieth wedding anniversary, Monday, June 1, 2015. He was buried with full military honors at Spring Grove Cemetery in Cincinnati.

My dad was my hero

Kim Brockhoff

Honor Flight Ambassador

In 1970, the Cincinnati Reds were having a very good year. As a present when I came home on leave from boot camp, my father bought a couple of tickets for a game and wanted me to wear my dress white Navy uniform. During the game some things were said to me about my service during the Vietnam conflict, and it wasn't "Thanks for your service."

Dad was much more upset about it than I was, and it took years for me to be angry about the treatment I received for serving my country, and to realize why he was so upset. My dad – who earned a Combat Infantry Badge, Bronze Star and Purple Heart during World War II – was my hero. He came home to no ceremonies or parties. He just helped to save the free world and went to work and raised a family.

I'll work for Honor Flight until it's over or one of my sons pushes me around D.C. in a wheelchair on my own Honor Flight.

I wanted to honor what he had done for me, so years later, after he passed away, I read about the World War II Memorial opening, and decided to send his name and picture along with his sister's name and picture – she was also a World War II veteran of the WAVES (Women Accepted for Volunteer Emergency Service) – to be recorded in their archives.

As a Vietnam Navy veteran, I'm active with the USO and American Legion, and I decided that our family foundation should donate money to the Honor Flight to get these World War II heroes to

Washington, D.C. to see their memorial before they're gone. So I persuaded my stepbrother to donate his money, and I donated my money and arranged for a flight to take my stepfather, who was also a World War II veteran.

I went along as a guardian for another World War II veteran. And that was all it took for me. I saw the faces of these guys and talked to them and heard them say that it was the best day they had in years, or in some cases since the war. I just had to help and do more.

Now, five years later, I still enjoy working to get these guys ready to go in the morning. Every time they come marching out of the tunnel at CVG behind those drums and bagpipes, I get all teary-eyed.

Kim Brockhoff

My stepfather now has Alzheimer's and does not communicate with us anymore. But one of the last things he did when he still could, was to point to the eight-by-ten picture of me, my brother and him on the morning of his Honor Flight. That picture is always kept in his room.

Talk about bringing tears to your eyes. That's why I'll work for Honor Flight until it's over or one of my sons pushes me around D.C. in a wheelchair on my own Honor Flight. I've told many people that I wish time could have been different, so I could have gone with both my father and my aunt on an Honor Flight. And when I do go as a guardian, I make a point of telling my assigned veteran, "You're my dad for today, as my dad didn't live to do this. So enjoy!"

The greatest gift was an Honor Flight

Scott Kuhr
Honor Flight Ambassador

My connection to Honor Flight Tri-State began as a 50th birthday present from my family. Knowing my interest in history and that a memorable experience would make for a unique gift, they signed me up to be a guardian. Little did we know what an inspired gift it turned out to be.

It's rare to be able to point to a date on a calendar that changes your life, but that's what happened to me on September 25, 2012, the day I was privileged to be the guardian for World War II veteran Herman "Hap" Whalen.

Hap and I met the morning of the flight, and there was an instant connection. Our pairing was random, but I believe fate

"Hap" Whalen with his guardian Scott Kuhr

played a part in bringing us together. Hap was a last minute replacement. And as it turned out, we had things in common nobody could have predicted.

Hap had a son named Scott (my name) who had tragically died years earlier. Had Scott lived, he would have been a little older than I was and likely would have been Hap's guardian. I felt honored to be part of a memory that Hap would have shared with his own son.

> ### *Hap was smiling and laughing as tears ran down his face. I knew at that moment how special the day had been for him... and for me.*

We also discovered that before moving to Northern Kentucky to be near family, Hap and his wife had lived near Melbourne, Florida – where my wife, Brenda, was born, and where her family lives.

Every stop we made that day was so moving and came with a wonderful memory. I especially enjoyed sharing the World War II Memorial with Hap, given his role as a mapmaker in the Army. At one point, a young lady and her friends came up to Hap. In broken English, they asked if they could shake his hand and take their picture with him. Hap, of course, was only too happy to oblige. These were total strangers who wanted to thank him for his service in a most genuine way. The young lady gave Hap a few kisses on his cheek, leaving him with a big smile on his face. I laughed and told him, "Whatever happens in D.C. stays in D.C."

The tremendous "Welcome Home" celebration when we got back to Cincinnati that evening caught us by surprise. Hundreds applauded and cheered us. Hap was smiling and laughing as tears ran down his face. I knew at that moment how special the day had been for him... and for me.

The entire day was the parade these deserving veterans never got when their tour of duty ended. The experience warmed my heart and filled my soul. I felt so blessed to have been a part of it.

I took pictures that day and created a photo album for Hap. My family and I delivered it to him a few weeks after the flight so he could share it with friends. I still stay in touch with Hap, and we have visited him and his wife, Barb, on many occasions.

Since that trip, I actively, passionately and proudly serve every veteran on every flight. As a history lover, I treasure their stories. I discovered that my uncle, Dan Hahn, had served in the Army during World War II, and was able to get him information that led to his own Honor Flight near his home in Florida. Our family wrote cards and letters for "Mail Call" to thank him for his service. As he put it, "I thought people forgot." But now he knows there are many, many people who appreciate what veterans have done to serve our country. His heart was touched and it will be a memory he will forever cherish.

I'll never forget the gift I received for my 50th birthday. It's the gift that keeps on giving.

To all the veterans: Semper Fi!

Ken Ludwig
Honor Flight Ambassador

I'm the youngest of thirteen children in my family. We were very poor, but I didn't know it. Growing up in Delhi is one of the best memories of my life. But I never knew my dad was a veteran of World War II until later in life. By then he was gone. He died when I was in the eighth grade at St. Williams, and I never had the opportunity to talk to him about the war.

Ken Ludwig

My brother Bob was in the Army Air Corps and was at Normandy on D-Day. I was too young to appreciate what he did. Years later I took him to Wright Patterson Air Force Base Museum and he showed me gliders that he built during the war. He wanted to fly them, but he was not qualified as a pilot.

Bob never finished high school until he received his GED when he was 65, but he was the smartest man I ever met. He could build anything. When he was in Normandy, my mother sent him a letter that she had given birth to my sister Carol. He told me he cried like a baby.

My mom and I said a prayer every night while he was a POW.

My brother Anthony was my true hero. He was a POW in Korea for thirty months and suffered unspeakable atrocities. I was 5 when he was released, and I remember the joy for my family and all of Delhi. They held a parade in his honor. My mom and I said a prayer every night while he was a POW and I believe he survived because of my mother's faith in God and her love for her children.

Before Tony died in 2005, I interviewed him for the Library of Congress Veteran's History Project. Before that, he had never spoken about his POW experiences. Now his six children can hand it down to their future generations so they will know what he went through to keep this country free.

I love being with the vets on Honor Flights. They remind me of my brothers. I am especially proud to share the honor of folding our American Flag with my friend Ray Frey. I savor the moment every time. I am still a United States Marine and damn proud of it. Semper Fi!

From two little flags to thousands

Lisa Houser
Honor Flight Ambassador

When my husband, Greg, went on one of the earliest Honor Flights, he had to drive to a Northern Kentucky church about forty-five minutes from our home at 4 a.m. He met twenty veterans and the five guardians who would spend the day together. They took a bus to Louisville to catch their flight. After a day touring the memorials, they flew back to Louisville for a bus ride home to Northern Kentucky. He finally got home in Maineville around 2 a.m. It was an extremely long day, but he couldn't wait to share stories with me.

Lisa Houser

From these humble beginnings, Honor Flight has now expanded to five charter flights a year, carrying 150 passengers on each flight, because of the dedicated volunteers and generous donors.

One time I decided to meet them for their late-night return. I got to the airport at 10 p.m. for their 11p.m. arrival, with two little American flags and my "Welcome Home" sign. Camera crews from local news stations started to arrive. I was excited about being on local TV, so I asked the cameraman, "Are you here for the Honor Flight?" He looked at me with my flags and sign and said, "No ma'am." My heart sank. What could be more newsworthy than veterans and their day in Washington?

Another reporter told me, "We're waiting for a prisoner who is being extradited back to Kentucky from Mexico." Sure enough, a heavily guarded, shackled prisoner walked by. As they hurried him past, I heard laughter and stepped out to see the veterans heading my way. Our heroes were home!

Alone, I clapped and cheered and waved my little flags. The veterans smiled and laughed, full of energy. My husband and the other guardians were totally worn out. But my husband said it had been a great day.

"Dear War Hero, my grandpa was in Korea. Do you know him?"

I was so proud of Greg and his passion for this group. That was the beginning of my love affair with Honor Flight. I decided that I wanted to get involved, and I was soon managing nametags. It was an opportunity to be one of the first people to welcome these veterans and guardians. We arrive at the airport at 5 a.m. on flight days, and there are always a few veterans waiting for us. I hate getting up early, so I'm a little grumpy – okay, a lot grumpy – until I walk in and see the first veterans waiting. Being with them just makes me smile. I am happy to play a small part in their special day.

Every Honor Flight veteran receives a "mail call" envelope on the return flight home – just like in the movies. We wanted to thank the veterans again for their service, and they love the letters they get.

I e-mailed teachers and group leaders in our region asking them to submit "thank you" letters to the veterans. My goal was five thousand – and I am happy to say that was easily achieved! This allowed us to give five letters to each veteran for a year of Honor Flights.

The younger schoolchildren colored pictures of soldiers and tanks, while high school students used it as a writing assignment. It was really amazing how many students wrote heartfelt thank-you letters. Some of my favorites:

"Dear Extinguished Veteran… "

"Dear Veteran, you have expired me so much…"

"Dear Sir, I'm so glad you are still alive!"

"Dear War Hero, my grandpa was in Korea. Do you know him?"

"Dear Veteran, I don't know anyone more braver than you."

Although I'm not on the flights when these are distributed, I hear about the veterans with tears in their eyes as they open their envelopes. And that's one more reason why I love volunteering with Honor Flight Tri-State.

Early morning preparations:
nametags and T-shirts

Every Honor Flight carries a crew of medics, stationed on each bus throughout the day to make sure the veterans, guardians, board members and volunteers have immediate medical attention if needed.

I can feel the fear and horror he experienced

Larry Cole
Honor Flight Medical Advisor

I learned of Honor Flight Tri-State from Sam Keller, my lifelong friend and Mayor of the City of Cheviot, where I have been a firefighter for more than thirty-two years. Little did I know my life would soon be changed forever.

My journey began in June of 2009, when I was asked to volunteer as a medic on the first flight from Cincinnati/ Northern Kentucky International Airport. I was excited to meet so many amazing people, such as Cheryl and Tom Popp, Nathan Bachrach, Ed Finke and Earl Morse, to name a few. The most amazing group on our flight was the seventy-one veterans of World War II who helped save our world.

Medic Larry Cole

I returned home late and realized I needed to be more involved. Six years later I am helping to recruit our forgotten heroes so we can provide them with "one day they will never forget."

They're not looking for an explanation, just someone to listen. God put me in this very place for a specific reason.

My role is to ensure that the medical needs of veterans and guardians are addressed during our trip. When I return home I can't wait to share all the stories with my wife, Donna. Eventually, Donna couldn't resist and traveled as a guardian with Bob Flaig, a World War II veteran, in September 2011. She was hooked. Donna and I became ambassadors and volunteered to call veterans and guardians to schedule their trips. I also now serve as Medical Advisor and continue my role as a medic on each flight. Donna has been appointed to the board of directors and leads Bus Three during our trips.

Each trip holds special memories, as no two are alike. I do not have military experience, but I did have an uncle who served in the Army for twenty years. Volunteering with Honor Flight Tri-State affords me the opportunity to personally thank veterans for their service. I feel privileged to serve them and cherish the conversations we have. At times I find myself sitting quietly with one of them on a bench at one of the memorials as he tells his story, sometimes for the first time since the war. The details are so vivid I can feel the fear and horror he experienced. I offer a hug, a hand on their shoulder, hold a hand and sometimes share the tears. They're not looking for an explanation, just someone to listen. God put me in this very place for a specific reason.

I read about our wars in history classes. Now as an adult I truly understand what sacrifices where made and I can put a face with the names of these heroes. I am truly blessed.

Medic Robert Klein

You realize how the war has haunted veterans

Cheviot Fire Chief Robert Klein
Honor Flight Medic

I love being affiliated with Honor Flight Tri-State because it's such an amazing opportunity for me to serve my true heroes. It has become a great passion in my life.

You can try to understand the casualties of war through movies and interviews on screen, but until you hear a firsthand account of a man who has faced death, witnessed the loss of his brothers, as well as other atrocities of war, it is hard to fathom. The way a man's face completely changes from a smile to a blank stare as he relives his experience with a quavering voice makes you realize how the war has haunted veterans. I've made more than thirty trips. Each time I am reminded just how blessed I am to live in this great country, and how important the "Greatest Generation" was and still is.

The Honor Flight team is second to none.

The Honor Flight team is second to none. Cheryl and Tom Popp, Mayor Sam Keller, Nathan Bachrach and Ed Finke organize, raise money and handle every detail with precision and professionalism. In 2009, Cheryl asked me if I would be the lead paramedic, and I was honored to accept. We have recruited several top area paramedic/firefighters, such as Assistant Chief Scott Souders, District Chief Ed Thomas, Lt. Rob Wolfrom, and Lt. Alan Boyle from Green Township Fire and EMS; Captain Scott Scherpenberg, Captain Larry Cole, Engineer Chris Lakeberg, Engineer Eric Sullender of Cheviot Fire and EMS; Battalion Chief Steve Conn, Colerain Fire; Chief Otto Huber, Loveland-Symmes Fire and EMS; and Nancy Van Rotz, RN, University of Cincinnati.

Every trip I am reminded of Mother Teresa's quote: "Not all of us can do great things. But we can do small things with great love."

'Bombs were falling all around the hospital'

Nancy VonRotz
Honor Flight Medic

Being involved in Honor Flight Tri-State is a small way to say thanks to those who served in our military, and to honor both of my parents, who served in World War II. Dad was in the Navy Seabees in the Pacific Theater, and my mom was a registered nurse in the Atlantic Theater. Growing up as the youngest of eight children, I didn't hear war stories. They felt it was their duty to serve. That humble attitude was reflected in Mom's journal entries:

> *Honoring those who served is a feeling deep in my soul.*

"We felt that it was no more than a job to be done," she wrote. And, "We (nurses) rolled up our pant legs and jumped into water, walking through a two-foot wide, roped-off, cleared path between a mined beach."

Another entry: "Today we spent hiding under steps with buildings shaking and bombs dropping all around – the machine guns pounding – then awful silence. The next night was in surgery with planes overhead and bombs falling all around the hospital." She was awarded four bronze service stars. We didn't know until seventy years later, when we requested a burial flag for her casket.

Honoring those who served in our military is a feeling deep in my soul. Being involved with Honor Flight Tri-State is an opportunity to honor those who have given so much to preserve our precious freedoms.

In loving remembrance of Lt. Alice M. Huber & Lt. Herbert J. Schutte.

Medic Nancy VonRotz

I treat the veterans as I would treat my father

Edward Thomas
Honor Flight Medic

When I heard about Honor Flight about nine years ago, my goal was to take my father and uncles on the flight before it was too late. I was not successful. But I felt that I still needed to go for them.

More than I could ever repay.

I went the first time as a guardian and experienced the love and respect given to every veteran on the flight. I knew that flight would not be my last. When asked to go as a medic, I was honored.

Medic Ed Thomas

On every flight I treat the veterans as I would have treated my father and uncles. I personally owe that generation more than I could ever repay. I love talking and spending time with them and being a small part of their very special day.

Medics are always prepared for medical emergencies during Honor Flight missions.

'I was so choked up I couldn't get a word out'

Nathan Bachrach, Simply Money
Honor Flight Donor

I didn't go looking for Honor Flight. It found me. I was going about my business as a partner at Simply Money, hoping to grow our firm, help our clients, and make a positive impact in the community. I wasn't looking for a "cause" or a "movement" to belong to. I just wanted to use our position in media to call attention to worthy organizations in our area. I certainly wasn't looking for a long-term relationship with a nonprofit.

When I was a younger man, and single, friends would tell me, "Love will find you when you aren't looking for it." Well, the love that found me was Honor Flight Tri-State.

Now, this romance with HFT didn't happen overnight. I was introduced to Tom and Cheryl Popp, heard about the flights, and assumed they had great community support. Who wouldn't support such a noble cause? The furthest thing from my mind was their need for cash.

Had I known they were conducting bake sales to raise money for each flight, I might have been scared off, thinking the task of helping would take more time and effort than I could afford. In military terms, I thought this would be a limited engagement.

*Nathan Bachrach
with Walter Steele*

*Ed Finke and Nathan Bachrach
on the Simply Money Media set*

We lent our Simply Money name to the cause, and raised funds to pay for a flight. That part was easy. Then on the morning of one of their flights my partner Ed Finke and I showed up at the 6 a.m. orientation to present an enlarged ceremonial check to HFT.

I have made countless public speeches over my media career. I've learned to control my emotions, my voice, and my expressions. None of that helped for what happened next.

As we presented the check, all the veterans, still mostly from World War II at that time, stood up and gave us a standing ovation. I started to tell them, "No, you don't applaud me, I applaud YOU. For all you've done, what I have contributed here is nothing." Only one problem. I was suddenly so choked up with emotion I couldn't get the first word out. I thought of my father, who passed away years before Honor Flight started. I was surrounded with memories of the holocaust survivors I grew up with. I recalled stories from my youth about the war, and its effect on so many of the members of the community I lived in. I was hooked.

Then I went on the flight, and watched men and women in their mid-80s drive to Columbus, then catch a plane to Baltimore and finally get on a bus and drive another hour to the World War II Memorial. They weren't exhausted, but I was.

Thus was born my first Honor Flight mission: to raise enough money so our heroes could fly from Cincinnati directly to Washington, D.C. on a charter flight. We've accomplished that, and many other goals on behalf of our veterans, and it's still a little embarrassing when people thank me for doing something so personally meaningful. I didn't go looking for Honor Flight, but it found me, and now it's part of who I am, and what I do.

Honor Flight donations impact each veteran

Scott Spicher
Honor Flight Donor

In November of 2014, we started the Honor Run Half Marathon in Florence, Kentucky. With the event on Veterans Day weekend, we wanted to benefit veterans. We found no better cause than Honor Flight Tri-State. To have the opportunity to give back to the brave men and women who fought and defended our freedom in World War II, Korea and Vietnam is truly an honor. Everyone involved with our Honor Run organization has a personal connection to a veteran of that era and knows the struggles and sacrifice they made.

 In May 2015 we had the privilege of serving as guardians on the Honor Flight trip that our event sponsored. That was the most rewarding experience of my life. To be able see the expressions of gratitude on the veterans' faces as we landed in Washington and visited memorials was priceless. To see people make it a point to go up to the veterans to shake their hand and say thank you was humbling. And then there was the welcome home party when we got back. My veteran served north of the 38th Parallel in Korea. He told me that when he got back to his hometown, he went back to the bowling alley where he used to hang out, and his friends wondered where he had been. They had no idea where Korea was. There was no fanfare or parade when he came home. But he received it at the Honor Flight welcome-home party, and that truly made his day and mine.

With a lot of charity events, you don't get to see exactly where your money goes or who it benefits. With Honor Flight Tri-State you get to see how your donation impacts each veteran. It is an honor and privilege to support Honor Flight Tri-State in its mission to keep our veterans flying.

'I'm a nurse, I've got this'

Bill Keating
Honor Flight Donor

Reflecting back on my Honor Flight experience as a guardian, my favorite memory was at Arlington National Cemetery after two veterans laid a wreath at the Tomb of the Unknown Soldier. As we were walking back to the buses, a World War II veteran, who must have been around 90, about five feet tall and maybe one hundred pounds, was pushing another veteran in a wheelchair.

I offered to push the wheelchair for her.

She smiled as she looked at me and said, "Hey, I'm a nurse, I've got this!"

It is moments like those that remind me that our World War II veterans are indeed the "Greatest Generation" – they believed and lived the motto, "Duty, Honor, Country," and they still do.

More than seventy years ago, our parents and grandparents risked their future to save ours. Now, generations later, we can honor our nation's veterans and stay connected to their legacy and life experiences through Honor Flight.

Great stories like these need to be shared. If April Kerley hadn't shared her guardian story with me I would not have been introduced to Honor Flight Tri-State. I thought the trip would be great, but it far exceeded my expectations. Honor Flight Tri-State, under the leadership of Cheryl and Tom Popp and its all-volunteer team, really knows how to thank our veterans by making it an experience of a lifetime for them.

To follow April's lead, I shared my personal experience with others. I sent out a challenge grant to my family, friends and

Bill Keating (right) with his vet

community with the goal to raise funds to sponsor three or four veterans on a future Honor Flight. The response was overwhelming. We raised enough to send almost twenty World War II and Korean War veterans on an Honor Flight.

May we all follow the lead of our Greatest Generation and live our lives with a sense of purpose, honor and service; and like them, protect the future of our children and grandchildren.

D-Day was one mission he never talked about

David Murray

It has been said that he may not have remembered everyone he met, but everyone he met remembered him. Dad was born in New Jersey and spent his early years in Stornoway, a small fishing village in the Outer Hebrides of Scotland, where he developed a love of ship and sea that never left him.

 Knowing neither his father nor his mother, he grew up cared for by relatives, and landed in Glasgow living with an aunt at the age of 10. For years he spent his time playing football (soccer) in the local parks of Partick near his White Street home and along Clydebank, watching the construction of some of the world's largest luxury liners and military ships. By 17, he was ready for the sea and enlisted in the British Merchant Marine.

Dave Murray, right, became known as the "Golden Vet" for after the introduction he facilitated between Simply Money and HFTS, when his son Martin worked for them.

He was greeted by Senator Bob Dole, (R.) Kansas, a veteran of World War ll who lead the drive for the World War ll memorial.

Soon after his enlistment, he got his chance to learn firsthand what perils the sea might hold – on November 5, 1941, just shy of his 18th birthday, his ship was attacked and sunk by a pair of German U-boats. He spent twelve hours in the North Atlantic waters, holding onto a capsized lifeboat with eleven other men. When they were finally picked up, he was given twenty minutes to live. In typical fashion, when asked about his ordeal by the Glasgow Times, his response was to focus on the skill of those who rescued him and thank them for their service. By the time he was 20, he was aboard two more ships that were sunk in the North Atlantic.

Dad spent about four years crisscrossing the North and South Atlantic, Mediterranean and Red Sea with the usual merchant cargo – fuel, grain, sugar, spare parts – as well as helping families in the early days of World War II smuggle themselves out of Italy to Morocco on their first step to safer lives in America.

His ports of call ranged from New York to Liverpool, Montevideo and Buenos Aries to Gibraltar, Aquba and Alexandria to Beirut, and Kingston to Baltimore – where he jumped ship to claim his U.S. citizenship.

Within weeks, he was back on the water in the U.S. Navy, mostly as a mechanic and gunner on various small boats. Dad spent D-Day off the coast of Omaha Beach on a recovery ship, ensuring that the bodies of less fortunate soldiers were not washed out to sea. Other than comments about being there, this is the one mission he never talked about. One of his last postings was on the President Warfield, a small unassuming ship that had little notoriety as a USN vessel but made up for that in 1947 when it was rechristened "Exodus," the ship made famous for its role in the creation of Israel.

After his military service, he settled in Chicago and took advantage of the G.I. Bill to earn a BA from Chicago Teachers College and an MA from DePaul University. He spent almost thirty-five years as a Chicago schoolteacher – often sharing some of his lighter stories of the Navy.

His relationship with Honor Flight was by chance. In 2005, he moved to Cincinnati to be closer to family. One day he noticed an ad in *The Cincinnati Enquirer* inviting World War II vets to participate in an oral history program sponsored by the Library of Congress. He hit it off with his interviewer, Ted Gardner, who invited him to join the Hornets group for its monthly breakfast.

That led to a sign-up sheet for an Honor Flight. We got a call on a Sunday night in August 2009 – someone wanted to know if dad wanted to take an Honor Flight – on Wednesday. It was an easy decision and the following Wednesday he was on his way.

It may have been the longest Honor Flight. The day was uneventful but the weather was not cooperative that evening. As the delay stretched into the night, they finally got back to Cincinnati around 2:00 a.m. But instead of being tired and worn out, dad and most vets on that flight were happy to have the extra time with each other. As I drove him home, his excitement was obvious.

He soon began to talk more about his time in the military, not just with stories of card games and shore leave, but sinking ships, battles, injuries and death. He often said, "The phrase 'war is hell' is an understatement." He also began writing about his time on the open seas and sharing it with his grandchildren.

I believe the Honor Flight gave dad some peace. He became comfortable sharing his experiences and began to exude pride in his military career. Before Honor Flight, they were just stories. After Honor Flight, he owned those stories as a legacy.

With his recent passing we've been sorting through things and two items show how important the Honor Flight was to him.

The first, hanging on the back of a chair he saw every day, was his Honor Flight nametag and faded boarding passes for August 18, 2009.

The second, in a shoebox that sat at his right hand virtually all day, every day, along with pictures of grandchildren, weddings, and close friends, was a photo of dad with Sen. Bob Dole. Every time he talked about his time in the service, he would eventually pull that picture out and tell someone, "I got to thank him for all he did to make that memorial real."

He was proud of what we've been able to give back to Honor Flight. When he passed away, it was an easy decision to request donations to Honor Flight Tri-State in lieu of flowers. Knowing that the guys in Honor Flight T-shirts handled his military honors and the flag-folding at his funeral would have made him even more proud.

Americans take too much for granted

Ken Scherzinger, Scherzinger Drilling
Honor Flight Donor

It seems to me that Americans take too much for granted. The rights we enjoy, earned in the Revolutionary War and every subsequent war, are still being defended today. Brave men and women served, sacrificed and died for our freedoms – without asking for glory or recognition, simply out of their sense of duty and patriotism.

Honor Flights are a great way to honor our veterans and educate the younger generation. We need to continually remind all Americans that freedom is not free – a heavy price has been paid.

I have sponsored several guardians from my company. They have told me when they returned that it was a once-in-a-lifetime experience. They were honored to give such a service to our veterans. Some had family members who were veterans, and it made them feel a part of their experiences. Others said they felt it was their patriotic duty since they did not serve.

When asked about the most memorable part of their trip, they say:

"I was most impressed by the respect shown to the veterans, even by the young children."

"I felt the pride that the veterans feel for our country, even after all these years."

"I was so amazed by the people who came to the airport in the morning and evening to welcome the vets and make them feel appreciated and honored."

Our employees who have gone on Honor Flights were proud to accompany them, and our company is proud to support Honor Flight Tri-State.

Giving veterans the honor they deserve

Shelly O'Neill, Emery Federal Credit Union
Honor Flight Donor

As I look back and reflect on Honor Flight, it's easy to remember why we chose to support them: They give veterans a chance to be part of the history they created.

Emery Federal Credit Union has had many employees with connections to the military, and that made it easy to decide we wanted to give something back. In today's world, many people don't realize what veterans go through and how important they are to our country. Supporting Honor Flight Tri-State is just one way Emery and our employees can show how much we appreciate our veterans. We hope to support this mission long into the future so that those serving today will be able to see and feel the honor they deserve.

Honor Flight is amazing. They make the veterans feel like they are the most important people on earth. Many of us at Emery have gone along as guardians, and every employee who has participated has praised the experience.

Veterans put their lives on the line in order to allow us to have the freedoms and privileges we have. By supporting Honor Fight, Emery has a direct role in giving veterans the gratitude they deserve. It is an honor to support this organization. Everyone should.

Old memories remembered, new ones made

Doug Oberklaus, Cors and Bassett LLC
Honor Flight Donor

On Tuesday, September 17, 2014, my bride, Jan, and I had the privilege to participate as Honor Flight guardians on a trip to Washington, D.C. One of our missions for our visit was to pay our respects at the Tomb of the Unknown Soldier in Arlington National Cemetery – a true icon of military sacrifice. The Sentinels who serve at the tomb are as dedicated as you will find anywhere. Their rules of conduct and duty to mission are a standard very few can match. The Tomb is guarded 24 hours a day, seven days a week, regardless of weather. There has been a guard at this post every day, without fail, since 1937.

The Changing of the Guard happens every thirty minutes. Once you see what a guard does during his shift, it's easy to understand the need for frequent changes. Their movements are precise, their uniforms are impeccable – not a wrinkle, not a piece of lint. Their gloves are white, their weapons are spotless, with shiny bayonets affixed. Each step, each move, each click of their heels is done in a very specific way. Even as they march back and forth, the placement of each foot is designed so that their head does not bob and their shoulders are constantly at the same level. They simply glide. It was a memorable sight.

Our group was given a distinct honor. Two individuals were chosen to place a wreath. This is the exact ceremony that we've seen the President do many times. It was very moving to watch our vets place the wreath at the Tomb of a fallen brother.

At the World War II Memorial there was a lot of activity – telling stories, remembering people and places and times long passed. Oddly, the veterans seemed to gather energy as they moved about the Memorial. They were very excited to be there. My veteran, Richard, was from Northern Kentucky and was anxious to have his picture taken at the Kentucky monument. The heroes who won World War II are dying at a rate of about one thousand each day. Time is running out for them to see their memorial.

Jan's veteran, Ed, was from the Korean War. One of the first things he noticed on the sculptures at the Korean War Memorial was the type of weapon one figure had. It was a carbine rifle. He remembered that he had trained with an M-1 rifle, but when he got to Korea they gave him a carbine and he didn't know how to use it. We got a chuckle out of that story.

There were stories all around, pictures being taken, friendships being formed, old memories being remembered and new ones being made. It was a pleasure to just observe and take it in.

One of our guardians who had recently lost her father, a Korean War veteran, was given the honor of placing a wreath at that Memorial. A short prayer, a thank you and a salute concluded the ceremony.

As we approached the Vietnam Wall Memorial, I found myself stuck in place. For an unknown reason, while Jan and our two vets proceeded down the path, I couldn't go. I didn't really know any of the people whose names were on the Wall, but I felt emotion welling up inside. Maybe it was because so much of my misspent youth was surrounded by the war. It was the lead story on the news every night for fifteen years. Guys I knew and grew up with had joined or had been drafted. My step-brother served two tours, and my brother joined the Army during the war. I don't know why, but it was surprisingly difficult.

When we got back to Cincinnati, we met the families of our vets. Tears were flowing, hugs were being hugged. It had to be as good as one could feel. Wow!

Jan said to her veteran Ed, "This is the welcome you should have had sixty years ago."

Ed summed it up: "It's just as sweet." Amen!

HONOR FLIGHT TRI-STATE

Welcome Home Veterans!

D-DAY   JUNE 6, 1944
YOU ARE ABOUT TO EMBARK UPON THE
GREAT CRUSADE TOWARD WHICH WE HAVE STRIVEN THESE
MANY MONTHS. THE EYES OF THE WORLD ARE UPON YOU...
I HAVE FULL CONFIDENCE IN YOUR COURAGE,
DEVOTION TO DUTY AND SKILL IN BATTLE.

GENERAL DWIGHT D. EISENHOWER

> "Goddam it, you'll never get the Purple Heart
> hiding in a foxhole! Follow me!"
>
> *— Captain Henry P. Jim Crowe, Guadalcanal, Jan. 13, 1943*

CHAPTER SIX
Legacy of History

Standing under a blossoming cherry tree surrounded by the stark white crosses at Arlington National Cemetery, a veteran paused to take in the rolling hills where America's war dead rest.

 "Nobody wants to pass the torch anymore," he said.

He was talking about history. About how a nation that forgets its heroes and their sacrifices is not worthy of the freedom they earned with blood, sweat, tears and their lives.

In 1940, the world population was about 2.3 billion. By the end of World War II in August 1945, more than 60 million people had been killed, including civilians and soldiers all over the world, from the most remote jungles of Asia to the most sophisticated cities in Europe.

The United States lost more than 440,000 American lives. Many of them volunteered to defend their country while the battleships still smoked and burned in Pearl Harbor. They fought to defend their own lives, they fought to defend each other, and they fought for an ideal: freedom from fascist, totalitarian tyranny.

One of the purposes of this book is to preserve their story and pass it along to future generations so that all Americans will know that when the world was in its darkest hour, being overrun by evil empires of hate, oppression and genocide, Americans ran to the rescue and gave their lives so that we can enjoy the peace and security we have today.

A U.S. Marine chaplain put it best: "It is the soldier, not the reporter, who has given us freedom of the press. It is the soldier, not the poet, who has given us freedom of speech. It is the soldier, not the organizer, who gave us the freedom to demonstrate. It is the soldier who salutes the flag, who serves beneath the flag and whose coffin is draped by the flag, who allows the protester to burn the flag."

It's not only our duty to remember our veterans. It is the key to our survival as a nation, which will remain the land of the free only as long as it is also the home of the brave. At the dawn of America, George Washington knew this well.

He said, "The willingness with which our young people are likely to serve in any war, no matter how justified, shall be directly proportional to how they perceive how the veterans of earlier wars were treated and appreciated by their nation."

All Americans need to make sure the torch is passed to future generations. Our nation has a rich treasure of honor and patriotism, but far too many don't know about it or take it for granted. Here, then, are stories, explanations and famous quotations about the meaning of America and the people who gave us our inheritance of freedom.

How it All Began

"What took so long?"

That's the first question most people ask when they learn about Honor Flight.

What took so long to finally build a memorial to the generation that won the biggest battle in world history? What took so long to get these soldiers, sailors, airmen and Marines to Washington so they can experience the monument that was built to honor them?

The story of the World War II Memorial sounds more like a monument to our federal government's inability to do anything without agonizing inaction and debilitating delay. It was first proposed in 1987, but was never brought to a vote despite repeated attempts. Finally, it was authorized in a law passed by Congress and signed by President Bill Clinton in 1993.

It took two years just to choose a site, which was one of the most valuable pieces of property in the nation's capital, with breathtaking views of the Washington Monument and the Capitol to the east, and the Lincoln Memorial and its Reflecting Pool to the west. Selection was delayed by objections that the Memorial would occupy open space that was used for protests and demonstrations. The irony was rich: If not for those WWII veterans, protests and demonstrations might be "verboten."

A design was finally chosen in 1998. Final approval was granted two years later. And construction began in 2001. It was dedicated and opened on Memorial Day, May 29, 2004.

It took more than twice as long to build a memorial for World War II than it took to win the war. While the veterans who saved the world from genocide and tyranny dwindled away, Washington dawdled and delayed, moving at the speed of a melting glacier. How many veterans died before they could see it?

Along the way, there were attempts by the ACLU and others to block a privately funded plaque to display a prayer by President Roosevelt on June 6, 1944, the morning of D-Day. That must have made many veterans wonder: Where was the ACLU at Normandy and Iwo Jima when brothers, husbands and sons were dying by the thousands? There were no objections to prayers then.

Here is part of FDR's prayer:

> *Almighty God: Our sons, pride of our Nation, this day have set upon a mighty endeavor, a struggle to preserve our Republic, our religion, and our civilization, and to set free a suffering humanity.*
>
> *Lead them straight and true; give strength to their arms, stoutness to their hearts, steadfastness in their faith.*
>
> *They will be sore tried, by night and by day, without rest-until the victory is won. The darkness will be rent by noise and flame. Men's souls will be shaken with the violences of war.*
>
> *For these men are lately drawn from the ways of peace. They fight not for the lust of conquest. They fight to end conquest. They fight to liberate. They fight to let justice arise, and tolerance and good will among all Thy people. They yearn but for the end of battle, for their return to the haven of home.*
>
> *Some will never return. Embrace these, Father, and receive them, Thy heroic servants, into Thy kingdom.*
>
> *And for us at home – fathers, mothers, children, wives, sisters, and brothers of brave men overseas – whose thoughts and prayers are ever with them – help us, Almighty God, to rededicate ourselves in renewed faith in Thee in this hour of great sacrifice.*
>
> *Thy will be done, Almighty God.*
>
> *Amen.*

Incredibly, the WWII Memorial was also delayed in part because of debates over funding. In the end, most of the $197 million cost came from private donations. The same nation that demanded and received the sacrifices of 16 million who served and 440,000 who gave their lives, was embarrassingly slow to sacrifice on their behalf.

Finally, Sen. Bob Dole, R-Kansas and co-chair Frederick W. Smith of FedEx led the charge to overcome opposition and get the Memorial built. He reminded others in the House and Senate that every year of delay meant more veterans who would never see their memorial. Years after it was built, when Dole was retired from public life, suffering from severe arthritis and nearly fatal wounds from machinegun fire in Italy, he still showed up at the World War II Memorial to greet veterans as often as he could.

But the question remains: What took so long?

Maybe the answer is that it took so long because the American people had to do what their leaders were unwilling or unable to do. Despite the support from Dole and others in Congress, the Memorial was almost entirely funded by hundreds of thousands of ordinary citizens, military organizations, veterans groups, fraternal and professional groups, corporations, foundations and school children across the nation.

As like the war itself, it was a gigantic victory by patriotic Americans who pulled together to win the battle – some on the front lines and many more giving support in whatever way they could.

The Honor Flights that swept the country are part of the same story. They did not start with a Pearl Harbor bang. They started slowly, modestly, with one man's dedication – then took off like a rocket launch.

Retired Air Force Captain Earl Morse, who was a physician's assistant at the local VA Hospital in Springfield, Ohio, noticed that his patients who had served in World War II loved talking about the new Memorial. He also quickly realized that although it was built in their honor, it was out of reach for most of them, because of advancing age, poor health or scarce finances.

When he asked if they would go see it, many had the same reply: With tears in their eyes, they told him they could not. Here was a generation that won the war, then built our nation, raised families, went to work every day, seldom boasted or asked for sympathy and almost never asked for thanks. They had no parades when they came home. Many never talked about the war with their own families. And now their tribute, finally built more than sixty years after the last shot was fired, was out of reach for most of them.

Morse was overcome with emotion and felt an irresistible obligation to do something about it. He decided to take several veterans in a small plane rented from the Wright-Patterson Air Force Base Flying Club. That group told other veterans about their exciting experience and word spread. Soon Morse's answering machine was swamped with messages from veterans asking how they could go to Washington with him.

So Morse did what any military man would do – he called in reinforcements. He took the idea to the Wright-Patterson Air Force Base Flying Club where he was a member, and eleven more pilots immediately signed up to help.

Honor Flight was off the ground.

As the effort grew, some veterans were unable to get into the small airplanes and weather sometimes caused trips to be cancelled or delayed. But the requests from veterans were still pouring in.

With a long waiting list just for the Springfield and Dayton area, Morse decided to book commercial flights as quickly as he could raise money. The first commercial Honor Flight took off from Dayton in 2005 and landed in Baltimore, then took a bus to Washington.

Soon the D.C. invasion by battalions of World War II veterans was making headlines, and groups across the nation began to get aboard. The Honor Flight Network was born with the addition of several flights from North Carolina that first year. It now includes more than 133 hubs in forty-two states; as of 2015, more than 140,000 veterans from all across America have taken Honor Flights for the trip of a lifetime.

All veterans fly free – and all contributions remain in the local area. The Honor Flight hubs have no paid staff. All hubs are managed by volunteers. Each veteran is accompanied by a guardian – a family member or someone assigned from a waiting list of volunteers. Guardians pay their own way for the privilege of being part of the experience.

Cheryl Popp, director of Honor Flight Tri-State in Cincinnati, started out as a guardian and got hooked. She speaks for many when she explains what it's all about. "Now is my chance to do something for my country. If I can make sure these men and women have a perfect day, that's what I can do."

The Cincinnati hub was the fourth in the nation. "When an Honor Flight Network of Springfield, Ohio sent someone to speak at our local pilot's club in Cincinnati, several of the club members volunteered to help and flew several flights as guardians that first year," Popp recalls. "With the commute to Dayton, and the long journey caused by landing in Baltimore, and busing the veterans to Washington, it was clear that we could serve our local veterans a lot better from a closer location."

Honor Flight Tri-State was launched and joined the national network in 2006.

"At first, the Cincinnati team took buses to Dayton, Louisville or Columbus to save on airfares, and low-cost, non-stop tickets were only available to Baltimore-Washington International. That required another hour-long bus ride. All that travel time meant less time at the memorials," Popp says.

"On one of the trips a guardian asked me, 'Why are you hauling these veterans all over the country for an Honor Flight?' When I explained that we couldn't afford a charter flight, he said, "Then let's raise the money. And I'm just the one to do it for you." In stepped Nathan Bachrach and Ed Finke and Simply Money.

He was right. With donations and grants from individuals and corporations, Honor Flight Tri-State was able to start charter flights, and now takes 380 vets per year on five separate flights from the Cincinnati Northern Kentucky International Airport.

As the years passed, even many of the World War II veterans who were still alive were unable to take a flight, so seats were opened to Korean War veterans in 2014. Many had been waiting two years or more for a chance to see their dramatic Korean War Memorial in D.C., which opened in 1995.

"We honor the most senior veterans first and they go to the top of the list immediately upon application," Popp explains. "Korean veterans and all of those in between will be selected in order of their birthdate. As of 2015, we now take applications from all veterans over age 65, whether they served overseas or stateside."

What began as an idea by one retired Air Force captain in one little Ohio town grew into the Honor Flight network nationwide. Although the World War II Memorial took nearly a dozen years, Honor Flights was going national just a year after the Memorial opened.

A big reason for that is the way Honor Flight works. "Capt. Morse's genius was not only to start the Honor Flight Network, but to allow each hub to operate independently," says Popp.

There's no bureaucracy – just individual hubs run by dedicated, unpaid volunteers and board members who bring unique perspectives, enthusiasm and vitality to each hub.

"Our goal is to get as many veterans as we can as fast as we can to see their Memorial. Honor Flights are a way to thank them for a job well done in gratitude for their incredible lives," says Popp. "This is a small gift from a grateful nation."

We Booked the First Flight on a Personal Credit Card

Greg Houser
Honor Flight Tri-State Founder

I am not a veteran. I never served in the military. The genesis for Honor Flight Tri-State stemmed from my love of World War II aviation and the veterans who served.

I always had a deep interest in the war, especially aviation. I had an uncle who was a bombardier on B-29s with thirteen missions over Japan. He sparked my interest and instilled in me my respect for veterans. As a general aviation pilot I got involved with the Cincinnati Warbirds, a squadron of the Warbirds of America. This

Greg Houser with Herb Heilbrun

group brought to Lunken Airport many historic aircraft, such as the B-17 Flying Fortress, B-25 Mitchell, B-24 Liberator, and a mighty B-29 Superfortress named "Fifi." It was a dream come true!

But I soon realized something was missing. Where were the veterans who flew the planes? Where were the bombardiers and "Rosie the Riveters" who assembled these aircraft? These veterans and their stories are more important than the planes.

We were going to get it done.

Earl Morse started Honor Flight in 2005 in the Dayton, Ohio area. He and his friends flew World War II veterans to D.C. in small, general aviation aircraft. In 2006, Earl started flying veterans out of Dayton International, and that's when I started talking to members of the Cincinnati Warbirds about starting an Honor Flight program.

I called Earl in the late fall of 2006. While Earl was sympathetic to my wanting to start a hub (chapter) in Cincinnati, he told me to sit tight – there was one in the works and he would be in touch with me once it was established. Then Earl contacted me to say that the primary contact for the Cincinnati hub had dropped out and it was mine to develop. While I was super excited, I had a full-time job and was raising a family. Could I take on such an immense project?

It didn't take too much soul searching. I was going to get it done! I contacted a great friend of mine, Jonathan Hardwick, a Cincinnati Warbird member. He was sold.

Our small group talked to any veteran's group that would listen. Not necessarily to raise money, but to get veterans on our flight list. Our first flight was October 17, 2007. Jonathan bought forty-seven plane tickets on his personal credit card, so we shopped for the least expensive airfare. We met at Lakeside Christian Church in Erlanger, Kentucky and boarded thirty veterans and seventeen guardians, medics and media on a charter bus for Louisville International Airport. We boarded Southwest Flight 636 to Baltimore. What a day it was! We stopped at the World War II Memorial, the Marine Corps Memorial and the Korean War Memorial. We arrived back at Lakeside Christian Church at 12:45 a.m. That's when I realized how important this was to our veterans.

It was a long day. Along with most of the guardians, I was pretty well worn out. The veterans were a different story. As the day wore on, they stood a little taller, their chest stuck out a little further, they walked a little straighter. It was almost like they were transported back in time. The Honor Flight group was hooked. We knew we had to make it succeed.

Looking back, early Honor Flight Tri-State highlights include helping Bluegrass Honor Flight in Louisville, Kentucky get started; partnering with the Experimental Aircraft Association for an Honor Flight from their annual Airventure Convention in Oshkosh, Wisconsin; and taking an Honor Flight with my wife, Lisa, and daughter, Katie, who served as guardians.

I stepped down from the board of directors in 2012. I am still involved, on the curb at the airport to welcome the veterans. I've been on more flights than I can remember. But, each one is different and it never gets old. I love seeing total strangers come up to our veterans and thank them. Rarely is there a dry eye. Lisa and I also return in the evenings for the Welcome Home Rally.

From our first humble flight from Louisville in 2007 until today, Honor Flight Tri-State has come a long way. From the few who got it started, I say to all of the wonderful folks who volunteer: Thank you!

World War II Memorial

True Stories from Honor Flight Veterans

Cheryl Popp
Honor Flight Director

Just Doing Our Job

My husband's Uncle Freddy was a good example of a typical World War II veteran. He didn't want to talk about the war. "That is in the past," he would say. "No need." In Uncle Freddy's last few years, Tom would stop by and talk to him about that time in his life. Tom asked a lot of questions and he finally opened up. Tom was honored that this man, whom he had the greatest respect for, would share things that had never been mentioned to others.

Maybe no one ever asked, or cared. But we learned so much. We learned about society, about the different generations and their priorities. He knew and we realized that as a nation we have lost respect for the past and those who lived it.

It hit us one day at Uncle Freddy's house. He was explaining how they went through France and Germany, describing the carnage they saw as they took back town after town. As we sat in the family room, we were surrounded by many paintings and prints from Henry Farny, Uncle Freddy's favorite artist, a Cincinnatian who specialized in scenes of the American West.

It was then that we realized what we, as a society have forgotten. We have forgotten how to listen. Several Farny paintings showed Indians sitting around their campfires telling stories. The elders were venerated, highly respected members of the tribe. The elders would tell stories about their hunts of long ago and other adventures. That was how knowledge was passed down from generation to generation. They didn't have schools, and of course no internet. Everything was passed along verbally, one generation to another.

Today, we have relegated the important duty of teaching and instructing our precious children to teachers who take their lesson plans from far removed boards of education that determine what they should learn and how they should think. Here we were, in the presence of a great man with an amazing life story, talking about his war experiences – and all the while he was teaching about life, and what is truly important about life.

Fred G. Popp went ashore as a medic at Normandy on D-Day. He wanted to be an Army Ranger, but an earlier injury discovered on the Ranger medical exam made him ineligible. So he became a medic. We always knew that what happened to him on D-Day was overwhelming. There was a good reason he didn't like to talk about it.

To me, he symbolized his generation, not only for what they went through but for what they accomplished after the war. They grew up in the Depression, went off to fight a terrible war, then came back home to marry their sweethearts. These men started families and led their lives with high moral values, built businesses like uncle Freddy did, and went on to build a great nation.

Tom begged Uncle Freddy to go on an Honor Flight many times. But every time he said he didn't deserve it, that others were more deserving than he was. Many veterans we talk to say the same sort of thing. "We were just doing our job." No amount of convincing worked. We lost Uncle Freddy in 2014. We buried him with full military honors and an Honor Flight Challenge Coin in his pocket.

Pilot's Certificate

The daughter of one veteran told us on the flight home that after her dad had started talking to other veterans, he opened his wallet and carefully took out several papers. He showed her his most treasured documents that he had carried ever since the war. To her great surprise, he carefully unfolded his pilot's certificate and pages from his log book that showed the missions he had flown during the war. That was the first time she learned that her father had been a B-17 bomber pilot. She had never thought to ask. With tears running down her cheeks she said, "I've known this man my entire life, and I never really knew him."

Cheviot Guys

Two veterans were sitting together on the tour bus, talking about their Honor Flight. It was the usual conversation between older vets: When did you go in, what branch did you serve in, where were you at such and such dates, etc. At each stop they returned to the same seats together, as if drawn to each other.

As they talked they made some remarkable discoveries. They both had served in World War II. Both came back home to Cheviot – which is a one-square-mile suburb of Cincinnati. They had lived only three blocks from each other their entire lives but had never met before their Honor Flight. As the rest of the bus laughed at the amazing coincidence, there was more to come.

One of the two veterans had received a "Dear John" letter from his sweetheart while he was overseas. He came home and married another lady after the war. Then as they compared notes, they found out that the woman who jilted him married his Cheviot seatmate. They couldn't believe that they had shared so much in common – same neighborhood, same service, even the same girlfriend – and fate finally put them together on the Honor Flight bus 70 years later.

Honor Flight Ambassador's Dad

Dee Daniels has been an Honor Flight ambassador for years. Her dad served in World War II and Korea. Her parents met while her mom served in World War II as an Army nurse. Her father was killed in Korea.

Dee grew up knowing her father only by a picture on the mantel. As a World War II veteran, Dee's mom went on an Honor Flight a few years back and Dee served as her guardian. While visiting the Korean Veterans Memorial, they were admiring the black marble wall where pictures of men who served in Korea were laser etched into the stone. And there before them was her father's picture, just like the one on the mantel.

It took Dee's breath away. Her mother broke down and cried. They wondered: Of all of the images on that Memorial, what brought them to that precise spot? How did they come to stand right in front of that picture among 2,400 images etched into the 164-foot slab of black granite?

It was a moment they never forgot. After all those years, they were reunited with their father and husband again, across time, across thousands of miles, across the boundaries of life and death.

Korean Veteran Sees a Familiar Face

He was relaxing in his wheelchair, being pushed along by his guardian when a Korean veteran was shocked to see a very familiar face – his own. He gasped and put his head in his hands. All of the memories rushing back in a flood. Yes, that was him, reproduced from a photo taken during his tour of duty in Korea, etched into the Memorial. And the most remarkable thing to others on the flight was how little he had changed.

In the picture he was wearing a hat, with the bill bent down on the sides, just so. As he sat there in disbelief, the hat he was wearing for his Honor Flight was bent in the same way, exactly like the one he wore in Korea. As others on the flight crowded in to take pictures, he smiled next to the younger version of himself – who also smiled, and looked back from the black granite wall.

Korean Embassy

The Korean Embassy in Washington, D.C. always makes sure there is a wreath of fresh flowers at the Korean Veterans Memorial. On one trip, the Honor Flight group was at the Korean Memorial when a large group of Korean men arrived with much drama and flourish. They carried a new wreath of fresh flowers and set up to make their presentation. The veterans stepped back as they Korean delegation read a proclamation in Korean. No one quite knew what to think.

I asked one of the men with the group, "Who are these people?" He bowed and told me they were from the Korean Embassy, and the Republic of Korea Defense Attaché to the United States was among their group. After their ceremony seemed to end, I told the man who appeared to be the highest ranking military officer that we had a group of Korean veterans present, and I would appreciate it if he said a few words to them.

He bowed deeply and said it would be his extreme honor. He announced to the other dignitaries that he was honored to be in the presence of such great men. He came over to a Korean veteran in a wheelchair, knelt down and thanked him for "saving my country." The Attaché then reached into his pocket and presented the veteran with his personal challenge coin. The veteran was overwhelmed.

The Korean War may have been the "Forgotten War" to many Americans who were not touched by it – but it will never be forgotten in Korea.

His Son's Name on the Vietnam Wall

"The Wall," as everyone calls it, is always a surprisingly powerful and emotional stop for veterans on Honor Flights, no matter what war they served in. On one trip, a World War II veteran told us his son was killed in Vietnam in 1966 when his helicopter was shot down. His name had to be on the Wall, but he had never been to Washington to see it.

Honor Flight Board Member Ed Finke and volunteer Ed Thomas escorted the veteran over to the Vietnam Wall and helped him get a rubbing of his son's name where it was etched into the Wall. It was a solemn and moving moment.

Finally, the father who fought in World War II was able to visit a memorial dedicated to the sacrifice of his son in Vietnam. It was a vivid reminder that when it comes to sacrifice for freedom, some families have gone above and beyond the call of duty.

'That Damned Rock'

Our first stop of the day for Honor Flights is the Iwo Jima Memorial. As we were gathering up the veterans to get back on the buses, one straggler stood very still, looking up at the famous statue of Marines raising a flag on Mount Suribachi. I quietly went up and stood next to him to ask if he was okay. He said yes, but he needed a few more minutes. That was easily granted.

When he was ready, he came over and said, "I had to say goodbye. I left my brother on that damned rock." He said nothing more but bowed his head and went over to board his bus.

Later, he talked about how he had been reluctant to go on an Honor Flight because he was not sure he wanted to face the loss of his brother again. But he said he finally felt at peace after all the years of mourning. Choking up with emotion, he said he was so glad he had finally come. He had said a final goodbye to the brother he loved and missed.

Sometimes you just have to be there to appreciate what we have in America.

The Intelligence Officer

A spry lady who served her entire World War II career "desk side" in Washington told us how much things had changed in the Capital in seventy years. She had been an intelligence officer during the war, but during the Honor Flight tour, she was a tour guide from the past.

She told fascinating stories about the Washington area, and was full of energy. I asked her about her work in the Intelligence Department. With a gleam in her eyes that said she knew plenty, she said, "Oh honey, I never looked at any of that stuff." The secrets of World War II were still safe with her. Loose lips may sink no ships today, but she was not taking any chances.

School Trip

As our buses pulled up to the Iwo Jima Memorial, we arrived at the same time with a group from an all-girls school on a field trip. It was a good match for both groups.

The girls found out that our World War II woman veteran had served as a nurse during the war and later had a career as a school teacher at an all-girls school. They crowded around her and asked if it was okay for their bus to follow us for the next two stops so that they could hear more of her stories. They all wanted to get their picture taken with her. She was totally thrilled to be such a star on her Honor Flight. And those girls may have found a new hero in a woman who served her country as valiantly as all the men.

The Golden Vet

They say "plans are the first casualty of war." The same is true on Honor Flight trips. No matter how we plan everything to the minute, we are still at the mercy of weather and flight delays. We learned that in 2009 on what became known at the time as "the flight from hell." Little did we know that it would also turn into one of our biggest wins for Honor Flight Tri-State.

Everything went well all day. But then as we headed home to Cincinnati, our plans were blown away by a big storm in Florida. We used the Baltimore and Dayton airports back then, to get the lowest airfares on AirTran. As we got to the Baltimore airport for our departure, we found out our evening flight was still stuck in Florida by bad weather.

As we anxiously watched the weather, it got worse. Our flight that was supposed to take off at 8:00 p.m. was delayed until after 11:00 p.m., and soon we were all stranded in a vacant terminal, watching all the shops and restaurants close.

Fortunately, McDonalds helped us out and brewed coffee and served shakes for everyone before they closed too.

While we worried, the veterans seemed to take it in stride. They enjoyed their extra time to talk and swap stories, while our Honor Flight board members started calling anxious relatives to let them know their loved ones were fine, sitting at the departure gate, waiting for news.

The airline tried to get us a plane from another location, but that flight was scrubbed because of maintenance issues. Then we realized that a lot of the contact numbers we had were daytime office phone numbers that were going to voice mail. Some of the veterans gave us family home numbers, but many did not have them.

We had started our day's journey in the early hours of the morning, as we gathered in the parking lot of a movie theatre north of town. That's where all of the relatives would gather – waiting to pick up veterans who would not show up as expected.

We frantically called board member Jonathan Hardwick, and he agreed to go to the meeting place to reassure the relatives and keep them in touch with us.

As Hardwick arrived, he found several family members anxiously looking for their long overdue vets. Some of them had decided to wait in an all-night Waffle House. And that was the unlikely beginning of a very long and wonderful relationship with a generous sponsor for Honor Flight Tri-State.

Martin Murray, who worked for Simply Money at the time, was waiting for his father, veteran David Murray. Hardwick joined Martin Murray at the Waffle House and they spent hours talking about Honor Flight and its mission. At the time, fundraising was just beginning and the future looked uncertain.

We finally managed to catch a flight to Dayton, and took a bus back to the theater parking lot as tired guardians and veterans either slept or waited anxiously to get home. Most finally made it home about 2:00 a.m. But I took a stranded veteran home, so I didn't get to bed until 4:00 a.m. It felt like I had barely fallen asleep when the phone rang at 8:00 a.m. with a very excited Martin Murray on the line.

"Can you be at my office at 11:00?" he asked. "We would like to talk to you about Honor Flight."

I didn't know what to expect. But after the long delays the day before, I had good reason to expect the worst. Who could blame the families of the veterans for complaining about waiting all night?

I gathered our brochures and details and went to the meeting. As Martin Murray asked me questions, he called in more and more people. Pretty soon the room was full. Everyone wanted to hear about our mission. They had been looking for just such a charity where they could make a difference.

By the time the meeting was over ninety minutes later, they had decided that Honor Flight was the group they were looking for. We had a mission they could believe in. They were excited about getting more veterans on Honor Flights, to share the success that was written on the face of every Honor Flight veteran. Martin's father, David Murray, could not stop talking to his family about his Honor Flight experience, and that had led Martin to make the early morning call.

As the relationship with Simply Money, Emery Community Foundation and Honor Flight grew, World War II veteran David Murray became known affectionately as "The Golden Vet," who helped us ramp up our efforts in an astounding way. He was proud to help so many veterans enjoy the day that he had experienced.

'If Only I Had Asked…'

One veteran I will never forget was a medic who went ashore on D-Day and traveled throughout Europe, ending up in Germany on V-E Day (Victory in Europe Day). I was interested in his stories because they sounded a lot like Uncle Freddy's experiences in France and Germany.

Several months later I met his daughter, who had been his guardian on the flight. She told me her dad had talked about his Honor Flight ever since and told her many stories that she had never heard before. She learned more about him and his character from those stories than she had ever known. She wondered out loud why he didn't tell her those stories before.

"Did you ever ask him?" I said.

The color drained from her face as she admitted she had never thought to ask.

The moral of the story is what we learned from Uncle Freddy: Just ask. The answers might be a gold mine of true stories of victory, adventure, miraculous survival, heartbreaking loss and vivid American history.

Just ask.

Detail from the Korean War Memorial

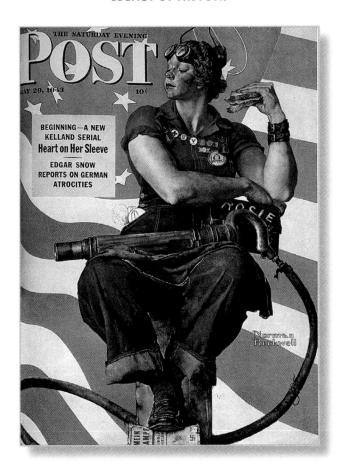

Women in the War

There were many heroes of World War II. Some stayed stateside. Some were not veterans, as they did not serve in the military. Many of these heroes were women.

"Rosie the Riveter" became the symbol of millions of women who joined the workforce for the first time during World War II. Her well-known poster was adapted from a Norman Rockwell illustration that appeared in the May 29, 1943 Memorial Day edition of the Saturday Evening Post. Her rivet gun was on her lap as she took her lunch break, eating a sandwich as her foot smashed a copy of Hitler's "Mein Kampf." As usual, Rockwell's symbolism was perfect.

The poster artist, J. Howard Miller, thought he had found the perfect Rosie when he spotted a 17-year-old metal press operator at American Broach and Machine, named Geraldine Huff. His poster for the Ad Council showed her in a polka dot bandanna, flexing her muscle over the caption "We can do it!"

Many women did not use a rivet gun or a welding torch. They cooked meals in defense plant cafeterias, raised money for war bonds and worked in offices for defense contractors as stenographers, bookkeepers, telephone operators and hundreds of other jobs. Women rolled up their sleeves like Rosie and made gas masks for the Army, life rafts for the Navy, ammo belts for the Marines and parachutes for the Army Air Corps. They learned how to read blueprints and some were among the math geniuses who worked on the Manhattan Project that created the atomic bomb.

Rosie the Riveter was never meant to be the symbol of the modern women's movement. She only wanted to promote changes in society to allow women to work outside the home to support the war effort. As the draft and enlistments caused labor shortages, industrial jobs that had been for men only were opened up to women. And once millions of Rosie's proved they could handle the rivet gun and lots more, those jobs stayed open to women after the war.

While the men went off to war, women farmed the fields, built the weapons of war, manufactured planes and tanks, worked in intelligence, made guns and ammunition, built ships and did whatever was needed. Many single women moved far away from home to work for the war effort. Others shipped out to the war zones to work as nurses and hospital aides.

They all made do during food shortages, often growing their own vegetables in "victory gardens." They fashioned clothes for their kids out of old cast-offs and volunteered for Civil Defense.

These brave women took on jobs they had never done before and broke the old stereotypes. They put on their overalls, tied their hair up in scarfs and laced up their steel-toed boots, proving there were very few jobs that could not be done by women.

Other posters encouraged them:

"Your country needs you."

"Your husband would be proud of your efforts to do your part."

"This is your way to serve – just like when your son or husband enlisted."

"There is work to be done and a war to be won."

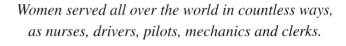

Women served all over the world in countless ways, as nurses, drivers, pilots, mechanics and clerks.

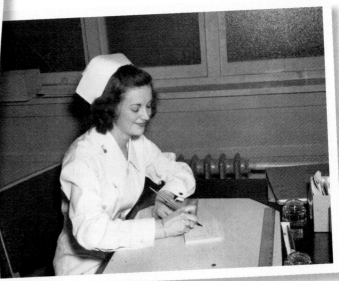

*The work of women in the war effort
freed up men for the front lines.*

Rosie the Riveter was way ahead of her time. Her "We can do it!" attitude empowered all women. When women realized they could work and maintain a proper home and contribute to the family finances, they just kept going – as they blazed a trail for generations of women to follow.

With the D-Day invasion looming, President Roosevelt called for accelerated industrial production. He asked women to help join in this effort. He implemented the Women in Necessary Service and the Women in War campaigns in preparation for an all-out push to crush the enemy.

- By 1944, 36 percent of all workers in prime defense contractors were female.

- Even in iron and steel factories, 23.3 percent of the workforce was female.

- In 1943 alone, 310,000 women were employed in the aircraft industry, making up 65 percent of the labor, compared to just 1 percent before the war.

The song "Rosie the Riveter" became their theme. It was written by Redd Evans and John Loeb in 1943. The lyrics described how "All day long whether rain or shine, she's part of the assembly line. She's making history working for victory."

After the war, 3.5 million women left the labor force. Most married and started families with returning veterans. But the power of women in the workforce would never again be underestimated.

Women who ran the arsenal of democracy were not working for equality. They were too busy hopping buses to punch a time-clock at 5 a.m. Many lived three or four to an apartment, sometimes with children, splitting shifts to share child care. Their dream was to be reunited with their fathers, brothers, sons, husbands, fiancées and boyfriends.

Their nightmare was to be the one who received the dreaded telegram or visit from men in uniform to inform them that their loved one had been killed or wounded. Just like the men who fought in Europe and the Pacific, they served and suffered and answered the call of their country.

The Navy WAVES and Coast Guard SPARS

In 1919, there was a small group of women who served in the U.S. Navy as nurses. Twenty-three years later, with a little push from Eleanor Roosevelt during World War II, Commander Mildred McAfree was commissioned to head up the Women Accepted for Volunteer Emergency Service (WAVES). The use of the word "emergency" meant that after the war they would all be de-commissioned. The common feeling was that women did not belong in the Navy. But they served brilliantly as nurses and medical personnel and were recruited for Navy intelligence and many other jobs.

By 1943, more than 27,000 American women were serving as aircraft mechanics, control tower operators, and in intelligence. By late 1944, the WAVES began accepting African-Americans, who accounted for one to every thirty-six enlistees. By the end of the war, 84,000 women had served in the WAVES, with eight thousand rising through the ranks to become officers. They were only 2.5 percent of the total Navy, but they made an impact.

After the war, Congress passed the Women's Armed Service Integration Act in June of 1948, to let women enlist in the regular Navy, although the Navy still referred to them as WAVES.

Women in the Coast Guard were called SPARS, from the Coast Guard motto, "Semper Paratus" – Always Ready. More than 11,000 women joined the Coast Guard as clerks, storekeepers, photographers, pharmacist mates, cooks and various other jobs. The term SPAR was abandoned after World War II and most enlisted in the Navy WAVES or regular Navy.

Women served courageously in many capacities. In World War II, two hundred Navy nurses were among the casualties. Many were killed trying to bring injured servicemen to hospitals as the Japanese bombed Pearl Harbor. When Corregidor fell in 1942, many were captured by the Japanese.

Women were actively recruited with War posters and served both stateside and overseas, allowing men to go into combat or wherever they were needed most.

Who Were the WACs?

World War II was being waged on land, sea and in the air on both sides of the world, in the Pacific and European Theaters. Nearly every man who could serve was in the military and the women were doing their share stateside. Women got started slowly in the war effort, but by the time the war was over, they were serving in many capacities.

More than 150,000 women served in the Women's Army Corps (WACs) during World War II. They were the first women, other than nurses, to serve in the United States Army. The public and the Army had problems accepting women at first. But it quickly became clear that women were a powerful resource.

Congresswomen Edith Nourse Rogers of Massachusetts met with Gen. George Marshall, the Army Chief of Staff, in early 1941, and told him she intended to introduce a bill to establish the Women's Army Auxiliary Corps (WAAC), to be separate from the existing Army Nurse Corps.

Rogers knew that women had worked overseas with the Army, under contract and as volunteers during World War I, as communications specialists and dietitians. They had served the Army with no benefits and had to obtain their own food and housing, without legal protection or medical care. When they returned from their assignments they had no disability benefits or pensions as veterans. Rogers was determined that would change in World War II.

She was persistent in her requests to make sure women who served would get full benefits. It was an uphill battle against the Army's ingrained culture. But her bill introduced in May 1941 was given serious consideration after the Japanese attack on Pearl Harbor six months later. Gen. Marshall thought that fighting on two fronts would stretch the U.S. manpower so thin, women could make a significant contribution. Opponents in Congress asked, "Who will then do the cooking, the washing, the mending, the humble homey tasks to which every woman has devoted herself, and who will nurture the children?" Over their objections, President Roosevelt signed the bill and set a goal of 25,000 recruits. That goal was met almost immediately.

Oveta Culp Hobby was the first director of the WAACs. She had extensive experience in both the private and government sectors. She was competent and efficient, as a former editor of a Houston newspaper and parliamentarian in the Texas Legislature.

The WAACs immediately began to recruit clerical workers, teachers and telephone operators needed by the Army. They would have to wear uniforms, including slacks, which were not considered feminine in the 1940s.

Hobby said, "The gaps women will fill are in those noncombatant jobs where women's hands and hearts fit naturally. WAACs will do the same type of work which women do in civilian life. They will bear the same relations to men in the Army that they bear to the men in civilian organizations for which they work. Women will help the men at war the same way they helped men achieve success before."

Initially, applicants had to be American citizens between the ages of 21 and 45, with no dependents. More than 35,000 women applied for one thousand positions. They started out as file clerks, typists, stenographers and motor pool drivers, but soon took on new assignments such as weather observers and forecasters, cryptographers, radio operators and repair, sheet metal workers, parachute riggers, trainer instructors, bombsite maintenance specialists, aerial photograph analysts and control tower operators.

They also worked on statistical control tabulating machines (the precursors of modern day computers) to keep track of materials and personnel. Some were assigned flying duties and served as radio operators on B-17 bombers.

The WAACs were a volunteer group. In 1943, Congress opened hearings to include them in the regular Army. The Women's Army Corps (WACs) was formed, and recruitment goals were increased.

With the WACs now a part of the regular Army, they were available for overseas assignments. Several served with Gen. Dwight Eisenhower in Africa. Two WACs who could speak French were assigned to Allied Headquarters as executive secretaries. They had harrowing experiences aboard a ship that was torpedoed and had to be rescued from the burning wreckage by a British destroyer.

WACs involved with secret intelligence worked around the clock during the planning for D-Day. Plans changed almost hourly and the WACs typed both critical and alternate plans and routed them through Allied Command.

In late 1945, a battalion of black WACs received a long awaited assignment. Organized as the 6888th Central Postal Battalion, the eight hundred women were stationed in Birmingham, England, responsible for the redirection of mail to all U.S. personnel in the European Theater of Operations. Those included Army, Navy, Marines, Civilians and Red Cross Workers, a total of more than 7 million people. When mail could not be delivered to an address, it was redelivered to the 6888th Postal Battalion, which sorted sixty-five thousand pieces of mail each day.

The Pacific Theater was the last to request WACs, whose duties there were often clerical, although some worked in communications, stockrooms and supply depots, as mechanics or in motor transport pools.

When they arrived in the Pacific, they were issued uniforms of wool pants, earmuffs and twill coveralls. The coveralls were too hot for the tropical climate and many women developed skin diseases. The commanders required that they wear the long pants to protect them from disease-bearing mosquitos, but the heat and humidity kept their clothing damp and stifling.

Most WACs were demobilized along with the rest of the Army after the war ended in Europe. But after petitioning Congress in 1946, the WACs were allowed to remain in the Army as regular enlisted personnel – proving their contribution to the war effort.

The WACs had changed the way women were treated in the military. Their perseverance and dedication to their duties also changed the attitude of men toward women in the workplace – forever changing the role of women in American Society.

WASPs:
Women Airforce Service Pilots

Although usually outnumbered by men as they were during the war, many women have taken part in Honor Flights. The first all-women Honor Flight was on September 22, 2015. Women veterans from World War II and Korea, along with guardians who included veterans of Afghanistan and Iraq, made a special stop at the National Women's Combat Memorial at the gates of Arlington National Cemetery.

The war effort touched everyone in the U.S. in the 1940s, and women helped in many ways. The Women Airforce Service Pilots (WASPs) was started by two female pilots, Jackie Cochran and Nancy Love, who submitted proposals to help fly planes and free up male pilots for combat duty.

WASPs were civilian female pilots, employed by the military to fly under the direction of U.S. Army Air Forces. During the war, 1,900 women were certified as WASPs to ferry planes to the combat zones and tow drones and aerial targets. More than 25,000 applied, but only women with experience or pilots' licenses were chosen.

The women were required to complete the same primary, basic and advanced training courses taken by Army Air Corps pilots. Many went on to specialized flight training. A typical WASP had 1,400 flying hours and a commercial pilot rating.

One black woman applied, but withdrew her application. Two Chinese applicants were chosen, Hazel Ling Lee and Maggie Gee. WASP Lee was killed in a runway collision. Ola Mildred Rexroat, a Sioux Indian, was commissioned as a WASP and joined the Air Force after the war.

WASP wings and women pilots
before a mission

Flight planning (left);
ready for takeoff

WASPs flew 60 million miles in every type of aircraft. They were not granted veteran status until 1977 and were not given the Congressional Gold Medal until 2009, so many WASPs did not consider themselves veterans. They were classified as civil service and did not receive military benefits. Records of their accomplishments were sealed for thirty-five years, inaccessible to historians until 1975, when the campaign to give them veteran status was launched.

Thirty-eight WASPs died in the war: eleven in training, twenty-seven on active duty. They were buried at their families' expense without military honors. The Army would not allow U.S. flags to be placed on the coffins of the fallen WASPs.

On July 1, 2009, President Obama and Congress awarded the WASPs the Congressional Gold Medal. Three of the three hundred remaining WASPs were there to take part, and many of the rest came to the U.S. Capitol to accept their medals a year later.

President Obama said, "The Women Airforce Service Pilots courageously answered their country's call in a time of need while blazing a trail for the brave women who have given and continue to give so much service to this nation since. Every American should be grateful for their service, and I am honored to sign the bill to finally give them some of the hard-earned recognition they deserve."

Editor's note: Ernie Pyle was America's most admired and widely read war correspondent during World War II. As a Scripps Howard reporter, he told the story from the foxhole, slogging along with the G.I.s through North Africa, Europe and then to the Pacific. He was killed by an enemy machinegun bullet during the battle of Okinawa, just a month away from his birthday. He would have been 45. Nobody told what it was really like on the frontlines as well as Ernie Pyle. His columns are reprinted with the generous permission of the Scripps Howard Foundation.

The Horrible Waste of War

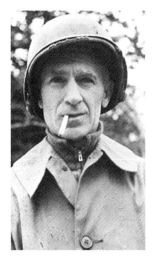

Ernie Pyle

By ERNIE PYLE

NORMANDY BEACHHEAD, June 16, 1944 - I took a walk along the historic coast of Normandy in the country of France.

It was a lovely day for strolling along the seashore. Men were sleeping on the sand, some of them sleeping forever. Men were floating in the water, but they didn't know they were in the water, for they were dead.

The water was full of squishy little jellyfish about the size of your hand. Millions of them. In the center each of them had a green design exactly like a four-leaf clover. The good-luck emblem. Sure. Hell yes.

I walked for a mile and a half along the water's edge of our many-miled invasion beach. You wanted to walk slowly, for the detail on that beach was infinite.

The wreckage was vast and startling. The awful waste and destruction of war, even aside from the loss of human life, has always been one of its outstanding features to those who are in it. Anything and everything is expendable. And we did expend on our beachhead in Normandy during those first few hours.

*

For a mile out from the beach there were scores of tanks and trucks and boats that you could no longer see, for they were at the bottom of the water - swamped by overloading, or hit by shells, or sunk by mines. Most of their crews were lost.

You could see trucks tipped half over and swamped. You could see partly sunken barges, and the angled-up corners of jeeps, and small landing craft half submerged. And at low tide you could still see those vicious six-pronged iron snares that helped snag and wreck them.

On the beach itself, high and dry, were all kinds of wrecked vehicles. There were tanks that had only just made the beach before being knocked out. There were jeeps that had been burned to a dull gray. There were big derricks on caterpillar treads that didn't quite make it. There were half-tracks carrying office equipment that had been made into a shambles by a single shell hit, their interiors still holding their useless equipage of smashed typewriters, telephones, office files.

There were LCTs turned completely upside down, and lying on their backs, and how they got that way I don't know. There were boats stacked on top of each other, their sides caved in, their suspension doors knocked off.

In this shoreline museum of carnage there were abandoned rolls of barbed wire and smashed bulldozers and big stacks of thrown-away lifebelts and piles of shells still waiting to be moved.

In the water floated empty life rafts and soldiers' packs and ration boxes, and mysterious oranges.

On the beach lay snarled rolls of telephone wire and big rolls of steel matting and stacks of broken, rusting rifles.

On the beach lay, expended, sufficient men and mechanism for a small war. They were gone forever now. And yet we could afford it.

We could afford it because we were on, we had our toehold, and behind us there were such enormous replacements for this wreckage on the beach that you could hardly conceive of their sum total. Men and equipment were flowing from England in such a gigantic stream that it made the waste on the beachhead seem like nothing at all, really nothing at all.

*

A few hundred yards back on the beach is a high bluff. Up there we had a tent hospital, and a barbed-wire enclosure for prisoners of war. From up there you could see far up and down the beach, in a spectacular crow's-nest view, and far out to sea.

And standing out there on the water beyond all this wreckage was the greatest armada man has ever seen. You simply could not believe the gigantic collection of ships that lay out there waiting to unload.

Looking from the bluff, it lay thick and clear to the far horizon of the sea and beyond, and it spread out to the sides and was miles wide. Its utter enormity would move the hardest man.

As I stood up there I noticed a group of freshly taken German prisoners standing nearby. They had not yet been put in the prison cage. They were just standing there, a couple of doughboys leisurely guarding them with tommy guns.

The prisoners too were looking out to sea - the same bit of sea that for months and years had been so safely empty before their gaze. Now they stood staring almost as if in a trance.

They didn't say a word to each other. They didn't need to. The expression on their faces was something forever unforgettable. In it was the final horrified acceptance of their doom.

If only all Germans could have had the rich experience of standing on the bluff and looking out across the water and seeing what their compatriots saw.

Permission to distribute and re-publish Ernie Pyle's columns was given by the Scripps Howard Foundation.

A Long Thin Line of Personal Anguish

By ERNIE PYLE

NORMANDY BEACHHEAD, June 17, 1944 - In the preceding column we told about the D-day wreckage among our machines of war that were expended in taking one of the Normandy beaches.

But there is another and more human litter. It extends in a thin little line, just like a high-water mark, for miles along the beach. This is the strewn personal gear, gear that will never be needed again, of those who fought and died to give us our entrance into Europe.

Here in a jumbled row for mile on mile are soldiers' packs. Here are socks and shoe polish, sewing kits, diaries, Bibles and hand grenades. Here are the latest letters from home, with the address on each one neatly razored out - one of the security precautions enforced before the boys embarked.

Here are toothbrushes and razors, and snapshots of families back home staring up at you from the sand. Here are pocketbooks, metal mirrors, extra trousers, and bloody, abandoned shoes. Here are broken-handled shovels, and portable radios smashed almost beyond recognition, and mine detectors twisted and ruined.

Here are torn pistol belts and canvas water buckets, first-aid kits and jumbled heaps of lifebelts. I picked up a pocket Bible with a soldier's name in it, and put it in my jacket. I carried it half a mile or so and then put it back down on the beach. I don't know why I picked it up, or why I put it back down.

Soldiers carry strange things ashore with them. In every invasion you'll find at least one soldier hitting the beach at H-hour with a banjo slung over his shoulder. The most ironic piece of equipment marking our beach – this beach of first despair, then victory – is a tennis racket that some soldier had brought along. It lies lonesomely on the sand, clamped in its rack, not a string broken.

Two of the most dominant items in the beach refuse are cigarettes and writing paper. Each soldier was issued a carton of cigarettes just before he started. Today these cartons by the thousand, water-soaked and spilled out, mark the line of our first savage blow.

Writing paper and air-mail envelopes come second. The boys had intended to do a lot of writing in France. Letters that would have filled those blank, abandoned pages.

Always there are dogs in every invasion. There is a dog still on the beach today, still pitifully looking for his masters.

He stays at the water's edge, near a boat that lies twisted and half sunk at the water line. He barks appealingly to every soldier who approaches, trots eagerly along with him for a few feet, and then, sensing himself unwanted in all this haste, runs back to wait in vain for his own people at his own empty boat.

*

Over and around this long thin line of personal anguish, fresh men today are rushing vast supplies to keep our armies pushing on into France. Other squads of men pick amidst the wreckage to salvage ammunition and equipment that are still usable.

Men worked and slept on the beach for days before the last D-day victim was taken away for burial.

I stepped over the form of one youngster whom I thought dead. But when I looked down I saw he was only sleeping. He was very young, and very tired. He lay on one elbow, his hand suspended in the air about six inches from the ground. And in the palm of his hand he held a large, smooth rock.

I stood and looked at him a long time. He seemed in his sleep to hold that rock lovingly, as though it were his last link with a vanishing world. I have no idea at all why he went to sleep with the rock in his hand, or what kept him from dropping it once he was asleep. It was just one of those little things without explanation that a person remembers for a long time.

*

The strong, swirling tides of the Normandy coastline shift the contours of the sandy beach as they move in and out. They carry soldiers' bodies out to sea, and later they return them. They cover the corpses of heroes with sand, and then in their whims they uncover them.

As I plowed out over the wet sand of the beach on that first day ashore, I walked around what seemed to be a couple of pieces of driftwood sticking out of the sand. But they weren't driftwood.

They were a soldier's two feet. He was completely covered by the shifting sands except for his feet. The toes of his GI shoes pointed toward the land he had come so far to see, and which he saw so briefly.

Permission to distribute and re-publish Ernie Pyle's columns was given by the Scripps Howard Foundation.

Ernie Pyle files his newspaper column in Europe.

They Were Good Boys

By ERNIE PYLE

IN NORMANDY, June 17, 1944 (By Wireless) —Lieut. Orion Shockley came over with a map and explained to us just what his company was going to do.

There was a German strong point of pillboxes and machine-gun nests about half a mile down the street ahead of us.

Our troops had made wedges into the city on both sides of us, but nobody had yet been up this street where we were going. The street, they thought, was almost certainly under rifle fire.

This is how we'll do it," the lieutenant said. "A rifle platoon goes first. Right behind them will go part of a heavy-weapons platoon, with machine guns to cover the first platoon.

Then comes another rifle platoon. Then a small section with mortars, in case they run into something pretty heavy. Then another rifle platoon. And bringing up the rear, the rest of the heavy-weapons outfit to protect us from behind.

We don't know what we'll run into, and I don't want to stick you right out in front, so why don't you come along with me? We'll go in the middle of the company."

I said, "Okay." By this time I wasn't scared. You seldom are once you're into something. Anticipation is the worst. Fortunately this little foray came up so suddenly there wasn't time for much anticipation.

***

The rain kept on coming down, and you could sense that it had set in for the afternoon. None of us had raincoats, and by evening there wasn't a dry thread on any of us. I could go back to a tent for the night, but the soldiers would have to sleep the way they were.

We were just ready to start when all of a sudden bullets came whipping savagely right above our heads.

It's those damn 20-millimeters again," the lieutenant said. "Better hold it up a minute."

The soldiers all crouched lower behind the wall. The vicious little shells whanged into a grassy hillside just beyond us. A French suburban farmer was hitching up his horses in a barnyard on the hillside. He ran into the house. Shells struck all around it.

Two dead Germans and a dead American still lay in his driveway. We could see them when we moved up a few feet.

The shells stopped, and finally the order to start was given. As we left the protection of the high wall we had to cross a little culvert right out in the open and then make a turn in the road.

The men went forward one at a time. They crouched and ran, apelike, across this dangerous space. Then, beyond the culvert, they filtered to either side of the road, stopping and squatting down every now and then to wait a few moments.

The lieutenant kept yelling at them as they started:

Spread it out now. Do you want to draw fire on yourselves? Don't bunch up like that. Keep five yards apart. Spread it out, dammit."

There is an almost irresistible pull to get close to somebody when you are in danger. In spite of themselves, the men would run up close to the fellow ahead for company.

The other lieutenant now called out:

Now you on the right watch the left side of the street for snipers, and you on the left watch the right side. Cover each other that way."

And a first sergeant said to a passing soldier:

Get that grenade out of its case. It won't do you no good in the case. Throw the case away. That's right."

***

Some of the men carried grenades already fixed in the ends of their rifles. All of them had hand grenades. Some had big Browning automatic rifles. One carried a bazooka. Interspersed in the thin line of men every now and then was a medic, with his bags of bandages and a Red Cross arm band on the left arm. The men didn't talk any. They just went.

They weren't heroic figures as they moved forward one at a time, a few seconds apart. You think of attackers as being savage and bold. These men were hesitant and cautious. They were really the hunters, but they looked like the hunted. There was a confused excitement and a grim anxiety in their faces.

They seemed terribly pathetic to me. They weren't warriors. They were American boys who by mere chance of fate had wound up with guns in their hands sneaking up a death-laden street in a strange and shattered city in a faraway country in a driving rain. They were afraid, but it was beyond their power to quit. They had no choice.

They were good boys. I talked with them all afternoon as we sneaked slowly forward along the mysterious and rubbled street, and I know they were good boys.

And even though they aren't warriors born to the kill, they win their battles. That's the point.

Did You Know?
Facts About World War II

Everyone in the United States was involved in the war effort. Pearl Harbor united Americans as never before. While the GI's fought, their families on the home front did what they could. Some joined Civil Defense groups or the Red Cross; others sold war bonds to finance the war or collected useful resources, from tinfoil to old tires. "Victory gardens" were a patriotic way for civilians to cope with shortages, including rationing of sugar, meat and gasoline. Being involved and "doing your part" of the war effort boosted morale and made all Americans feel like they were in the fight together.

Did you know?

- Because of its industrial contributions to the War, Cincinnati and parts of the Midwest were identified as targets for enemy attacks, even though they were far away from the coastlines.

- The Selective Service Act of 1940 drafted men between the ages of 18 and 45. With the huge numbers who enlisted and were drafted, new housing was needed, and the Ft. Thomas barracks were built in Northern Kentucky.

- Blood drives in Cincinnati alone collected 335,000 pints of blood.

- Rubber was restricted because it was needed by the military.

- Metal and tin cans were "recycled" for airplane construction.

- The Boy Scouts collected tons of paper, newspaper and magazines for the war effort.

- Over fifteen million people moved during the war, most to find jobs in factories. Many women took jobs outside the home for the first time, as the men deployed overseas. The government even set up day care centers in the factories.

- Ten-thousand factories were converted to military support.

- As the Midwest boomed with war manufacturing, workers came from Tennessee, Kentucky and West Virginia. General Motors auto plants were quickly transformed to make tanks and airplanes. The Willow Run factory in Detroit was turned into a B-24 Bomber assembly line, producing a new bomber every hour.

- Posters were everywhere, recruiting, encouraging and warning workers that

"Loose Lips Sink Ships." Some posters were so large they hung from buildings and were made into banners.

- President Roosevelt asked for 45,000 tanks, 20,000 guns, 60,000 planes and 8,000 ships for the war effort.

- The Crosley Radio company was the "nation's station" with the most powerful transmitter of its day. It was over 500,000 watts and was constructed in Mason, Ohio. The tower is still in use today.

- A remote factory in Kings Mills, Ohio – now famous as the home of Kings Island Amusement Park – was one of the most prolific ammunition factories for the war. Most of the ammunition was packed by women at the Kings Mills Cartridge Company.

- Wright Trainers, a two-seater airplane, was built by Wright Aeronautical Company near Dayton, Ohio. Another small airplane, the Aeronica, was built at Lunken Airport in Cincinnati. Both were called "defenders" because so many World War II pilots trained in them.

- With everyone anxious to hear news of the war, movie theaters became the "living room" of America, where families could watch movie newsreels from the front before the regular feature.

- Newspapers provided the details of battles, victories and defeats in Europe and the Pacific. One of the most beloved and famous war correspondents was Ernie Pyle, of Scripps Howard News Service. He courageously accompanied the G.I., across Europe and then transferred to the Pacific when Germany surrendered. He was killed in the Pacific and the nation mourned him. *The New York Times* reported:

> Ernie Pyle died today on Ie Island, just west of Okinawa, like so many of the doughboys he had written about. The nationally known war correspondent was killed instantly by Japanese machine gun fire. The slight, graying newspaper man, chronicler of the average American soldier's daily round, in and out of foxholes in many war theatres, had gone forward early this morning to observe the advance of a well known division of the Twenty fourth Army Corps.

- When the war ended on VE Day and VJ Day, it was announced with some of the biggest headlines ever used.

- Over 300,000 GI's were served in the USO at Union Terminal. Many other USO locations were located throughout Cincinnati.

- As a security measure, more than 120,000 Japanese Americans were arrested and interned in "relocation" camps after the attack on Pearl Harbor.

213

- From 1942 to 1944, the United States went from zero aircraft available in Europe to 12,200.

- Germany lost 1,060 warships, including battleships such as the Bismarck, cruisers, destroyers and submarines. The United States lost 157. Germany lost 994 submarines; the U.S. lost 52.

- Oil production in the United States during the war was 223 million tons. Germany produced 6.4 million tons.

- More than half of all the aircraft in World War II were made in America.

- The U.S. produced 60,973 tanks.

- Production of aircraft went from 2,141 in 1939 to 46,000 in 1945.

- More than 400,000 Americans died in the War

- The Normandy Invasion on D-Day had the most casualties of any battle in Europe, with 12,000 Americans killed. That is more than have been killed in Afghanistan over the past thirteen years.

- The bloodiest battle of the Pacific War claimed 12,500 American lives on Okinawa during an 82-day siege.

- The Russians had the most military casualties in World War II: More than 8 million perished. The Germans lost 2.3 million military casualties.

- Civilian deaths were far greater. Hundreds of thousands died in bombing raids on Japan and Germany. Entire cities were wiped out with atom bombs that were dropped on Nagasaki and Hiroshima to force Japan to surrender. Another 6 million, mostly Jews, were killed in Hitler's Holocaust. Men were killed first to reduce the risk of revolt in concentration camps such as Auschwitz and Dachau.

- Sixteen percent of the population of Poland was lost.

- Even though Germany never invaded the United Kingdom, the British lost more than 60,000 civilians to German air raids.

- World War II caused more deaths than any war in human history. Worldwide, 70 million were killed. China lost 6 million, many killed by Japanese war crimes.

- There has not been a war between the forty-four richest nations since the end of World War II.

- The Korean War claimed 36,000 Americans and 105,000 wounded. Technically, it never ended; there was never a peace treaty. About 7,800 Americans are still missing in action.

- There were 415,000 South Koreans killed and more than 429,000 wounded. The Chinese lost 1.5 million in the Korean War. The United States spent more than $67 million on military operations in the Korean War.

A Soldier's Dictionary: World War II

- Ack-Ack: Anti-Aircraft fire.

- Ash Can: Depth Charge.

- BAR: Browning Automatic Rifle.

- C-rats: C-rations, canned meals.

- Crud: Jungle rot.

- Dear John: Bad news letter from girlfriend at home.

- Dogface: Soldier.

- Dugout Doug: Gen. Douglas MacArthur got this nickname from Marines who noticed his preference for being in bunkers, far from the fighting.

- Fubar: Fouled Up Beyond Repair (or Recognition).

- G.I.: Soldier/ground infantry.

- Girene: Marine.

- Jeep: General Purpose Vehicle.

- Mae West: Lifejacket.

- Milk Jug: P-47 Thunderbolt fighter, shaped like a milk bottle.

- Old Blood and Guts: Gen. George Patton.

- Pineapple: Hand grenade.

- Potato Masher: German hand grenade.

- Ronson: Sherman Tank, nicknamed after a popular cigarette lighter for the way it would easily ignite.

- S.O.S.: 'Stuff' on a Shingle, aka chipped beef on toast.

- Tin Can: Destroyer.

- Woolworth flattop, Jeep carrier: Escort Carriers. The crews said they were designated CVE because they were Combustible, Vulnerable and Expendable.

A Soldier's Dictionary: Korea and Vietnam

- Airborne: Refers to soldiers qualified as parachutists.

- Air-Cav: Air cavalry, airborne Infantry.

- A-team: Team of 10 U.S. Special Forces.

- B-52: High altitude bomber.

- Band- aid: Call for a medic.

- Bird: Helicopter or any aircraft.

- Bird Dog: Forward air traffic controller.

- Cache: Term for hidden supplies.

- Charlie: Viet Cong guerilla fighters.

- Chop-chop: Slang for food.

- CP pills: Anti-malarial pills.

- Deuce and a half: Two-and-a-half ton truck.

- DMZ: Demilitarized zone.

- E-tool: Folding shovel carried by infantrymen.

- Fatigues: Green standard combat uniform.

- Flak jacket: Heavy fiberglass-filled protection vest.

- Gook: Derogatory term used for Asian enemy.

- Grids: Maps broken into numbered, thousand-meter squares.

- Grunt: Infantryman.

- Hot: Area under fire.

- Huey: Nickname for the UH-1 helicopter.

- In country: Vietnam.

- KIA: Killed in action.

- MASH Unit: Mobile Army Surgical Hospital.

- MIA: Missing in action.

- OR: Operating room.

- P-38: Small collapsible can opener.

- Rack: Bed or cot.

- Recon: Reconnaissance mission.

- Rock and roll: Firing a weapon on full automatic.

- Ruck: Backpack issued to the infantry in Vietnam.

- Sky crane: Huge double-engine helicopter used for heavy lifting.

- Spider hole: Camouflaged enemy foxhole.

- Steel pot: Standard U.S. Army steel helmet.

- Tracer: A round of ammunition that glows when fired.

- Tunnel rat: Soldiers who volunteered to crawl through enemy tunnels.

- VC: Viet Cong. Also "Charlie."

- Wake up: Last day of Vietnam tour.

- Wood line: A row of trees at the edge of the forest.

- Zapped: Killed.

They Said It:
Famous Quotes About War

"As life is action and passion, it is required of a man that he should share the passion and action of his time at peril of being judged not to have lived. Combat is an incommunicable experience."

– Oliver Wendell Holmes, veteran of the Civil War

"Combat is a 'test of character,' it makes bad men worse and good men better."

– Joshua Lawrence Chamberlain, Battle of Gettysburg

"My spirit bled each time one of my men fell."

– Confederate Gen. Robert E. Lee

"You have conducted yourselves 'with no remorse for the past, confident regarding the present and full of hope for the future.' You can sleep 'the sleep of the brave.'"

– Alexander Dumas

"As in war you have been good soldiers, so in peace you will be good citizens."

– Gen. William Tecumseh Sherman

"This war is not an ordinary war. It is the war of the entire Russian people. Not only to eliminate the danger hanging over our heads, but to aid all people groaning under the yoke of fascism."

– Soviet Dictator Josef Stalin, June 1941

"A gigantic fleet has massed in Pearl Harbor. This fleet will be utterly crushed with one blow at the very beginning of hostilities. Heaven will bear witness to the righteousness of our struggle."

– Japanese Rear-Adm. Ito, November 1941

"No amphibious attack in history had approached this one in size. Along miles of coastline there were hundreds of vessels and small boats afloat and ant-like files of advancing troops ashore."

– Gen. Dwight Eisenhower, July 1943, Sicily

"The world must know what happened, and never forget."

– Gen. Eisenhower, visiting Nazi death camps, 1945

"Sure, we want to go home. We want this war over with. The quickest way to get it over with is to go get the bastards who started it. The quicker they are whipped, the quicker we can go home. The shortest way home is through Berlin and Tokyo. And when we get to Berlin, I am personally going to shoot that paper hanging son-of-a-bitch Hitler. Just like I'd shoot a snake!"

– Gen. George S. Patton, addressing troops on June 5, 1944

"I have returned many times to honor the valiant men who died. Every man who set foot on Omaha Beach was a hero."

– Lt. Gen. General Omar Bradley, Commander of the US First Army

"We shall defend our island whatever the cost may be. We shall fight on beaches, landing grounds, in fields, in streets and on the hills. We shall never surrender."

– British Prime Minister Winston Churchill

"I believe it is peace in our time."

– British Prime Minister Neville Chamberlain, 1938, on his deal with Hitler.

"You cannot invade the mainland United States. There would be a rifle behind each blade of grass."

– Adm. Isoroku Yamamoto

"I fear all we have done is awaken a sleeping giant and fill him with a terrible resolve."

– Adm. Yamamoto, after the attack on Pearl Harbor

President Franklin Roosevelt's prayer on D-Day:

"Almighty God: Our sons, pride of our Nation, this day have set upon a mighty endeavor, a struggle to preserve our Republic, our religion, and our civilization, and to set free a suffering humanity.

Lead them straight and true; give strength to their arms, stoutness to their hearts, steadfastness in their faith.

They will need Thy blessings. Their road will be long and hard. For the enemy is strong. He may hurl back our forces. Success may not come with rushing speed, but we shall return again and again; and we know that by Thy grace, and by the righteousness of our cause, our sons will triumph.

They will be sore tried, by night and by day, without rest-until the victory is won. The darkness will be rent by noise and flame. Men's souls will be shaken with the violences of war.

For these men are lately drawn from the ways of peace. They fight not for the lust of conquest. They fight to end conquest. They fight to liberate. They fight to let justice arise, and tolerance and good will among all Thy people. They yearn but for the end of battle, for their return to the haven of home.

Some will never return. Embrace these, Father, and receive them, Thy heroic servants, into Thy kingdom.

And for us at home – fathers, mothers, children, wives, sisters, and brothers of brave men overseas – whose thoughts and prayers are ever with them – help us, Almighty God, to rededicate ourselves in renewed faith in Thee in this hour of great sacrifice.

Many people have urged that I call the Nation into a single day of special prayer. But because the road is long and the desire is great, I ask that our people devote themselves in a continuance of prayer. As we rise to each new day, and again when each day is spent, let words of prayer be on our lips, invoking Thy help to our efforts.

Give us strength, too – strength in our daily tasks, to redouble the contributions we make in the physical and the material support of our armed forces.

And let our hearts be stout, to wait out the long travail, to bear sorrows that may come, to impart our courage unto our sons wheresoever they may be.

And, O Lord, give us Faith. Give us Faith in Thee; Faith in our sons; Faith in each other; Faith in our united crusade. Let not the keenness of our spirit ever be dulled. Let not the impacts of temporary events, of temporal matters of but fleeting moment let not these deter us in our unconquerable purpose.

With Thy blessing, we shall prevail over the unholy forces of our enemy. Help us to conquer the apostles of greed and racial arrogancies. Lead us to the saving of our country, and with our sister Nations into a world unity that will spell a sure peace a peace invulnerable to the schemings of unworthy men. And a peace that will let all of men live in freedom, reaping the just rewards of their honest toil.

Thy will be done, Almighty God.

Amen."

Flag-Folding Ceremony

The American Flag has been the symbol of the United States of America since the birth of our nation. It waves on the winds of our history – on the ground, in the air and on the sea, on every continent, representing the dreams of our nation.

It has been torn, tattered and shot through with bullet holes in battle, and then draped over the caskets of our fallen. It decorates our lawns and front porches and puts the thrill of patriotism in our parades. It has been draped over the shoulders of athletes and defiled, desecrated and burned by those who seek to destroy what it symbolizes. The flag represents all Americans. It has healed the wounds of warriors and is saluted by them with pride.

Ever since it was named the "Star Spangled Banner" in our National Anthem, the flag is our country's most recognized and inspiring symbol in every corner of the world, where it represents freedom and our founding principles.

On each Honor Flight day, the veterans are celebrated with an emotional ceremony in which an open flag is passed over the heads of everyone, to show how all Americans "serve under the flag."

At each welcome ceremony, the American Flag is passed back to the front of the room, then folded in a unique and specific manner, following American Flag etiquette:

- The folded flag makes a triangle to symbolize the tri-cornered hats of colonial patriots during the War for Independence and honor the soldiers who served under General George Washington.

- The red and white stripes are always folded into the blue field.

- The flag is folded at waist level and the surface of the flag is kept parallel to the ground. No part of the flag is allowed to touch the ground.

- The flag is folded lengthwise, to cover the blue field of stars.

- Then folded again lengthwise with the blue field on the outside.

- Next, the ribbon of folded flag is again folded into a triangle by bringing the striped corner of the folded edge to meet the open edge.

- The triangular folding continues inward, moving from stripes to stars, lining up with the open edge until the flag is completely folded and the blue field of stars is all that is visible. The last corner of the flag is tucked inside, creating a perfect star-studded triangle.

- Each fold represents part of our heritage.

- The first fold stands for liberty and the pursuit of the American Dream. The white stripes symbolize liberty.

- The second fold represents unity. Quoting from the Bible (Mark 3:25), Abraham Lincoln said, "A house divided against itself cannot stand."

- The third fold represents justice. The blue field behind the white stars stands for justice.

- The fourth fold represents the perseverance of our countryman even after defeat.

- The fifth represents hardiness that our enemies often underestimate.

- The sixth fold represents valor, symbolized by the red stripes that stand for the blood shed by all Americans who sacrificed for our freedom.

- The seventh fold is purity. The path to freedom was lit by the Declaration of Independence, and still shines to beckon all seeking asylum from persecution and oppression.

- The eighth fold represents our innocence. George Washington once said, "The love of my country will be the ruling influence of my conduct."

- The ninth fold is sacrifice, to honor all military personnel and everyone that sacrifices for our freedom, including public servants.

- The tenth stands for honor, to respect all who have conducted themselves with honor on behalf of all citizens.

- The eleventh is independence. America stands as a lighthouse of freedom and independence for the oppressed of the world.

- The final fold represents truth. America was founded on the God-given truths written in the Declaration of Independence, "That all men are created equal, that they are endowed by their Creator with certain unalienable rights, that among these are life, liberty and the pursuit of happiness."

Each flag folding is a pledge that every American will remain forever free. When the flag is completely folded, the stars that shine from a deep blue background remind us that "In God we trust."

Adapted from the National Flag Foundation.

The Purple Heart is America's oldest medal, first awarded as the Badge of Merit by Gen. George Washington in 1782.

The Story of the Purple Heart

The oldest military medal given by the U.S. military is the Purple Heart. The heart-shaped decoration has a profile of George Washington and hangs from a purple ribbon. It is awarded in the name of the U.S. President to "those wounded or killed, against any enemy of the United States or as a result of an act of any such enemy or opposing armed forces, while serving with the U.S. Military."

The original Purple Heart, designated as the Badge of Military Merit, was established by George Washington in 1782 when he was the commander-in-chief of the Continental Army. The Badge of Merit was awarded to only three Revolutionary War soldiers. It was not used again until it was revived on the bicentennial of George Washington's birth in 1932.

The Purple Heart differs from all other decorations in that an individual is not "recommended" for it, but earns it by meeting specific criteria. When contemplating the award of this medal, commanders must take into consideration the degree to which the enemy caused the injury. The wound for which the award is made must have required treatment by a medical officer, and records of medical treatment for wounds or injuries received in action must have been made a matter of public record. The Purple Heart is not awarded for non-combat injuries.

Injuries or wounds that justify the Purple Heart include: injury caused by an enemy bullet, shrapnel or other projectile created by enemy action; injury caused by an enemy placed land mine, naval mine or trap; injury caused by enemy-released chemical, biological or nuclear agent; injury caused by vehicle or aircraft accident resulting from enemy fire; and concussion injuries caused by an enemy-generated explosion.

From 1942 to 1997, civilians who served with or were closely affiliated with the armed forces – such as government employees, Red Cross workers, war correspondents and the like – were eligible to receive the Purple Heart. Among the earliest non-military recipients were the nine firefighters of the Honolulu Fire Department who were killed or wounded while fighting fires at Hickam Field during the attack on Pearl Harbor. One of the most famous recipients of the Purple Heart was Ernie Pyle, the newspaper war correspondent who was given the medal posthumously by the Army after being killed by Japanese machinegun fire in the Pacific during World War II. Civilians are no longer eligible for the Purple Heart.

The criteria to receive a Purple Heart has changed many times during its history. During World War II, nearly 500,000 medals were manufactured in anticipation of the estimated casualties resulting from the planned Allied invasion of Japan. To put that number in perspective, it is greater than the total combined American military casualties during the sixty-five years following the end of World War II – including the Korean and Vietnam wars. In 2003, there remained 120,000 Purple Heart medals in storage. The surplus allowed combat units in Iraq and Afghanistan to keep Purple Hearts on hand for immediate awards to soldiers wounded in the field.

The Distinguished Flying Cross

The oldest military aviation medal was created after World War I, when the first combat aircraft proved their value for reconnaissance and weapons platforms. Pilots of those early airplanes showed outstanding courage and endurance on their combat missions. The Distinguished Flying Cross was created to recognize their gallantry.

It "may be awarded to any person who, while serving in any capacity with the Armed Forces of the United States, distinguishes himself, or herself by heroism or extraordinary achievement while participating in aerial flight. The performance of the act of heroism must be evidenced by voluntary action above and beyond the call of duty."

The golden medal contains a cross made by a four-bladed propeller, symbolizing sacrifice and flight, against a square of rays. It hangs on a ribbon of red, white and blue stripes.

By an act of Congress during President Calvin Coolidge's administration, the Distinguished Flying Cross was designated to be awarded to anyone in the Army Air Corps (now the Air Force), Navy or Marine Corps after April 6, 1917, who "distinguished himself by heroism or extraordinary achievement while participating in aerial flight."

Because the DFC was established after World War I, it could not be given to World War I pilots, who were the first pioneers of military aviation who used biplanes for dogfights, scouting, bombing, artillery spotting and ground attacks. The award is not limited to combat heroism. The purpose is aerial achievement, in war and peace. The DFC has been awarded to pilots who set distance and endurance records.

The first DFC was presented to a Pan American flight crew on May 2, 1927, by President Coolidge, for their five-ship, 22,000 mile flight. The medal had not even been struck yet, but was hurriedly prepared for the presentation.

The first Naval aviator to receive the DFC was Commander Richard E. Byrd, for his transatlantic flight from New York City to the coast of France. The DFC was also awarded to Charles Lindbergh, an Army Reserve Captain, on June 11, 1927, for his famous transatlantic flight in the Spirit of St. Louis, and to Amelia Earhart, who set numerous aviation records before being lost on an attempt to fly around the world.

Earhart was the first and last civilian to receive the medal. It has since been confined to military aviators.

Special legislation permitted Orville and Wilbur Wright to receive the DFC posthumously for their first powered flight at Kitty Hawk, NC, on December 17, 1903.

Famous DFC recipients include:

- Army General Douglas MacArthur

- General Jimmy Doolittle, USAF

- General Thomas Stafford, USAF – flew to the moon on Apollo 10

- Rear Admiral Alan Shepherd , USN – one of the original seven American astronauts

- Brigadier Gen. Michael Collins, USAF – Command Module pilot, Apollo 11

- Brigadier Gen. James DeVitt, USAF – commander of Gemini 4 and Apollo 9

- Col. Buzz Aldrin, USAF – Lunar Module pilot, Apollo 11, and second man on the moon

- Col. Frank Borman, USAF, commander of Apollo 8

- Col. Eileen Collins, USAF – first woman commander for two space missions

- Col. Gordon Cooper, USAF – commander of Faith 7 and Gemini 5 – original seven astronaut

- Col. John Glenn, USMC – first American to orbit the earth

Numerous other astronauts are recipients, except Neil Armstrong. The first man on the moon was ineligible. Although he served in the Korean War and was a Naval officer and test pilot, he was a civilian during his career with NASA.

Political figures who received the DFC include:

- President – Lt. George H.W. Bush

- Senator – Capt. John McCain

- Senator – First Lt. George McGovern

- Senator – Capt. Joseph McCarthy

- White House aide – First Lt. John Ehrlichman

From the flyboys of the Greatest Generation, who flew propeller driven fighter planes and bombers during World War II, to the men and women who pilot sophisticated jet aircraft over the skies of Iraq and Afghanistan, military aviators have captured a special place in the hearts and minds of all Americans. While they all fly with honor for our country, only those who have distinguished themselves with extraordinary valor and achievement are awarded the Distinguished Flying Cross.

Missing Man Formation

The Missing Man Formation

The most magnificent and solemn aerial maneuver is an aerial salute performed as part of a flyover of aircraft at a funeral or memorial event, in memory of fallen pilots or veterans. It has been used for presidents, astronauts and others to show love, respect and camaraderie.

The most common Missing Man Formation is based on the "finger four" combat formation, in which aircraft are staggered like four fingers in a salute. As the group passes over, the number-three aircraft executes an abrupt pull-up and turns to the west in the direction of the setting sun, representing that one has died as the others carry on the mission.

Legend says it began with British fighter pilots flying over the funeral of Manfred von Richthofen, The Red Baron, as a sign of respect. With eighty combat kills, he was the ace of all aces in World War I. It was used infrequently and privately during World War I, never for the public.

It was seldom used in the United States until after the Vietnam War, when the USAF Thunderbirds used it for the first time to honor Vietnam POWs. Antique "warbirds" and aircraft of all kinds are now used for this solemn tribute.

Members of the Cincinnati Warbirds, the Trojan Horseman and other flight teams perform this moving formation for the funerals of veterans upon request, subject to aircraft and pilot availability and weather conditions.

Stainless steel columns at the United States Air Force Memorial represent the Bomb Burst Formation

What are
Blue and Gold Star Mothers?

Nobody suffers in wartime more than mothers whose sons are on distant shores in harm's way. To provide support to all the mothers who had sons and daughters on active duty, Blue Star Mothers of America was formed after World War I.

There was hardly a block in America without at least one Blue Star home, which was recognizable by the handmade flag displayed proudly in a front window — a blue star on a white field with a red border. Many windows had more than one flag because many families had more than one child serving.

The Blue Star flag was a symbol of national unity, as mothers supported each other and united behind their children who were serving. Those flags were displayed with patriotic pride, to remind everyone of the sacrifices being made in defense of freedom.

Blue Star mothers also teamed up to work in hospitals, served as guides in train stations and prepared packages for the service members. The organization faded after World War II, but when the United States was again attacked on September 11, 2001, there was a resurgence of Blue Star organizations throughout the nation.

As families lost their children to the war, Blue Star flags were replaced by Gold Star flags and another organization was born to support Gold Star Mothers who shared their grief and supported each other. The Gold Star flags were hung in the same windows, all over America.

Nothing could replace the loved ones who were lost in battle. But Gold Star Mothers offered comfort to each other in the most trying times any family can face.

Gold Star Mothers continue to provide emotional support by doing volunteer work with veterans and at Veterans Administration hospitals. They have paid the highest price any parent can imagine. Their patriotism and respect for other service members deserves our nation's deepest gratitude.

Legacy of Freedom: From Valley Forge to Fallujah

The message carved in stone on the Korean War Memorial says, "Freedom is Not Free." But how many Americans know the true cost of liberty? The answer can be found by counting the Americans who have given their lives in wars since the nation's founding.

By far the worst war in our history was the Civil War, from 1861-65, when all the casualties were Americans. War statistics become less reliable as they reach farther into the past. But according to most estimates, about 620,000 were killed in the Civil War. More than 50,000 were killed in just three days at the Battle of Gettysburg.

In the 1860s, 620,000 was about 2 percent of the nation's population of 31 million. The same percentage today would equal more than 6 million deaths. But take away women and children and the elderly, and the death percentage would be much higher. According to some estimates, one in every five young men in the South was killed.

By comparison, the Revolutionary War (1775-1783) was far less deadly with an estimated 25,000 killed.

The War of 1812 (1812-1815) claimed 20,000.

The Mexican-American War (1846-48) caused 13,283 American military deaths.

World War I (1917-18) accounted for 116,516 American war deaths.

In the modern era:

- World War II (1941-1945): 440,000 killed. According to the Department of Veterans Affairs, among the 16 million who served in World War II, about 1.7 million were still living in May of 2015.

- The Korean War (1950-1953): 36,574 American lives. Of 5.7 million who served in the Korean War era, 2.2 million were still living in May 2015.

- The Vietnam War (1964-1975): 58,220 killed. More than 8.7 million served during the war; 7.3 million were still living in May 2015.

- Desert Shield (1990-1991): 383 killed. Most of the 2.3 million who served are still alive.

- The War on Terror: 4,486 Americans have been killed in Iraq; 2,345 killed in Afghanistan. Adding civilian deaths and other military actions, 9,655 Americans had been killed as of mid-2015.

With the end of the draft, fewer and fewer Americans have friends and family who have served in the military. During World War II, 60 percent who served were drafted. By the time the draft ended during the War in Vietnam, about a quarter who served were drafted. In today's all-volunteer military, less than half of one percent of all Americans serve.

Taps

The simple, haunting sound of "Taps" played on a bugle seems to hang in the air and echo in the heart long after the song has faded away.

The twenty-four melancholy notes are played every evening before dusk as the flag is lowered on U.S. military bases, to signal "Lights out, the day is done."

"Taps" is also played at military funerals and memorial services, as a final, solemn tribute. It's the most easily recognized tune in the world.

Honor Flight veterans hear "Taps" during a moving ceremony at the Tomb of the Unknown Soldier in Arlington National Cemetery.

Although popular legend says the notes of "Taps" were found in the pocket of a fallen bugler boy during the Civil War, most historians agree that the origin is an adaptation of the French final call "L'Extinction des Feux" ("Putting out the Fires"). The final call of the French military was called a "tattoo," to mark the end of the evening's drinking and send soldiers back to their garrisons. It was sounded an hour before the final bugle call, to end the day by extinguishing all fires and lights. The final five measures of the French tattoo resemble the American version of "Taps."

Part of the American legend is true: "Taps" did originate during the American Civil War. As Union General Daniel Butterfield was camped at Harrison Landing, near Richmond, Virginia, he thought the French bugle call was too formal for the troops in the field. In July 1862, he hummed the tune he had in mind and had one of his aides write down the music. Then they played the notes and lengthened and shortened it while trying to keep the original melody.

The music caught on and was even adopted by Confederate buglers. It was made the official Army Bugle Call after the Civil War, but was not known as "Taps" until 1874.

Now it is the final salute to America's fallen. The poignant notes echo sadness and grief at memorial services, accompany the lowering of the flag, and signal "lights out" at day's end.

There are no official words to the music, but soldiers know the popular verse that accompanies the lonesome bugle call:

Day is done, gone the sun.

From the hills, from the lake,

From the sky.

All is well, safely rest.

God is nigh.

A national organization called Bugles Across America has a network of more than eight thousand volunteer horn players who will play "Taps" at funerals, memorials and other ceremonies, upon request.

Memories

Memories

Memories

Memories

Memories

Memories

Memories

Memories

KILROY
WAS
HERE